FISHER'S FACE

Captain John Fisher of HMS *Excellent*, 1883.
Courtesy of The Masters and Fellows
of Churchill College, Cambridge.

FISHER'S FACE

OR, GETTING TO KNOW
THE ADMIRAL

JAN MORRIS

Random House
New York

Library of Congress Cataloging-in-Publication Data
Morris, Jan.
Fisher's face / Jan Morris. — 1st ed.
p.   cm.
ISBN 0-679-41609-9
1. Fisher, John Arbuthnot Fisher, Baron, 1841–1920. 2. Great
Britain—History, Naval—20th century. 3. Great Britain. Royal
Navy—Biography.   I. Title.
DA89.1.F5M67 1995
359'.0092—dc20
[B]   94-34174

Manufactured in the United States of America on acid-free paper.
24689753
First American Edition

Book design by Oksana Kushnir

For

JACKY

a *jeu d'amour*

Contents

INTRODUCTORY

Suppose one summer day in the 1880s you and your spouse, or your lover, are invited for drinks with the captain on board HMS *Inflexible*, 11,880 tons, Queen Victoria's guardship during Her Majesty's holiday sojourn at Menton in the south of France. What a thrill! The ship is the Royal Navy's latest and largest battleship, probably the most powerful single weapon of war in the world, and she lies there in the still blue bay of Villefranche, swarmed about by yachts, Mediterranean skiffs and picketboats, with an air of monstrous authority.

To anyone brought up in the heyday of the sailing navies—anyone, that is, over thirty or so—she hardly looks like a ship at all, but more like a machine out of the Industrial Revolution, a floating mass of painted iron lying surly at her anchor. There is no elegance to her, just armored swagger. At first sight it is hard to know which is her bow and which her stern, and she seems all ungainly bump and protrusion, like a mill or a foundry, with two graceless funnels above a muddled superstructure. Only her heavy wooden masts and riggings pay a kind of lip service to the centuries of naval architecture that have gone before. Her four 16-inch muzzle-loading guns, weighing 80 tons each and mounted in turrets like enormous barnacles, are the heaviest ever put in a British ship—"portentous weapons," Mr. Gladstone once remarked of them, "I really wonder the human mind can bear such a responsibility." Her 24-inch iron armor, backed by layers of teak, cork and stacked coal, is the thickest ever made. Her reciprocating engines develop 8,400 horsepower, and are good for 14.75 knots.

Every last device of naval technology equips the *Inflexible.* Two 60-foot steam torpedo boats are mounted on her upper deck. A torpedo-launching gear droops in a sinister way from her bows. Electric lights illuminate the ship, electric alarms ring in the captain's quarters when anything goes wrong. Ballast tanks are designed to keep the vessel steady at sea, and the mazelike passages belowdecks are color-coded for clarity. When those guns have fired their projectiles, they are swiveled inboard and hydraulic machinery rams the next shells up their muzzles. *Inflexible* is an altogether modern instrument of violence, breaking from tradition in a hundred ways. It is not by chance or rote that she is the royal guardship this year; she is seen around the world as the prime contemporary talisman of British naval and technical power—the supreme power, that is, of the age.

For the British Empire is approaching the climax of its brief but spectacular career as the only real superpower. Industrially supreme, thanks to its early mastery of steam, financially secure, socially stable, Queen Victoria's island kingdom has extended its dominance around the world in a manner unexampled since the time of the Romans. Britain now governs about a quarter of the earth's surface. The empire is far more than a mere geopolitical unit: it is an elaborate abstraction of ideas, loyalties, fancies, bluffs, aspirations, exhibitions, deceits and contradictions. The queen of England, now *so much* enjoying her holiday in the south of France, is Empress of India too, and commands the genuine allegiance, together with the compulsory subjection, of hundreds of millions of people of every color in almost every part of the globe. A vast ramshackle thing of infinite nuance and many self-delusions, the British Empire feels itself to be unassailable.

This insolent but alluring assurance, together with the begrudging respect that goes with it, is sustained by the Royal Navy, the oldest and greatest of the world's fleets. It traces its origins to Henry VIII, or Henry V perhaps, or, as romantics claim, to King John, or to the fleet that Alfred created to fight the Danes: but its high-Victorian power is really based upon its successes during the Napoleonic Wars at the start of the century, and in particular to Horatio Nelson's annihilating victory at Trafalgar in 1805. Trafalgar indirectly decreed the shape of nineteenth-century Europe, and proclaimed its peace—only broken since then, in a peripheral way, by the Crimean War of the 1850s. Finding itself beyond challenge, the Royal Navy has developed into an institution of colossal self-esteem. It is a self-appointed arbiter of world affairs, its squadrons scattered throughout the seas maintaining the discipline of the empire and frequently interfering in the affairs of foreigners: "Tell these ugly bastards," Captain William

Pakenham, RN, once instructed his interpreter, having disembarked in Turkey to end a dispute among local bandits that was none of his concern—"tell these ugly bastards that I am not going to tolerate any more of their bestial habits."

By and large, the nineteenth century accepts the Royal Navy at its own valuation. It really does maintain the general tranquillity, after all, besides performing many useful services—charting the ocean, servicing lighthouses, fighting pirates, hindering slave traffic, helping in natural emergencies and often preventing calamities by its mere presence. People still recall with gratitude its Nelsonic days of glory, and around the world there is pleasure when a British squadron sails in, with its flags and bands and glitter, the decorous formality of its protocol, and the balls and entertainments which it arranges with such panache, more than making up for the drunken revelries of its seamen. The navy is the showiest possible display of political strength, far more colorful than any parading army, and there is nothing more magnetic than power exhibited with style: among the admiring visitors to the British battleship *Warrior*, when she first went on display in the 1860s, were six foreign princes, a grand duke, the Turkish viceroy of Egypt, Garibaldi and the entire diplomatic corps of Lisbon.

So it is that the *Inflexible* lies there with that overbearing air, the very exemplar of the Royal Navy's meaning, and a kind of historical cynosure. Horribly wonderful though she is, she is hardly more interesting than your host her captain. At thirty-nine John Arbuthnot Fisher, "Jacky" to his seamen and to the fleet at large, is already an ambivalent legend. His origins are said to be dubious, perhaps half-Oriental. He is as clever as a monkey, and notoriously devious. He has charmed the queen, who loves having him at her villa dinner table. He has apparently bewitched the Lords of Admiralty, who have given him this magnificent command to the chagrin of many seniors. His admirers say he is the most striking personality to have emerged from the Royal Navy since Nelson himself. His enemies call him a schemer, an upstart, a womanizer and a dago, and say he is as brashly alien to the gentlemanly mystique of the service as his ship is to the lovely sailing aesthetic of the past. Already there are few officers of the navy who do not recognize his name, whether in admiration, envy or resentment, and the ugly but fascinating HMS *Inflexible* suits his reputation precisely.

The captain's cutter takes you smartly to the battleship, seamen in wide sennit hats at its oars, burly coxswain at the tiller. The accommodation ladder is down. The lieutenant of the watch courteously salutes and a sprightly midshipman, wearing a starched wing collar but apparently about thirteen years old, officiously takes you in charge. "Follow me, please"—and away you go, rather too fast for comfort, beneath the muzzles of that portentous artillery, down a narrow companionway, along passages painted in bright blues, reds and yellows, through bulkhead doors, squeezing past barefoot respectful sailors, until at last the midshipman, visibly stiffening himself, knocks upon a cabin door. "Captain Fisher, sir," he calls, "your visitors are here"; and in a surprisingly high-pitched and rasping voice from inside we hear the instant response: "Bring 'em in, boy."

A stocky clean-shaven man, inclining to stoutness, rises to his feet as the door opens, in a uniform stylishly cut but informally worn: a big white handkerchief droops from its breast pocket, old-fashioned gold cuff links show below its jacket sleeves. *"Loyal au mort,"* it says on them, "Faithful unto Death." An air of potent oddity surrounds him. His hair falls in a cowlick over his high forehead. His skin is yellowish. His ears are remarkably small. His prominent eyes are a pale gray-brown with unusually small pupils, and his lips are rather thick. His expression looks at first sight supercilious, or arrogant, or possibly voluptuous, but relaxes into a peculiar suggestion of skeptical self-amusement. His mouth is not exactly mocking, but astringent, and with his high cheekbones and slightly slanted eye sockets he really does look a little Asiatic. His presence is *ex officio* commanding, but when he rises light-footed to greet you a smile of quite extraordinary sweetness crosses his face, and the midshipman beside you, the white-coated steward in the corner of the cabin, both smile too, in an almost proprietorial way, as if to say, "What d'you think of our Jacky?"

Well, and what *do* you think of him? If you are a woman, you are likely to be charmed off your feet, but puzzled. At first you wonder if he is really anything more than an extension of his ship, with no life of his own outside that plated labyrinth. Could there be any tenderness in such a man? Would you ever be sure of him? Is there cruelty to his charm, or is he the sort who would always need comforting? There's something disconcerting to those eyes, which sometimes glaze into utter blankness. On the other hand, he does seem stupendously sure of himself. How he flaunts his rank and authority. A lot of merriment is there, too— look at those laugh lines—and the smile is undeniably engaging, even kind. A man worth knowing better, you may decide. A man (though you hardly like to admit it even to yourself, with your own dear one beside you) it might well be fun to love.

If you are a man, suspicion will be your first response. A very odd fish, you may think. A bit of a schemer. That face is decidedly strange—a touch of the tar brush perhaps? One does not like that queer withdrawal into the expressionless. Hardly your English gentleman, and not quite what one expected of the commander of Her Majesty's guardship. A womanizer? Or even, the navy being what it is, a sodomite? And yet, one must admit, the fellow has style. He wears his command like a birthright, whatever his origins. He seems excused the petty anxieties and inconveniences of existence, here on his great ship, secure in his vocation. All in all, you conclude, a man worth the meeting; and though you would never confess it for a moment to your beloved, by Jove, if the truth were told you wouldn't at all mind yourself being Captain J. A. Fisher, Royal Navy, HMS *Inflexible*.

So the pair of you swiftly and silently respond to Fisher's face: but you have little time to think about it, for in a moment he has seized one or the other of you around the waist, and whistling what sounds like some sort of hymn tune, is waltzing you exuberantly around the cabin furniture to the table, where the steward, laughing now, is already pouring the champagne.

A century and more later, almost all these responses to Jack Fisher go through my own mind every morning when I am home in Wales, for tacked inside my closet door is a very large photograph of the man just as he was in 1881: dressed in that same well-tailored, loosely worn captain's uniform, sitting one leg across the other in a posture of inexpressible conceit, and looking over my right shoulder with an air compounded about equally of the suave, the sneering and the self-amused. The face no longer comes as a surprise to me. Apart from those of my family it is the face I know best, far more familiar to me than the features of statesmen, actors, artists or even old friends. Anywhere in the world, by a flick of my fancy, I can summon that picture into my mind, and rehearse once more the mingled emotions that our imaginary visitors felt long ago on the great battleship (whose guns, by the way, were to prove less devastating than they looked, whose ballast tanks did not work, whose masts and riggings were eventually discarded as useless, whose electric circuits repeatedly gave men shocks, and whose career ended ingloriously at the breaker's yard in 1903).

Although Fisher died six years before I was born, he has been one of my life's companions. I first set eyes on him in a photograph sometime in the late 1940s, and knew at once that he was the man for me; and when in a secondhand bookshop I came across a set of his memoirs inscribed in his own hand, his grand and unmistakable calligraphy sealed the conviction. In 1951 I determined to write a book about him, and in letters to magazines and newspapers solicited the help of relatives, colleagues, shipmates or acquaintances. Many of his contemporaries were still living then, and material rained upon me. I heard from people who loved Jack Fisher, and people who detested him, women who were crazy about his memory, men who loathed his guts. I heard from people into whose lives he had briefly brought a glimpse of the unforgettable, and from people who merely remembered his reputation. I was sent letters of his, newspaper cuttings, invitations to reminiscent teatime chats. I was offered evidence of his British Israelite convictions, and promised, from his seagoing days in the Mediterranean, "yarns and anecdotes that would not be suitable for publication." I was given a faded photograph of his aunt Fanny, who could be as rude as Jack, said an accompanying note, but never so charming.

From Bermuda came a memory of the days when meeting a British admiral on an imperial station was like meeting royalty—"the British Empire *was* an Empire then. . . ." An embittered old admiral, quoting a eulogy of Fisher as "a great Christian gentleman," wondered sarcastically if "relentlessness, remorselessness and ruthlessness were really Christian virtues." A former signals officer sent me an expletive signal of Jacky's that he had treasured for half a century. A nonagenarian who kept a curio shop in Cornwall recalled with pride that he had once been Fisher's private cook. An eminent man of letters told me that Fisher was the most remarkable man he had ever met, a naval contemporary characterized him as "a brilliant bastard," a superannuated colonial governor promised me all manner of intimate insights.

Fisher, it seemed, was a Great Englishman, a disgrace to his uniform, a manipulator, a hobgoblin, a damned socialist, a crook, a paragon of kindness, a parvenu, a cad, a genius, a fraud, a delight. Only one thing all were agreed upon: he had a marvelous face.

The more I heard, the more I was enthralled. I was intrigued to discover, too, a series of petty coincidences connecting Fisher's life with mine—places, dates, incidental references that overlapped our two experiences, and made me feel curiously close to him. I was puzzled by the peculiar fascination he seemed to hold for me. Even so, I somehow sensed that I was not ready to write my Fisher book. I repeatedly introduced his name into works of mine on other subjects, and frequently snared people into my interest—as we labored together up the icefall of Everest in 1953, I discover from the autobiography of the mountaineer Michael Ward, I was talking about Jack Fisher. So I was at the Omani hamlet of Firq in 1955, Brigadier Malcolm Dennison of the Muscat and Oman Field Force has recently reminded me—and I made a Fisherian of him, too. But I never got down to the book. From time to time I heard of the death of one or another of my correspondents, who must have thought me horribly ungrateful, and with a pang of guilt learnt from the obituary columns about brave services at sea in World War I, or distinguished contributions to the political and diplomatic life of the 1930s. Fisher's generation was fast disappearing, and when I reread those letters from my informants they began to seem like messages from another society altogether, their values and assumptions remoter every year; but still I stored away their confidences in a pile of box files that acquired, as the decades passed, a patina of age and mildew, and I cherished the project in my heart for the better part of a lifetime.

Not that Fisher has been short of biographers. The destiny of the *Inflexible* was perhaps a little bathetic, but the promise of its captain was fulfilled in just the complex and disturbing way one might have guessed from his appearance. Fisher's whole life was devoted to the Royal Navy. It was his pride and his passion from boyhood to old age, and in its service he was to become an internationally famous man, an Admiral of the Fleet, a peer of the English realm. a member of the Order of Merit and one of the world's powerbrokers. His first full biography appeared in 1926. There was another in 1956, a third in 1970 and a biographical study in 1991. Fisher himself wrote the two volumes of highly idiosyncratic memoirs that I found in the bookshop (five shillings a volume, I see now); he figures in many autobiographies by public men and women of his period, and in innumerable historical works; in the 1950s and 1960s an American academic in Honolulu, Hawaii, published a five-volume analysis of his contribution to naval history, and a three-volume edition of his letters. Nowadays the general public may have forgotten his name, but in his time—a time when admirals were celebrities, and navies full of glamour—"Jacky" Fisher was a star.

. . .

Here are the bare bones of his career, as you might find them in the *Dictionary of National Biography* (where his entry falls, properly enough I think, between those of John Neville Figgis, divine, and Henry Fitzalan-Howard, fifteenth Duke of Norfolk).

He was born in 1841 in Sri Lanka, then the British colony of Ceylon, was sent to England when he was six, and joined the Royal Navy as a cadet when he was thirteen—one of the last to get his officer's training entirely at sea. He did not often go into battle, his being the century of the Pax Britannica, but he served all over the world: in the Baltic during the Crimean War, on the China station during the Opium Wars, in the Mediterranean and the West Indies, at dockyard, gunnery and torpedo establishments in Britain. He commanded frigates, cruisers and battleships. He was at one time or another in charge of the navy's guns, its ships and its personnel. In 1897 he took command of the North Atlantic station, and in 1899 he became commander in chief of the British Mediterranean Fleet, the most influential naval force on earth. Finally Fisher was, for two periods of office, First Sea Lord, the professional chief of the Royal Navy. He died in 1920. In the course of this long career Fisher exerted a profound influence on all the fleets of the world, and transformed his own from a complacent instrument of empire into the modern fighting force that won, or at least did not lose, World War I. Thus he permanently affected all our histories.

He did it with a contempt for the past, a ruthlessness, a disrespect for convention and a capacity for intrigue that made him innumerable enemies. He was accused of nepotism, vengefulness, warmongering, stridency and hubris. He was said to have wrecked the romantic comradeship of the navy, inherited from Nelson's fraternity of captains, the Band of Brothers. If it were not for Fisher's crazed belligerence, it was suggested, the Great War might never have happened. Fisher affected not to care, storming his way through all hazards with a hyperbolic energy, and he was supported by an unshakably loyal coterie of aides, friends and admirers—"the Fishpond": but he was not as invulnerable as he pretended, and in the end something cracked in him, his career petered out in pathos, and an admiral who had seemed a brazen epitome of success finished his life impotently neglected by the navy he adored, and by the state he had served for sixty years.

He married when he was twenty-five, young for a naval officer then, and the union lasted until his wife's death fifty-two years later. They had a son and three daughters ("Fishcakes," the navy called them), and Fisher spoke and wrote lovingly of his Kitty until the day she died. He was, however, a famous philanderer, if only in a platonic kind, flirting shamelessly with women from queens to secretaries, and in the end living apart from his wife with an adoring duchess of his acquaintance. One of his greatest pleasures was dancing, a more suggestive enthusiasm in those days; but another was listening to sermons, for Fisher was fascinated by the Bible, quoting it constantly and colorfully all his life, though more obviously influenced by the Old Testament than the New. He was a radical in many ways, despising class differences or hereditary privileges, having no feel for empire, considerate always for the common seaman; but especially in old age he loved the company of the great, and when he was made a baron, complained that he ought really to be a viscount. Professionally he could be vicious, vindictive and unfair, but in personal affairs, as almost all my informants agreed, Fisher was essentially a kind and sweet-natured man. Women did not invariably love him, but children did.

This life of mingled accomplishment and disappointment, remembered with such ferociously mixed sentiments and summed up in such an unforgettable face, has kept me thinking about Jack Fisher for forty years. Now that at last I am writing my book about him, it will be like declaring my emotions after a secret infatuation. Fisher is still alive for me, and in these pages I shall go wherever he goes, as infatuates do, eavesdropping upon his conversations, reading over his shoulder, picking his brains, seeing what he sees in the fact or in the fancy, gossiping about him as others gossip, interesting myself in his interests and shamelessly trying to feel his feelings. For I know now the nature of Jacky's hold over me. Like the couple assessing him at his cabin door, long ago in the bay of Villefranche, one half of me wants to be loved by him, and the other half wants to be him.

I

SHINING MORNING FACE

Spoiled Boy

King Alfonso XII of Spain was once so pleased by something Fisher said that, if we are to believe Jack, he threw his arms around his neck, kissed him, popped a chocolate into his mouth and cried "You darling!" Jack Fisher was born to be spoiled, and in his maturity he liked to quote the nautical ballad writer Charles Dibdin: "There's a sweet cherub that sits up aloft that looks after the likes of poor Jack." On his very first evening in the navy, he claimed, the first lieutenant of the ship of the line *Calcutta* gave him an orange, and if the fruit was really no more than figurative, the implication was certainly true. "I . . . take so many people in by my manner," Fisher was later to write, and he was never shy in recalling the favors he enjoyed.

The captain and commander of the *Calcutta* "loved me till they died." The captain of the *Pearl* "wants to keep me on board here altogether." The officers of the *Warrior* "kindly spoiled me as if I was the Baby." The captain of the *Furious*, who claimed to have committed every crime in the book except murder, wrote of Fisher that "as a sailor, an officer, a navigator and a gentleman I cannot praise him too highly." The captain of the *Highflyer* was so captivated by him that he gave him a pair of cuff links: they had the captain's own motto on them, and Jack wore them for the rest of his life— we glimpsed them below his coat sleeves on board the *Inflexible.*

Admiral Sir Geoffrey Hornby invited Fisher to live on his flagship while the cabins of his own ship were being painted, and Lady Hornby sent him presents of apples inscribed "To Little Jack Fisher." Admiral Sir Frederick Seymour urged him, when Fisher was convalescent from an illness, to take a battleship wherever he liked. Admiral Sir James Hope promised "he would take care to look out for me always." Vice Admiral Sir Henry Kellett said that "as long as he has me by him to take care of him, he doesn't care what happens." Admiral Sir Leopold McClintock's kindness to him was "unforgettable." When Fisher took lodgings in England as a young officer, the landlord was "like a Father to me," and when the captain of a tramp steamer give him a lift from Malta to Constantinople, "that man and I, till he died, were like David and Jonathan."

Admiral Hope, who was Fisher's commander in chief on the China station, introduced him to the phrase "Favouritism is the Secret of Efficiency," perhaps to excuse his own blatant partisanship for the young lieutenant. Fisher adopted it as his own, and it became one of his most notorious sayings. He meant by it that people of particular ability should be frankly encouraged above their contemporaries: in the beginning he was doubtless thinking chiefly of himself.

. . .

He probably first realized this gift in himself, and realized its advantages too, when at the age of six he was sent alone from Ceylon to live in England. We hear very little about his childhood impressions of the country. He recalled having had "seven hard years" of it there, but in his memoirs he skims somewhat imaginatively over the circumstances, and his biographers are none too specific either. He went to live with his maternal grandfather, Alfred Lambe, a wine merchant living at 149 New Bond Street, London. The site was then next door to a fishmonger's (it is now occupied by Louis Vuitton, the leather-goods people) and Jack must have seemed a quaint little waif indeed, straight from the unimaginably exotic Ceylon, turning up there with his few chattels in the very heart of the West End. Mr. Lambe, so Fisher wrote in his old age, had been deprived of a fortune in Portugal "through the artifices of a rogue"—a sufficiently romantic explanation, perhaps, for the fact that he took in lodgers. The diet he provided his grandson, Jack alleged, consisted of nothing much but boiled rice with brown sugar, except when kindly boarders supplemented it with bread and butter.

When Jack was sent to a boarding school in Coventry, however, he spent some of his holidays at a sumptuous country house, Catton Hall, on the banks of the River Trent in Derbyshire. I visited this place once, and it happened that when I drove up to its entrance on a lovely autumn afternoon, and rang the bell in search of Fisher's memory, who should open the door, with some difficulty, with a certain reaching for knobs and fumbling inside, but a small boy—eight or nine years old. He was very confident and amiable. He told me his parents were out hunting but that I could try later if I liked, he shared my amusement as we said good-bye, he waved me away down the drive, and though he didn't know it himself, for those few moments he had been metamorphosed for me into little Jack Fisher, just the same age, with just the same obliging quick assurance, 140 years before. For Jack doubtless felt more to the manner born at Catton Hall than ever he did in the hard-up wine merchant's lodging house beside the fish shop in Bond Street.

It was Anne Beatrix Wilmot-Horton, widow of a late governor of Ceylon, who thus introduced him to the pleasures of stately living, and so became the first of his innumerable patrons. She was Jack's godmother, although she had never met him until he came to England, and she it was that Byron apostrophized in the lines "She walks in beauty like the night / Of cloudless climes and starry skies; / And all that's best of dark and bright / Meet in her aspect and her eyes." Lady Wilmot-Horton was hospitable, too, and good-natured, and clever, and rich, and in all ways a most desirable surrogate for an absent mother.

At Catton, Fisher was first exposed to the sources of patrician confidence. He was to become something of a swell himself, with a weakness for the grand style, and he probably acquired the taste in the company of Lady Wilmot-Horton, together perhaps with a touch of social resentment and radicalism. He enjoyed for the first time the pleasures of the

English countryside, messing about in the gardens, watching the herons and the rabbits, fishing for perch in the Trent, and he doubtless opened the front door with increasing boldness, like my little host 140 years later, when he could beat the servants to it.

We must suppose him a fascinating child, odd to look at, curiously precocious, with a comical turn of phrase and an enchanting smile. I am sure Lady Wilmot-Horton, whose own children were grown up by then, took pleasure in showing him off to her friends and guests, and when he decided that he wanted to join the navy, she was soon able to fix it. She got in touch with another Derbyshire landowner, Admiral Sir William Parker, who happened to be not only the last survivor of Nelson's captains, but also the admiral in command of the naval base at Plymouth. This job gave him, *ex officio,* the right to nominate two cadets for entry into the Royal Navy, rather as squires held patronage to livings in the Church of England. One nomination he had passed on to a surviving niece of Lord Nelson, to bestow it as she would, but the other, when Lady Wilmot-Horton asked him, he happily gave to Jack Fisher.

It so happened that the Nelsonian niece was also a neighbor at Catton, and she too was persuaded to nominate Jack. Why he plumped for a naval career he was never to explain. He had no family connection with the sea, and no experience of it except the voyage from Colombo, but he had been reading Southey's life of Nelson, and perhaps that inspired him. Whatever the motive, sustained by these illustrious sponsors, hastened by the affectionate string-pulling of Lady Wilmot-

Horton, within a few weeks he was sitting before a naval board of examination at Portsmouth.

Its members were undoubtedly dazzlingly braided—majestically whiskered, too, ample beards and imposing sideburns being almost de rigueur among senior naval officers then. They must have looked formidable indeed to the small boy who, opening the door of the examination room, saw the scene awaiting him there: a bare deal table with books upon it, a single empty chair, a blaze of medals and gold lace and three stern faces looking down at him. Presently, though, the sternness surely relaxed into amusement as the candidate's character revealed itself, and then Jack knew he was home and dry. All successfully spoilt children can recognize that instant: the moment when they have won over the adults, or the interviewers, or the bosses, or the senior officers, just as performers know precisely the moment when they have captured their audiences.

By his own account all that Fisher had to do to join the Royal Navy was to write out the Lord's Prayer, say the three times table, jump over that chair and join his interrogators in a glass of sherry. Is it true? Not in the fact, for there had already been a written test and a medical examination, but true certainly in the import, for Fisher's ability to charm his superiors was to be crucial to his career. Very soon afterward he was charming another. He formally entered the service in HMS *Victory*, Nelson's old flagship, afloat still as a headquarters ship at Portsmouth, but his first seagoing vessel was the 84-gun *Calcutta*, lying along the coast at Plymouth. Before boarding her he was invited to dine with his nominator, Admiral Parker, the commander in chief. The admiral's house still stands, a fine Georgian mansion looking over the Devonport roads toward the dockyards on the western bank, where the warships lie now as then; it is pleasant to fancy the thirteen-year-old on the edge of his chair in its dining room, enjoying an urbane evening of good food and naval reminiscences with the old sailor and his wife.

After dinner Jack said in all gravity that it was time he "joined his ship," but the Parkers persuaded him to stay the night at Admiralty House, and so it was in the admiral's own picketboat that he went off next morning, with his bag and his Bible, to become a sailor himself.

Concerning Origins

Fisher was always to boast, nevertheless, that he entered the navy "penniless and forlorn," and it was true that his good luck he chiefly created for himself. His origins were not much help, in his own as in the navy's eyes. He was really hardly more than an orphan of empire, sent home from the colonies to make his own life, and by his own abilities he did it.

His mother seems to have been the snag. She was Sophy Lambe, a Londoner who had the misfortune to marry a coffee planter in Ceylon at the very moment when the Ceylonese coffee boom collapsed. She had gone out to the island to keep house for her brother Frederic, another planter—a common practice in those days, saving "many a young fellow," as a Victorian moralist put it, "from drink and ruin," and offering young women a good chance of finding a husband. Sure enough, in 1840 Sophy married Captain William Fisher, an army officer serving as aide-de-camp to the governor of the colony, Sir Robert Wilmot-Horton.

Hardly were they wed than Captain Fisher quit the army and bought himself two coffee estates in the central highlands of the island. Coffee had first been planted in Ceylon in the 1820s, and had inspired a kind of running mania among speculators. For years every Briton on the island wanted a part of it, even governors, and William Fisher joined the craze at its tumultuous height, in 1841. In the very same year the bubble burst, and from then on life for the Fishers was downhill all the way. They were condemned to scrape a living ever after, the properties making such losses that William was obliged to accept a temporary and ill-paid job as chief superintendent of police, while Sophy proceeded with her wifely duties of producing eleven children, four of whom died in infancy.

In photographs Fisher *père* looks handsome enough, in a raffish way, but ineffectual. He was said to have come from a line of English landed gentry and clergymen that had once been very grand. In the seventeenth century Sir Clement Fisher, Baronet, lived at Packington, in Warwickshire, on a truly magnificent estate (now incorporating a championship golf course). Later the family splendors evidently declined. The Fisher baronetcy went into abeyance, the estate was lost, and by the early nineteenth century the family was represented more modestly, and more certainly, by the Reverend John Fisher, rector of Wavendon in Buckinghamshire, so archetypal a village of the shires that along the road was a pillar traditionally claimed to mark the very center of England. It was from here that William Fisher, son of the rector and incongruously a captain in Her Majesty's 78th Highlanders, went out to seek his fame and fortune in Ceylon.

He found neither, and he died in Ceylon from a fall from a horse after thirty-five years in the country. Jacky Fisher saw his father for the last time when he was six years old, but remembered him tenderly always, preferring to recall him as a handsome, brave and soldierly figure of the frontiers. The few letters that William wrote to the little boy are wan but endearing, urging young Jack to work hard and say his prayers, advising him not to care about other men's opinions and apologizing that he could send so little pocket money— "You have a great many brothers and sisters . . ."

His father's memory was important to Jack, surrounded as he was to be in the Royal Navy by colleagues steeped in English heritage. He knew very well that rivals regarded him as an upstart, an oddball or even a half-caste, and he doubtless felt obliged to compensate, if only in his own mind. He liked to remember the Warwickshire baronets, their tombs at Packington "going back into the dark ages"—the four generations of Fisher clergymen at Bodmin in Cornwall (not recorded, I may say, in the list of rectors in the parish church)—the Fisher whose motto was *Ubi voluntas, ibi piscatur*, "We fish where we like"—the Fisher who was "over 60 years a fellow of Magdalen College, Oxford"—his great-uncle mortally wounded at Wellington's side at the Battle of Waterloo—his grandfather at Wavendon, whom he wishfully characterized (they never met) as "a splendid old parson of the fox-hunting type"—his father the 78th Highlander and ADC to the governor of Ceylon. They were English gentlemen all.

His mother was another matter. She sprang from the London commercial classes. Jack unconvincingly maintained that William had married her for her beauty, and he liked to claim that her grandfather was John Boydell the eighteenth-century engraver, who was also lord mayor of London. She was more probably his great-niece (Boydell had no children, not in wedlock anyway), and her beauty must have been in the beholder's eye. In photographs she looks terrible. An elegant painting of her is reproduced in Admiral Sir Reginald Bacon's biography of Fisher (1929), but I strongly suspect the picture to be of somebody else altogether, and in his text Bacon can only bring himself to say that Sophy was "of strong build and determined appearance." This she certainly was, and I would guess that she was the commander of the Fisher family in Ceylon. There is to her presence some of Jack's own compelling assurance—it is not impossible to fancy her hitching up her black skirts and throwing back her veil to issue the orders on a quarterdeck. She reminds me sometimes of Truganini, the last Tasmanian aboriginal, and sometimes of Liliuokalani the final queen of the Hawaiians: there is something at once regal and condemned to the heavy-jowled calculation of her face.

But who would not look condemned, saddled with an improvident husband in early-Victorian Ceylon, enduring more or less constant childbirth in the tropics? Even those of her children who survived were taken from her, sent back to England to be educated and find their own place in the world. Jack, the eldest, went when she was twenty-seven, and one after the other his four brothers and two sisters went too. Captain William Fisher died when Sophy was forty-six, broken one feels by all the mischances of the colonial life: she then followed her little ones to England, impecuniously.

Jacky Fisher's earlier years were spent at Wavendon, the first of his father's coffee plantations. It was named after Captain Fisher's boyhood village, and formed part of the scattered settlement of plantations called Rambodda, some 3,500 feet up in the hills. In those days the district was almost inconceivably remote, a countryside of wild ravines and waterfalls, impenetrable forests and cloud-enveloped hills. There were no proper roads, and the plantation houses were only one stage removed from the log cabins of pioneers. The whole place swarmed with wildlife—monkeys, tortoises, deer, leopards, jackals, wild elephants, cranes, parakeets. The cicadas were deafening in the afternoon. Glowworms flew about in showers, butterflies in multitudes, fruit bats stank in the woods. It was not an easy place to raise a family. Years ago, poking around in the old British churchyard at Pussellawa, close to Rambodda, I came across the graves of three siblings, aged four, three and nearly two, who had all died within two days, September 14 and 15, 1866: they were thought at the time to have been accidentally poisoned by viper grass in a rhubarb tart, but they had really all died of cholera, and it was only long afterward that I realized them to have been the children of Fisher's own sister Alice.

There were to be Fishers in Ceylon for several generations, and some are remembered in the Anglican church in the hill station of Nuwara Eliya. Three of Jack's own siblings are commemorated there, and so is Captain William Fisher himself. Wavendon still exists, too, though it would hardly be recognizable to its founders. Behind it the hills still rise rugged and forested into the clouds, but the wildlife has mostly made itself scarce. Tea is the crop now, and the land-scape below is a thick green carpet of shrubs, so well tended as to look almost suburban. The original plantation house has been repeatedly altered and extended, its rooms all swal-lowed up; the simple coffee sheds of Jack's childhood have long been replaced by a big tea factory. The Fishers are alto-gether forgotten there, nobody has heard of Jack and nobody remembers how Wavendon got its name. One of my corre-spondents told me that in the 1930s, at least, a patch of land there was still known as *fishermalai*—"fisherfield"; but hard though I tried, I could catch no glimpse of the little boy's stumpy figure playing among the tea gardens.

Jack's younger brother Frederic, "Billy" to the family, re-called life in this outpost of empire cheerfully enough, if in a stereotyped colonial way: climbing trees, riding horses, watching his father hunt elephants, swimming in rock pools, playing barefoot in the wild. Jack recorded almost nothing of it. He was never greatly interested in nature, he was not a sportsman and he seems to have had no feeling for animals, so possibly the images of primitive Ceylon made little im-pression on him. As it happens my own life's partner was born on a plantation not far from Wavendon, and she too was sent away in her seventh year: judging by her experience, Jack Fisher's adult memories of Ceylon were perhaps just a blur of shade and sunshine, heat and lemonade, horses, tea things on the veranda, a pet baby elephant, a bird in a wooden cage—all of them presently becoming, parents, animals, home, bird and all, little more than shadows in the memory.

In Fisher's case the faded recall may have been half deliberate. He viewed his immediate family equivocally, and in later life preferred on the whole to have little to do with it. Two of his brothers followed him into the Royal Navy, Frederic becoming an admiral too, Philip drowning at sea as a young lieutenant. The two others, Bertram and Frank, returned as civil servants to Ceylon, where Bertram committed suicide in middle age. Alice, the elder sister, married another coffee planter in Ceylon. Lucy, the younger, married an army officer. There was only one occasion, it seems, when these seven children were all together—in England in 1865, when they assembled to have a group photograph taken.

In it Jack, the eldest, looks properly proud of himself as head of the family, and when his brothers and sisters were young he seems to have been kind and helpful to them all. He encouraged Frederic to join the navy. He was distressed when Philip's ship, the training ship *Atalanta,* vanished without trace in the Caribbean in 1880. On his only return visit to Ceylon, with the frigate *Ocean* in 1872, he was immensely taken with Frank—a perfect specimen of a man, he said, with "a sort of bold careless proud way about him." He corresponded regularly with his sisters, and kept a keen eye on the family finances.

Gradually, though, he drew away from them all, beginning with Alice, whose children's graves I stumbled across at Pussellawa. After that terrible loss she and her husband returned to England, where he took Holy Orders but presently died. Alice went on to marry a first cousin, and this peculiarly antagonized Jack Fisher; supposedly because he disapproved of such incestuous unions, he swore that he would never again speak either to Alice or to her husband, and he never did. The marvelous Frank he appears to have lost all touch with. Lucy left his life. Unhappy Bertram he never mentioned. Frederic grew up to be a cheerfully successful officer in the standard mold, known to the navy as Uncle Bill because of his genial habits and avuncular attitudes to young women, but in later life he learnt to steer clear of the disturbing virtuoso that Jack was to become. When Fisher came to have children of his own, he kept them strangely in ignorance of all their aunts and uncles, except the unavoidable Billy.

But it was Sophy who brought out the most neurotic in Fisher. I hesitate to mention Jack and Sigmund Freud in the same sentence, so fiercely would they have distrusted each other, but I have to say that Fisher seems to have suffered from a severe maternal complex. He loved to boast that he was weaned very late—the secret of his vigor, he claimed— but he was never close to his mother. After saying good-bye to her when he was six, he claimed to have "not the slightest recollection of her" by the time he met her again twenty-five years later, and said he had none of the feelings of a son for his mother. He hastily dissuaded her when she once thought of visiting him in Hong Kong, admitting frankly enough that he was "in a horrid fright of my Mother some day turning up unexpectedly." Enviously moved by other men's maternal loyalties, and horrified to imagine what it would be like if his own children did not love him, nevertheless when the widowed Sophy returned to England needing money, Fisher was not pleased.

I fear he was haunted by the guilt of this inadequate affection, making up for it only, it appears, with a financial allowance in Sophy's old age and extravagant fictions about her beauty in his own. When he was a lieutenant on the China station there reached him through the mail from Ceylon a photograph of Mrs. Fisher, evidently on glass. It was thirteen years since he had set eyes on her, but when he removed the wrappings his mother's severe face looked back at him in fragments. I can imagine the sad symbolism of the moment filling his eyes with regretful tears. He stuck the picture together again, and wrote of the experience: "I can hardly believe it is my mother when I look at it. She seems so young . . . Well! women are very deceptive in everything. I have found that out in the short time I have been in the world."

Poor Sophy lived out her days very modestly in London, seldom intruding upon Jack's progress toward fame and power: and when the time came, in 1895, she slid out of his life almost imperceptibly, and is buried who knows where.

There were always other women to see him through. In his eighteenth year, as a lieutenant on the China station, he was detailed by his admiral to call upon Lady Robinson, wife of the governor of Hong Kong, in the brand-new Government House above the harbor (the colony, coincidentally the subject of another of my books, was born in the same year as Fisher himself). While he was there, a Mrs. Coutts was announced. "I was off like a shot," he wrote the same day, "just fancy facing two strange females all by myself . . ." But I don't believe a word of it. He was in his element—the fascinating young lieutenant, already marked out as a man of promise, so easily delighting those middle-aged colonial ladies, while Chinese servants shuffled and bowed around the drawing room with cakes and fresh hot water.

He knew how to please women, and he needed them. He felt the absence of a mother, however ambiguous his feelings about Sophy. He no doubt missed the attentions of Lady Wilmot-Horton and the doting chatelaines of Derbyshire. It was hardly surprising that he found for himself, during his first long tour of foreign duty, a woman confidante so obviously a mother substitute that he actually addressed her as Mams, or as Mammy. Mrs. Edmund Warden was the wife of the P&O manager in Shanghai, and as such she often met officers of the British warships operating in Chinese waters. Many looked to her for auntly affection—treats and parties when they put into Shanghai, the odd service that she could arrange for them through her husband's office. Jack Fisher demanded rather more, and the letters he wrote to her are full of poignancy between the lines.

How proud he is to tell her when he is promoted, how upset when she asks somebody else to do some shopping for her in Japan, how touchingly eager to let her know when a captain commends him, a dispute goes his way, he wins a competition or passes an examination! "Dear Mams," he writes when he is promoted to lieutenant, "You should see me in my scales and full-dress coat, such a beauty! One can't help hearing as one walks along people saying 'Who's that? By George, a handsome fellow!' " Or: "I say, Mams, I am not proud, you know, but mind you don't get making a mistake and address to J. A. Fisher, Esq., instead of *Lieut. J. A. Fisher,* R.N. Now you need not laugh!!" Or: "Hurrah! Well done, Mams, you are a real, jolly, good, good, good old party. I got your letter yesterday and the parcel . . ." Or: "I forgot to tell you that I was very nearly SEASICK. Just fancy a fine Lieutenant being seasick . . . If you say anything to anyone, I will never speak to you again, *there!"*

These are the earliest known letters of Jack Fisher, who was to become one of the most prolific, original and entertaining of English letter writers. We know of none to his mother, and it was to Mrs. Warden that he confided his feelings when that photograph of Sophy arrived shattered through the mail. Beneath the full-dress coat he was only a child—"the great child," the London *Times* still called him when he went to his grave sixty-two years later.

II

LOOK ON THIS FACE
YE MIGHTY

The Pageant

With the infatuate eye we can see John Fisher at the very moment when, in Victorian theory anyway, he became a man. His baptism of fire, his first taste of action (and almost his last), occurred in his sixteenth year, in 1857, on a waterway called the Fatshan Creek near Guangzhou in China. There the Chinese, resisting Western encroachment in what came to be called the Opium Wars, had massed a fleet of more than 100 well-armed war junks; and there the British Navy set out to destroy them.

They sent seven paddle-gunboats up the river, towing behind them rowing-boats full of sailors, and if we go up there now on the hydrofoil from Hong Kong to the spanking new ferry-port of Pingzhou, we can see it happening still. There stand the towering junks, blocking the stream in two massed flotillas. Here come the gunboats, firing left and right. The rowing-boats are slipped for the assault, each flying a huge White Ensign at its stern, armed with a big brass cannon in the bows, and commanded by a midshipman with drawn sword. We hear a great cheer go up—"one of those British cheers so full of meaning," says a participant, "that I knew at once it was all up with John Chinaman"—and furiously the sailors throw themselves upon those junks. There is a frenzy of esoteric war cries, signal rockets, gunshots, whistles, shouted commands, explosions. Captain Thomas Shadwell, Fellow of the Royal Society, readies himself for the fight in his blue tailcoat, yellow waistcoat and tall white hat, and belligerently brandishes an umbrella. Commodore Henry Keppel, approaching the battle in a ship's gig together with his Irish setter Mike and His Royal Highness Prince Victor Hohenlohe, a nephew of Queen Victoria, finds the boat shot away beneath him, and shaking a fist at the enemy yells, "You rascals, I'll get back at you for this!" The junks are stormed, set on fire, sunk and scattered. Captain the Honorable Arthur Auckland Leopold Pedro Cochrane, son of the founder of the Chilean navy, chases the last of them hell-for-leather upstream and out of sight. Commodore Keppel and Prince Victor are rescued. Mike rejoins the fleet.

And in the middle of the melee, "armed to the teeth like a Greek brigand," we see young Jack Fisher, in command of one of the rowing-boats, yelling like everybody else, blowing his whistle, brandishing his saber, clambering over junks, chasing Chinese, cheering again as victory becomes clear and returning to his ship, the paddle-sloop *Highflyer*, sweaty and exhilarated, if not actually bloody with manhood.

A caustic historian of Hong Kong, G. R. Sayer, suggested of the Battle of Fatshan Creek that, there being a lively market at that time for lithographs of naval engagements, it was fought to provide a profitable subject. He had a point. As the nineteenth century passed the British Navy became more a

pageant than a fighting force. Spectacle was an important
tool of imperial dominion, expressed in architecture, in ritual, in bearing, in military display, in the show of history, and
above all, perhaps, in the swaggering and emotionally
charged confidence of the fleet. One of its own officers, in a
rare moment of poetry, summed the navy up as "a two-fisted,
free-living, implacable, tragic, jovial, splendid service," and
although Queen Victoria was not altogether enamored of
it, since it had declined to make her German-born husband
an Admiral of the Fleet, the nation as a whole thought it
splendid.

In the late 1850s, when Jack became a lieutenant, the fleet
numbered some 5,000 officers and 55,000 men. At the head of
it was the ancient Board of Admiralty in London, presided
over by four Naval Lords, occupying an exquisite series of
buildings in Whitehall, and so entrameled in tradition and
old privilege that it was (for example) patron to the church
living of Alston with Garrigill and Humshaugh. The navy
was disposed in eight main fleets, strewn around the entire
world, and in the year 1858 alone British gunboats were
called upon to display the spectacle of empire, as a pacific or
a punitive influence, in New Zealand, Panama, the Kuria
Muria Islands, Honduras, Thailand, Brazil, Sarawak, Egypt,
western Canada, Veracruz, Morocco, Newfoundland and the
coast of China.

The long saga of sail was coming to an end. The British
Admiralty had been quick to seize the advantages of steam,
and the needs of the Crimean War hastened the process. The
navy's ships had masts and riggings still, but almost all its

major vessels—some 425 of them—were equipped with steam engines too, and were driven by screws or paddles (only in 1981 did the Royal Navy's last paddle-tug go to the breaker's yard). It was a time of epochal transition in naval technique, and this made the pageant all the more colorful. Many of the big ships still looked more or less like the ships of the line at Trafalgar, their wooden hulls painted in the familiar checkerboard black and white, bristling with broadside guns, with painted figureheads and generally only a pair of black telescopic funnels betraying the presence of engines within. On the other hand, the steam gunboats, built of iron and mounting the biggest possible guns in the smallest possible hulls, were the very opposite of the wooden walls, and when one of these tough little craft splashed by the three-decker *Achilles*, for instance (built in 1798), or saluted an admiral in his stately sailing barge, it was like seeing the ages pass.

For the most part the navy preferred *Achilles* and the barge. Some of its most ambitious officers soon realized that an understanding of steam was the way to distinction, but the majority resented its arrival. For one thing the wooden sailing ship had been brought to a peak of technical perfection, and their mastery of it was legendary. For another the myth and beauty of sail was essential to their feeling for their profession: they were like cavalrymen, a century later, obliged to convert to tanks. They argued that the wind was free, that sailing ships needed no coaling stations, and that mechanical ships would always be unreliable. They agreed with the navy's standard instruction book when it decreed in 1862:

"There is no greater fallacy than to suppose that ships can be navigated on long voyages without masts and sails." Some captains preferred never to use their engines at all. Nearly all believed that the ability to handle a sailing ship was infinitely more gentlemanlike than a knowledge of steam engines.

Fortunately for them the captains were left largely to their own devices. They called the British Navy the best of all yacht clubs, but its ships were semiautonomous clubs of their own. Until 1857 there was not even a general uniform, at least for ratings, who were dressed according to the fancy of their commanding officers—the men of the *Caledonia* wore Scottish bonnets. Ships were painted in a variety of colors. Some had white waterlines, some yellow, some captains preferred their ships' boats blue rather than white, some spent large sums of money on gold leaf for ornamental purposes. Captains often took their own civilian chefs to sea with them, along with their domestic pets, and they decorated their quarters in the full Victorian elaboration of trinkets, potted palms, and antimacassars.

These idiosyncrasies could feed upon all manner of inherited custom, part of the very ethos of the Royal Navy: the giving of orders by drum and bos'n's pipe, the flying of innumerable flags, the music of shipboard bands—violins, violas, cellos, euphoniums, clarinets—or the free cask of ox-tongues, which, by immemorial tradition, was delivered to a captain upon the commissioning of his ship.

The ratings accepted all the flummery as part of the nature of their job. They were a rough-and-ready lot. I have beside me a photograph of the men of the warship *Coquette,* taken in 1855, and they look less like a military body than a group of hippies from the 1960s. Some are bearded, some are heavily side-whiskered, all are barefoot, and they are dressed in an easy variety of loose smocks and caps, with lanyards round their necks. One or two look piratical, and a few I would pre- fer not to bump into on a dark night in Portsmouth. At the side of the picture three men are making music, on violin, fife and drum, and in the foreground sits a villainous-looking pair of pet monkeys.

The captain of such a ship was paid £365 per annum, an able seaman got £23, and in every other way too the gulf be- tween officers and men was extreme. All the ratings were now volunteers, mostly from the seaport towns of southern England, but in many respects their lives had not much changed since the days of the press-gang. Their candlelit quarters were squalid, their hammocks were slung all among the guns, their food was monotonous and the peacetime mor- tality rate among them was more than twice the British na- tional average. They smoked and chewed a lot of tobacco, and they were notoriously prone to syphilis ("ladies' fever") and to drunkenness—the latter encouraged by the navy's hallowed custom of serving them one-eighth of a pint of rum at twelve-thirty each day, the equivalent of two double whiskeys. Years ago in South Africa I watched some colored workers on a Cape vineyard receiving part of their daily ra- tion of red wine—a bottle and a quarter a day, as the law then required: as they shambled blearily off, drinking the wine out of old baked-bean tins, I was reminded of the sailors of the Royal Navy, long before, returning to their duties after the daily splicing of the mainbrace. Minor mutinies were common, and desertion was always a temptation, especially in desirable foreign ports: when a British admiral went ashore in San Francisco during the 1848 gold rush, so the story goes, his entire boat crew ran away to the goldfields, and he had to find his own way back to his flagship. Flogging was still a frequent punishment.

Despite it all, they generally seem to have maintained an astonishing degree of cheerfulness and esprit de corps, and except perhaps for the Americans were generally agreed to be the best body of naval sailors in the world. They were usually proud of their ships, and of the navy itself, and since they signed on for at least ten years, and were likely to have served in every corner of the globe, in every kind of duty, they became as they grew older very repositories of naval lore, tradition and experience. Another photograph I have is a portrait, taken in 1859, of Able Seaman John Reeman, of the second-rate *London*. He looks a tough nut indeed, ready to take thirty lashes anytime or disappear into the goldfields if given a chance, but ready to fight well too, stick by a comrade, give a woman a good if tipsy night out, tie an utterly reliable knot or blasphemously take charge of a boat when all seems lost—in short, somebody I would much rather have as my friend than as my enemy.

There were men not unlike John Reeman among the officers too, for this was an age of feral adventurers, and all over the empire British gentlemen were demonstrating their ruthless contempt for convention or compromise. The navy's officer corps, when Jack Fisher entered it, was a marvel of variety and originality. Its average age was high, because promotion was nearly always by seniority; except for misconduct no officer could be forcibly retired. Her Majesty's ships carried many midshipmen hardly into their teens, but there were sixty-year-old lieutenants, too; Admiral Parker was still in command at Portsmouth when he was in his eighties, while the commander in chief on the China station in the mid-1850s had not previously been to sea for thirty-one years.

Traditionally the navy was not so much aristocratic as gentlemanly. It had been parliamentary rather than royalist in the English Civil War, and Nelson's Band of Brothers were mostly, like Nelson himself, men of the upper middle classes. By the middle of the century it had acquired a more patrician appeal, and though it still did not possess the social cachet of a Guards regiment, or the cavalry, nevertheless it was speckled with grandees. It was also rich in originals, expressing their pride and high spirits in every kind of bizarre behavior, in excesses of toughness or foppery, in peculiar dress and verbal affectation, in preposterous devotion to tradition or convention, in weird hobbies and pithy nicknames (of which my own favorites are The Swell of the Ocean Wave, given to the prodigiously urbane Admiral Sir Beauchamp Seymour, and Old 'Ard 'Art, which is what they called a stony-faced ascetic called A. K. Wilson).

They were nearly all fine seamen, though; they were often quick, witty and worldly, and among them there were many professionals seriously devoted to the science of their calling, and eager to advance it.

Such was the semiprivate world into which Jack Fisher was initiated halfway through the Victorian century, to spend the rest of his days in its ambiance. The same names recur throughout his career, and men who served with him in the days of sail and paddles were still part of his life in the twentieth century—A. K. Wilson, for example, Old 'Ard ' Art, who was to be his perennial familiar. Aesthetically, as it were, Fisher was wonderfully suited to the Victorian navy. Its ostentatious flair, its humor and its gossipy cussedness were just his style, and he precociously embraced it. By the time he was nineteen he had briefly commanded one of Her Majesty's warships, the paddle-sloop *Coromandel* (1,200 tons). I often used to see him when I lived beside the Lyman Channel in Hong Kong, where the traffic goes by for the Pearl River—among the myriad freighters and sampans, the foaming hydrofoils, the chugging lopsided ferries and the swarming fishing boats, elegant and immaculate the racing *Coromandel,* with Lieutenant Fisher in a snub-peaked cap and a mess jacket lording it on the bridge.

And I have been at close quarters with him on board HMS *Warrior,* to which he was appointed gunnery officer in his twenty-second year. This was a crucial turn in his career. The *Warrior* was the first oceangoing iron warship—not built of wood and clad in iron plate, but built of iron throughout—and she was the largest, fastest and most powerful ship of her time. I have known her for many years, because she ended her active service, stripped of all upper-works, forlorn and unrecognizable as a fueling hulk at Doc Penfro, Pembroke Dock in Wales. Whenever I saw her I thought of Fisher, but in the 1970s she brought him far more vividly to life for me when she was rescued from her degradation, miraculously restored and taken to Portsmouth, where she now lies beside a wharf almost at the very spot where Jack joined the navy. Boarding her today really is like reentering the nineteenth century. Everything is in place, engines to fire buckets, everything looks brand-new, and I know of nowhere, on land or sea, that offers a more palpable re-creation of the past.

The officers' cabins are aft, and are hardly more than cubicles. I picked one as Fisher's to my fancy's satisfaction, when I visited the ship in 1992; and I was picturing his few possessions there—that patched-up photograph of his mother perhaps, a portrait of Lady Wilmot-Horton, a prayer book, pen and ink, a print of Trafalgar—when above the clamor of the tourists and the scamper of schoolchildren I heard another sound, out of the past. It was the noise of an improvised band, and presently around the upper deck I saw a little procession prancing. J. A. Fisher, the gunnery lieutenant, led the way, playing a tune on a brown-paper kazoo. Behind him came the chaplain, banging on a coal scuttle, the doctor with a pair of tongs and a shovel, and in the rear the venerable paymaster clashing the lid on a tin kettle. *Thump thump, tootle tootle* they marched by, with Fisher waving a beat with his left hand and the laughter of seamen echoing all around the ship.

"What's that confounded noise?" I heard a voice shouting from the captain's cabin on the deck below—the familiar voice of Captain the Honorable Arthur Auckland Leopold Pedro Cochrane, victor of Fatshan Creek. There was a sudden silence. The procession halted in its tracks, Fisher's hand in midair. Then the duty sentry answered. "It's only Mr. Fisher, sir," he said.

The captain merely grunted, and the band struck up again.

A Fine Fellow

They may have treated him like a baby in the *Warrior*, but it was not for long. Fisher's pleasures would always be rather juvenile, his humor often adolescent, his conversations and even his official dispatches laced with fun. Nevertheless he soon developed a masterly and unpredictable presence that enthralled many people, and scared many others to death. "He prowled around with the steady rhythmical tread of a panther," a subordinate remembered not so many years later. "The quarterdeck shook and all hands shook with it."

As we know, by the time he assumed command of the *Inflexible* in 1881, he was a fine fellow indeed. He had perfected his voice of command, partly by drilling imaginary men on the hills behind Portsmouth, and he gave his authority showy nuances that were all his own. He always looked younger than his age, but even in his thirties he could appear astonishingly omnipotent when he wished, and the effect was accentuated by his unnerving habit of falling suddenly now and then into a mood of enigmatic abstraction. When he once took a squadron of ships to pay a call upon the governor of Tetuán, the governor later revealed what had most impressed him about the fleet. It was not the great guns, the discipline, the immaculate paintwork or the mighty reciprocating engines. It was Fisher's face.

The older he got, the more exotic that face became. Sometimes, when he twisted his mouth down in one of his scornful moments, and raised his eyebrows superciliously, it could look positively Chinese, and one could suppose him dressed in long brocades and gilded slippers. His enemies in the navy made much of this. It proved his unreliable origins, they claimed, and he was variously nicknamed the Half-Caste, the Oriental, the Mulatto, the Siamese or the Yellow Peril. The German naval attaché in London once described him in an official dispatch to Berlin as an "unscrupulous . . . half-Asiatic." Fisher seemed not to care about these insinuations, except when they upset his family; he used to joke about his oriental duplicity, and perhaps rather relished the popular rumor that he was the love child of a Singhalese princess.

He was certainly proud of his remarkable looks, molding them as an actor might into a sort of living art form. "A great painter," he wrote with satisfaction in his old age, "unsuccessfully attempted my portrait and tore up canvas after canvas and observed he could have done it had I only had a thick moustache! but my mouth was impossible to depict! At one moment diabolical—the next angelic!" There was a strong trace of narcissism to Jack Fisher, from his earliest days to his last, and if it contributed to his conceit, it also added to the disturbing magnetism of his presence. He was, thought the writer Esther Meynell, "a mixture of Machiavelli and a child, which must have been extraordinarily baffling to politicians and men of the world."

Everybody agreed that he looked like nobody else. I have studied his face for four decades, and it still puzzles me. For a time I thought the combination of slightly Mongolian looks and a naturally sunny nature might be signs of Down's syndrome, vestigially suffered, but doctors told me this was medically impossible. Then I considered the possibility that Fisher really was half-Singhalese. Sometimes I could fancy a sort of spectral resemblance in old pictures of noblemen of Kandy, some of whose faces were more or less the right shape, and who were certainly sufficiently striking of appearance, wearing as they did embroidered quadricorn hats, puffed sleeves and swathed ceremonial aprons that made them look distinctly pregnant; but I could hardly believe that Mrs. Fisher, wife to the ADC of the governor of Ceylon, would get away with such a mésalliance in the colonial society of the 1840s (and I could have no doubt that Captain Fisher was Jack's father—that photograph of Aunt Fanny of Wavendon, all the force but none of the charm, made it indisputable).

A less unlikely explanation, I have lately come to think, lies in later photographs of Sophy Fisher. If she looks an English rosebud in that apocryphal painting, later she grew to appear distinctly foreign—and in particular, perhaps, Iberian. I remembered Jack's tales about his maternal grandfather's being defrauded by some alien scoundrel, remembered too his talk of a lost property in Portugal; and so I reached the novelettish surmise that respectable Mr. Lambe, wine merchant of New Bond Street, had perhaps been ruined by an illicit relationship with some lady of Oporto. A dark little daughter, shipped off as soon as possible to her brother in the colonies, a marriage somewhat above her station to a gentlemanly Englishman, and lo! John Arbuthnot Fisher comes ethnically tantalizing into the world.

He was not a tall man, standing about five feet seven inches in his prime. For this he blamed the miserable diet of midshipmen in his youth—"their little bellies were never full." He held himself very erect, though, and adjusted his posture according to circumstance. There are pictures of him in later life with various figures of royalty, and there he has adopted a distinctly courtly pose; on the other hand there is a photograph of him as admiral-superintendent of Portsmouth Dockyard that makes him seem almost an impersonation of Isambard Kingdom Brunel, the engineer—the legs wide apart, the frock coat unbuttoned, the cap tilted like Brunel's stovepipe hat, a pair of gloves held aggressively in one hand as Brunel might hold a cigar, and a look on his face of down-to-earth, steam-whistle, double-shift determination.

His clothes were always smart, and do not seem archaic even now. At a time when naval officers could freely adapt their uniforms, Fisher's were always distinctive. He wore his jackets rather long, his cravats casually, and a handkerchief almost always protruded with a calculated flourish from his breast pocket. In civilian life he liked to wear double-breasted reefer jackets, spats which were sometimes blue, and a sort of cut-down top hat that was technically defined, so Lock's the hatters of St. James's Street kindly tell me, as a square-crowned bowler. Clothes were important to him, and contributed importantly to his persona. His grandson, the third Lord Fisher, once put on for me Jack's dark-blue great-coat, a magnificent ankle-length affair collared and cuffed in astrakhan, lined with gray squirrel and extremely heavy; and as he stood there in this splendid garment, offering me a family smile of particular gentle charm, it was miraculously as though I were looking at the old sailor himself, brought back to earth in one of his sweeter moods.

I find it hard to think of Fisher as a man among men in the full-blooded all-male society of the Victorian navy. The off-duty memories he recalls for us—playing the fool with the chaplain and the paymaster, taking tea with the governor's wife, going for walks—all seem remarkably innocuous. He smoked cigarettes and cigars, but never to excess. He drank moderately. He was no glutton, and he does not seem to have shared the puerile fondness for practical jokes common among his peers. He once told Esther Meynell that he had some stories unsuitable for her ears, but as he had just been telling them to the dean of Westminster I doubt if they were very shocking. In writing at least, his language was so fastidious that he would seldom even use the word "damn," only "d——n," and the nearest I have found to the Rabelaisian in his humor was a joke about The Souls, the Cambridge aesthetic and intellectual coterie: "Souls have no testicles *(That's copyright!)."* Fisher did not shoot, he played little sport and was a dedicated churchgoer.

Did he ever get really drunk? Did he ever visit a brothel? Did he swear? Did he ever tell a dirty story? Who is to know? There is a telling reference to Fisher's contemporaries in Ford Madox Ford's *The Good Soldier*: the "cleanest-looking sort of chap," says the book's narrator, might delightedly throw himself about in his smoking-room chair when he heard a gross story. Margot Asquith, wife of the prime minister, once reported Fisher as being "at his gayest and coarsest." I suspect, though, that his "coarsest" was no more than music-hall ribaldry. One of the reasons his shipmates spoiled him was his willingness to stand watch for them when they went roistering ashore; even as a young lieutenant he was happy to stay on board indulging his own appetites for astronomy, navigation, naval tactics and design. He was, as the old British Army used to say in disparagement, *keen*—the very opposite of a flaneur. He had known little in life except the Royal Navy, and he threw himself from the start heart and soul into his profession.

I have behind my desk a late-Victorian print entitled *Britain's Empire of the Seas,* depicting all the major ships of the Royal Navy afloat in the late 1890s. It is a thick mass of masts, sails and funnels, and spattered over the scene is a pattern of yellow marks by which I have identified the vessels of Fisher's seagoing career. *Highflyer* and *Coromandel* have gone, but right at the back is the old black *Warrior,* and there is the fully rigged steam battleship *Hercules,* and the

Bellerophon, known to the fleet as "Old Billy" and famous for her enormous bow wave, and the cruiser *Northampton* with her long, long bowsprit, and the once-paramount *Inflexible,* now obscurely in the middle of the picture, and the battleship *Minotaur,* which has five masts, and the graceful *Renown,* her twin funnels side by side, which was Fisher's first flagship. In themselves they are a history of nineteenth-century naval architecture, and Jack mastered and transcended them all.

It was in his forty-first year that he first became known to the British public. The occasion was an imperial intervention in Egypt, a country of particular importance to the British as the link between Africa and Asia, and as guardian of the Suez Canal. Egypt was theoretically subject to the sultan of Turkey, but it had its own monarch in the person of the Khedive Tewfik, and for some years had been essentially a financial colony of Britain and France. In 1882 a fiery Egyptian nationalist, Ahmad Arabi Pasha, led a military protest against foreign control of the country, making himself more or less dictator. Many Europeans were killed during riots in Alexandria, Egypt's principal port and the summer residence of the khedive, and British and French fleets were sent to intervene. The French wavered in their resolution, and withdrew: the British literally stuck to their guns, and in July 1882 Alexandria was bombarded by eighteen ships of the Mediterranean Fleet, commanded by The Ocean Swell himself, Sir Beauchamp Seymour, and including the greatest of all its battleships, Fisher's *Inflexible.*

It was a baleful sort of expedition. Smoke still arose from the riot-wrecked European quarter as the somewhat ragtag fleet assembled along the line of the city. Some of its ships lay offshore, some actually entered the harbor beneath the walls of the khedive's palace, Ras-el-Tin. The range was short, the bombardment prolonged, and in Alexandria they were always to remember the occasion with resentment; seventy-five years later I was reproachfully shown dilapidations in the former fortress of Kait Bey, on the site of the ancient Pharos lighthouse, and told the British had made them in 1882.

The navy's purpose was first to neutralize the city's powerful fortifications, and then to restore order in the city; at the same time it seized the chance to try in earnest, for the first time, the big new guns developed during the past twenty years of peace. The army would later take care of Arabi Pasha (he was exiled to Ceylon), and in the event was to stay in Egypt for another seven decades. The naval objectives were achieved without much trouble, and the *Inflexible* played a leading part in the action, firing more shells than any other ship and receiving more hits from the batteries on the shore. She was the centerpiece of the spectacle; when she fired one of her colossal guns she was entirely shrouded in yellow smoke, out of which the shell soared birdlike into the sunshine. Fisher's thunder was rather stolen, however, when the commander of a far lesser ship, Captain Lord Charles Beresford of the frigate *Condor*, dashed beneath the guns of one of the most contumacious of the forts to silence them in a few moments of skillful fire.

Jack was assuredly piqued, and he was not altogether pleased with the performance of the *Inflexible,* either. Her shooting, though accurate, was not as effective as had been expected, much of her gadgetry proved useless, and the concussion from her guns was so violent that some of her boats disintegrated—Fisher thought "the whole box of tricks" ought to be taken back to Portsmouth Dockyard and rebuilt. However, his own moment of glory came when he took command of the naval brigade that went ashore after the bombardment, his quarters being in the abandoned harem at Ras-el-Tin; for he then achieved the first of the Fisherisms that were eventually to make a national figure of him. He invented, with the help of an old acquaintance, the armored train.

Here it comes now, pounding out of the blistering heat on a preliminary run. There has never been such a weapon before in the history of warfare. Its locomotive, requisitioned from the Khedival Railways, is spouting smoke, steam and sparks in the middle, while in front and behind are wagons clad about with armored plate and sandbags, and bristling with guns—a Nordenfeldt machine gun, two Gatling guns, two 9-pounder field guns and a 40-pounder, all brought from vessels of the fleet and provided with their own crane for easy removal again. There is a wagon full of ammunition, heavily armored, and a "torpedo truck" containing "electric-contact torpedoes for use against trains"—early land mines, in fact.

Sailors in straw hats are crouched in warlike postures around the guns, officers in pith helmets are standing lordly in the engine's tender, and as this redoubtable equipage hisses by, ready for anything, proudly monitoring its passage are its creators: Old 'Ard 'Art and Jacky Fisher, the former displaying no emotion whatsoever, the latter in his Brunel mode—legs astride, jacket undone, his face fluctuating between the sneer of cold command and a small boy's irrepressible glee.

Concerning Women

The ironclad train, as they called it then, got Fisher's name into the London newspapers. The bombardment of Alexandria made him a Commander of the Order of the Bath. The flies and dubious water of the Ras-el-Tin harem gave him an attack of dysentry that plagued him for years to come, perhaps making his face extra yellow, and sparking his lifelong concern with his own and other people's health. He was obliged to give up his splendid command, and was invalided home into the arms of a loving wife.

She was born Katharine Josephine Delves-Broughton, but he always called her Kitty (though surely not in reference to the celebrated eighteenth-century prostitute of that name, who was said to have died from the abuse of cosmetics, and who was remembered in the nursery rhyme "Lucy Locket lost her pocket, / Kitty Fisher found it . . ."). Her paternal background was much like his own, for she was the daughter of an Anglican clergyman and had connections in the baronetage, but Fisher loved to boast in later life that she was related to kings. I greatly like the sound of her. When she was young she was pretty in a very English way, demure-looking, with wide brown eyes and a high forehead; when she was old she was matronly and very ample, and moved heavily about in thick black skirts, wearing lace collars. She was a few months older than Jack. They had three daughters and a son, all of whom seem to have had happy and successful lives—the son, after Charterhouse and Oxford, joined the Indian Civil Service, the daughters all married naval officers, two of whom became admirals in their time.

Kitty declared at the start of their marriage that she would allow nothing to stand between Jack Fisher and the fulfillment of his ambitions, and she kept her promise. She never let him down, and would have defended him fiercely, if need be, against the Lords of Admiralty themselves. She sounds the perfect naval wife, always ready to travel, socially adept at occasions ranging from the entertainment of midshipmen to the reception of royalty, and perfectly ready to lend a hand, with one or another of her daughters, in the furnishing and decoration of a captain's cabin (Prince Henry of Prussia, on an official tour of inspection, found her hard at work with a paintbrush on board *Inflexible*). She did not even object, it is said, if Jack woke her in the middle of the night and required her to jot down some thought of his in the notebook they kept beside their bed. Everybody seemed to like Kitty Fisher, even Fisher's worst enemies—even King George V, who was to become one of the worst of all.

For Jack she was also, no doubt, yet another mother. They married in 1866, when he was serving at the gunnery school in Portsmouth, and he was clearly head over heels in love with her—he only wished, he said, that they had married when they were twenty-one. When he went to sea again, to three more years on the China station, his letters are extremely loving, but are streaked less romantically with piety and self-pity. The present Lord Fisher has a huge stack of these letters from his grandfather to his grandmother, mostly written on board the *Ocean*. They are immensely long, page after page of closely packed handwriting, full of professional news, modest boasts and complaints, heavy with allusions to Providence and the One Above, and altogether less dashing than confiding. Sometimes, it seems to me, they are more like letters from one woman to another than letters from a sailor to his girl.

Later a suggestion not so much of disillusionment as of ennui creeps into their relationship. In the photographs taken of Kitty, as her life goes by, she seldom smiles: she seems proud of her brilliant husband, but underwhelmed by him. We see her once in the cabin of his flagship *Renown*, when he is an admiral. He sits foursquare facing the camera in a flowered armchair; she sits sideways next to the upright piano, looking at Jack affectionately perhaps, but a little cynically, as if to say that she knows him a lot better than we do. We see her again in the garden of a London house, when Fisher is a famous man and they are entertaining the grandest of guests—an English queen, a Russian empress, a princess. With a grandchild in his arms Fisher is obviously basking in the admiration of the great ladies, one of whom is taking the photograph; Kitty, by then very stout, is lumbering heavily across the foreground, keeping a weather eye on the baby, as though she is off to arrange for some sandwiches.

He loved her always, I do not doubt; he recognized her

fine qualities; he was grateful for her inflexible fidelity; but gradually, I fear, over the long decades of professional excitement and social advance, she came to bore him rather. She was not particularly clever, or very fashionable, or rich. She was just a good, kind woman. With Kitty as with Sophy, one fears, Fisher was periodically nagged by guilt. He was one of those people born to luck, born to be spoiled, who want everything; but who, having kind hearts themselves at bottom, are slightly ashamed of expecting too much of others. Not that he ever quite deserted his Kitty. He wrote to her constantly until the day she died, and he it was who composed the inscription on her memorial.

Fisher was easily at home with women, enjoying their company and sharing many of their interests. He liked gossip: "I met Mrs Markham on the Bund," he reported to Mrs. Warden when he was eighteen, "she hardly seemed to know me—*really*, I am not joking . . ." He was observant of clothes: "She wore a white-satin, low dress," he reported to Kitty about the queen of Greece when he was thirty-six, "trimmed with very fine transparent black lace, a very long train, and roses of all kinds embroidered around the top of the skirt and along the train . . ." He empathized with women's preoccupations: a method for preserving one's figure without dieting, for instance, was to soak a towel in soda water and wrap it round the stomach—"it is unfailing." He believed in universal suffrage, and when he read of a case of wife abuse in 1911, he said the woman ought to be allowed to shoot her husband, and get a pension afterward. He was interested in the upbringing of children: if a mother was always saying don't do this, don't do that, "Why! it puts the very idea of doing it into their little heads . . ." He had a favorite scent—verbena. He genuinely admired the traditional womanly qualities of strength with tenderness, and loved to say that Nelson himself, the greatest of all the admirals, was "three parts a woman!"

At the same time Fisher was extremely sexual, and his enemies indeed made him out to be an unprincipled libertine. A popular navy tale had a married captain confronting Admiral Fisher with an ultimatum: promotion for the captain, or divorce court for the admiral. In a puckish way he encouraged this reputation. He once told Edward VII that he had ravished every virgin in London ("Splendid if true" was the king's comment), and liked to quote the apothegm "Do right and fear no man, Don't write and fear no woman." When he was commander in chief in Bermuda, so one of my correspondents told me, he openly invited "a beautiful American" to move into Admiralty House, and assured her that "if his family gave any trouble he would pack them off home." From time to time I hear legends of people said to have been illegitimate offspring of Jacky Fisher.

Enigma surrounds his sexual activities, but I am inclined to believe that Fisher's innumerable affairs seldom if ever went beyond the lasciviously platonic. He was an addict of the Old Testament, and the seventh commandment must have been ingrained in him. "I must tell you the lovely story," he wrote to a friend once, "of a most beautiful woman in high circles in London, who told me her husband had been sitting on the doorstep waiting to shoot one of her men friends! *It wasn't me!* I told her I wished it was." But it wasn't. "What a man really likes," he said himself, "is to be a saint with the reputation of being a bit of a devil."

There was an element of conventional Edwardian boulevardism to his attitudes, together with strong infusions of the behavior traditionally expected of sailors, but I think he wore his heart genuinely on his sleeve, and he regularly reported to Kitty on his flirtations. His emotions were always impulsive, sensual and extreme, and he was as extravagantly demonstrative to male friends as he was to women.

It seems to have been Fisher's passion for dancing that first branded him a rake. Fellow officers were often shocked at his habit of dancing the whole evening with one woman, then considered fast behavior. Fisher himself admitted that "without any doubt, there's a good deal of temptation in it," and when he was commander in chief in the Mediterranean one of his rear admirals so disapproved of his conduct that he declined all invitations to Admiralty House. Fisher would waltz all night with a woman who danced well enough, or who was willing to be swept away by Fisher's fun. He apparently perfected his techniques during a stay on the North American station. There I suppose, on winter nights among the dark stone houses of Nova Scotia, while the snow lay deep on the streets outside and the ships were thick with ice, Fisher came like some genial goblin of the Old World into the hospitable homes of Halifax, and found in the whirl of the waltz the perfect outlet for his sex and sociability.

Dancing was an old pastime of the Royal Navy—in earlier times bos'un's mates used to pipe the order, "Hands to dance and skylark"—but Fisher gave it new meaning. He was ready to dance with anyone, male or female, and if there was no music to hand he would make his own, whistling or humming one of the simple melodies he liked—if not his favorite waltz, Benjamin Godard's immensely popular "Berceuse," then one of the jollier hymn tunes of the American evangelists Moody and Sankey. He expected all his officers to dance too, loved arranging impromptu shipboard balls, and when he became an admiral had the quarterdeck of his flagship especially reconstructed to serve as a dance floor. One of his Halifax partners said he would dance on the veranda, on the lawn or anywhere else, and he is variously recalled as having danced hornpipes on wardroom tables, entering dining rooms and in the presence of the czar and czarina of Russia. His style was extremely vigorous. When he went to a navy dance he generally took with him a couple of fit young midshipmen, in case he found no woman able to keep up. Violet Asquith, the prime minister's daughter, once reported dancing with him on his deck "for a very long time before breakfast": she said his staying power was formidable, "and as he never reverses I reel giddily in his arms and lurch against his heart of oak." "We were riding for a fall," remembered an officer seized by Admiral Fisher for a shipboard waltz, and indeed so madly did he whirl them both around the deck that they tripped and rolled over and over in the scupperway—"everyone was convulsed with laughter, including the Admiral."

He never stopped dancing, all his life. It kept him young, he said, and gave him "ginger." When he was in his seventies he boasted of dancing until three in the morning every night for three weeks, once dancing eight waltzes with the same partner without stopping (*"She was only 17, so it didn't signify!"*). In later years he especially liked dancing with Americans: now he is waltzing with "a sweet American," now with "a perfect [American] gem," now with "a merry widow from Michigan"—all in all "the most splendid women on earth for dancing! No women touch them!"

In 1904 one of King Edward VII's private secretaries, Sir Frederick Ponsonby, was going for a walk in the gardens at Balmoral when he encountered Admiral Sir John Fisher, First Sea Lord and His Majesty's principal naval aide-de-camp. They had not met before. For a moment or two they walked together in silence, Ponsonby suspecting that Fisher had only joined him out of politeness. Then the admiral spoke. "Do you like dancing?" he asked.

When I show people Fisher's face, most men find it over-whelmingly arrogant or supercilious, but most women are intrigued by its mixture of suggestions, and often place their hands over the forehead or the chin to analyze its several meanings—command here, humor there, softness around the eyes, contempt about the mouth. In life it seems to have been his strange mixture of the authoritative, the devious and the innocent—the childlike Machiavellian—that women liked best, together with an often-noticed streak of the feminine in him.

One of my correspondents, forty years ago, wrote to tell me of times when she was a saleswoman at Jays, the London store on Regent Street. Kitty Fisher bought her dresses there, and often while she was inside the dressing rooms Jack used to sit in the corridor outside and chat to my informant, sitting beside her on a velvet ottoman. Neither of them was very tall, and so they sat there together, the admiral and the shopgirl, dangling their legs side by side, laughing, and eating toffee from a bag—"I always thought what a funny little man he was, and now I am old and look back on the happy hours of those days, this is one of my memories..."

In his last years Fisher took on a private secretary, and her daughter sent me his various letters of engagement. They told her nothing but the worst. She would be a fool to work for him—it would be penal servitude—she would be a maid of all work, nurse, secretary, clothes mender, valet, "and nightly harried by being called in to write at any sort of unearthly hour just as you are with your dressing gown thrown about you ... all that on £10 a month and never a holiday ... is your health robust enough?" Mrs. Dorothy Loxton came to love the old man dearly, and treasured all his funny, impulsive and half-illegible letters until the day she died.

He had the knack of the sweet gesture. When he was one of the Lords of Admiralty, an officer's wife asked him to arrange a home appointment for her husband after three years on the China station. He told her to send him a slip of the blue ribbon she was wearing, and the man got his posting. In order to buy one of his friends a Christmas present of slippers, he secretly borrowed one of her shoes. One day, riding in an open carriage through London with the king of England, attended we may suppose by grooms and coachmen, Fisher caught sight of "a beautiful woman I thought was in America." Without a second thought, "carried away by my feelings," he jumped to his feet and waved to her: when the king remonstrated, Fisher said he had forgotten all about him.

Another elderly correspondent of mine, who had been in domestic service, remembered the pleasure Fisher gave to the maids of the household when he went to collect an honorary degree at Cambridge. Having dressed himself up to the nines in his full-dress uniform, ablaze with decorations, he invited them all to his bedroom to inspect him in his glory, and to have the wonderfully florid orders identified for them—from Spain, from Russia, from Japan, from Turkey . . . "On leaving and bidding farewell to an hostess," delightfully added the letter writer, "I believe it was customary of Sir John to kiss the lady's hand."

I bet it was! Ever since Catton Hall, Fisher had known just how to please *les grandes dames,* and some of them were very grand indeed. Queen Victoria, for example, most upset to hear that the entertaining captain of her former guardship had come home a sick man from Alexandria, commanded him to visit her at Osborne, her country house on the Isle of Wight, and thereafter he often did. We see him at his cockiest there—he loved sailing close to the wind when it came to dealing with grandees. "What are you all laughing at down there?" the queen-empress once asked of the guests at the far end of her dining room. "I was telling Lady Ely, ma'am," came the unmistakable voice of Captain Fisher, "that I've got enough flannel round my tummy to go all round this room!" Later Queen Alexandra became almost an intimate, first as Princess of Wales, then as queen of England. Fisher loved her for her grace and simplicity ("She don't paint"), enjoyed gossiping with her ("She put me up to lots of malignant doings") and adored dancing with her despite her limp and her deafness. She remained in touch with him all his life, writing him gentle letters of sympathy at times of trouble, and on one occasion at least, a bracing note of reproach.

Another noble favorite was the Grand Duchess Olga of Oldenburg, younger sister of the czar, known to the Russians as "Sunshine" and to Fisher as "a peculiarly sweet creature." We see him teaching her to waltz at Carlsbad, flirting outrageously with her on board the royal yacht and declaring himself in love with her. When she once told him, in a letter, that she had been bitten around the ankle by gnats, Fisher immediately telegraphed to say that he wished to God he had been one of the gnats; "Sunshine" in return said that she would walk to England for another waltz with him. There was an unnamed Polish countess, too, whom he described as "an apparition of extraordinary grace and loveliness," and the Duchess of Sunderland he defined as "my very close friend," and it was in the Duchess of Hamilton's company, if not her arms, that he was to end his days.

A woman writing soon after his death remembered first meeting him when he was a lieutenant, and feeling about him then a sense of romance that never left her. She was, she added, "four or five years old at the time."

· · ·

Nevertheless, there often sounds something tiresome about Fisher's philandering—another of my correspondents reported the almost statutorily Edwardian backstairs kiss—and it did not invariably work. Some women instantly disliked him, some distrusted him and many were hostile as a matter of principle, because he was a professional threat to their husbands. Just as he used the affection of women to advance his interests in the navy, so when he became one of the great men of the service he found that women were among those most angrily opposed to him. His purposes were often socially radical, and lofty Edwardian hostesses resented them. They reviled our Jacky as an arriviste or a half-caste, and he in return spat back at them generically as "the drawing-room brigade."

Violet Asquith, despite those prebreakfast dances, despised his table talk and said he told her a stock of anecdotes, puns, chestnuts and riddles that might have come out of Christmas crackers. Later she declared him a wicked old lunatic. Her stepmother, Margot, who thought his conversation coarse ("What it is to have a young heart!" Fisher retorted), once cut him dead at a Guildhall banquet; when one day she found herself grabbed around the waist in the prime minister's offices and treated to an impromptu waltz, she had to admit that "the old boy is a fine dancer," but Fisher said the experience *quite upset me.* Mrs. Winston Churchill hated Fisher, the writer Katharine Mansfield called him "a presumptuous self-conscious high-stomached old roarer," and he never succeeded with Alexandra's successor Queen Mary, wife of George V: indeed it is hard to imagine him waltzing that stern Teutonic dame around his quarterdeck, knocking her feathered toque askew and whispering sweet nonsense in her ear.

But he was never abashed, because in any case the navy came first. The fleet was his ruling passion emotionally, and his intellectual obsession. As a poet might neglect a mistress to write a sonnet, a politician to plan an election, so I am sure there was no liaison that Fisher would not instantly abandon if the British Navy called. Its ships across the oceans, its men, its history, its status in the world, its style, its underlying grim and brutal method—these were the loves that permanently seduced him.

Radical Jack

When Fisher was invalided home from the *Inflexible* in 1882, to spend much of the next few years trying to recover his health, he was presented with this letter from the crew of the battleship:

Sir:

We the ship's company of H.M.S. *Inflexible,* take the earliest opportunity of expressing to you our deep sorrow and sympathy on this sad occasion of your sickness, and it is our whole wish that you may speedily recover and be amongst us again, who are so proud of serving under you. Sir, we are all aware of the responsible duties you had to perform, and the great number of men you had to see to during your long stay on shore at Alexandria, which must have brought the strongest man to a bed of sickness; but we trust shortly to see you again amongst us and on the field of active service, where you are as much at home as on your own grand ship, and at the end may you receive your share of rewards and laurels, and your ship's company will then feel as proud and prouder than if it was bestowed on themselves.

Sir, trusting that you will overlook the liberty we have taken in sending this to you, We beg to remain, Your faithful and sympathizing ship's company, INFLEXI-BLES

I would rather have received such a letter than the most flattering of reviews, and Fisher declared it to be one of the most valuable things he possessed. He still heard from old Inflexibles forty years later, when he was an Admiral of the Fleet and the battleship had long been broken up, and there is no doubting the rapport he habitually established with the crews of his ships. He was ageless, and so got on well with young lieutenants and midshipmen. "Williamson and Paine pulled his leg and chaffed him in the most astounding way," wrote a midshipman about him when he was an admiral. "Repartee was bandied about, and Jackie used to go into convulsions of merriment and laughter." He was also relatively classless, and so readily at ease with English working-men. When he hitched that ride with the tramp ship to Constantinople, so he loved to recall, its master said to him: "There's only one bunk, and when I ain't in it the mate is, [and] we ain't got no cook." That was all right, said Fisher, he didn't want no bunk, he didn't want no cook, and so they sailed in perfect harmony to Turkey.

Fisher was a famous disciplinarian, but of an exciting kind. He wanted everything done instantly, dramatically, at double-time. He worked his sailors with a merciless enthusi-asm; "rare rousings up" is how one of his crew remembered it years later. When he took over a vessel everybody expected drastic consequences. It might only be a new way of painting ship—in the *Ocean* he distributed cut-down meat tins of paint to every member of the crew, and had the entire ship painted within an hour of docking, It might just be a new word of command—on the *Warrior* he introduced the order "Still," meaning that every man must freeze, and it remained on the navy's gunnery books until after World War II. Or it might be a revolutionary upheaval of almost everything: time and again we read of Fisher's capacity to change the style and reputation of a ship or a dockyard.

In the ship of the line *Donegal*, it is said, he knew the names of everyone—and not only their names, according to the perhaps overcolored memories of one of his ratings, but "where they were born and what religion they were supposed to be." *Donegal* was his first ship as a commander (dean, as it were, to the captain's bishop) and in her he first established his reputation as the Seaman's Friend. My files are full of imprecations from Fisher's fellow officers, but I have heard not a single complaint about him from the lower deck. His attitudes to his crews were essentially compassionate. He claimed as an old man to have fainted at his first sight of a flogging, and when he came to power at the Admiralty he was quick to abolish degrading punishments. The real meaning of the Nelson Touch, he liked to say, was Nelson's unfailing consideration to his men.

There are many examples of his kindness to the navy's ratings, and here is one of them. A lady sent me the tale of her husband, assigned to coast-guard duties on the west coast of Ireland, but dying to be moved to England to join his wife and their new baby. She had appealed in "a very simple but truthfully girlish letter (for I was only 21)" to the First Sea Lord, Sir John Fisher. "A fortnight later a letter came on His Majesty's Service. My Dad took it in, how his hand trembled he could not make it out. Oh, Dad I said that's for me, I wrote to Admiral Fisher, oh, dear, how he looked at me, I said, well, open it, and do you know that kind gentleman was going to cause my husband to be removed to a Station in England (provided my husband was desirous of this removal)."

Fisher greatly prized the esteem of the lower deck. On Christmas Day 1859, he reported in pleasure to Mams that about thirty bluejackets had "been doing nothing else but hugging me and wanting me to take their grog—I'd like to give them 2 dozen all round, the brutes." And when in 1902 he left the Mediterranean at the end of his term as commander in chief, he emerged from a farewell dinner to the deck of his flagship to be greeted by the entire ship's company with their own version of "Goodbye, Dolly Gray," the American hit song of the day—"Goodbye, Jacky, we must leave you . . ." Can't you hear their strong young voices still, and see the mist in the admiral's eyes?

Like so many of Fisher's attitudes, his care for the seamen was not all disinterested. "I know the British sailor to the very core! He has been my study all my life, and I have a deep affection for him." He also recognized, though, that being the Seaman's Friend would pay professional dividends. The purpose of the Nelson Touch, after all, was to win battles.

Jack was a modernist, and he realized that the social structure of the Royal Navy, like the hierarchy of England itself, was outdated. The ratings and warrant officers were treated as beings of a lower order. The officers were drawn overwhelmingly from the gentry classes, meaning (so Fisher loved to fulminate) that they represented a mere one-fortieth of the population. Snobbery was a curse of the service: "Buggins is first cousin of the Duke of Dankshire, and can't be passed over—he's an ass, but he must have his turn." Also the executive officers, concerned with navigation, tactics and gunnery, were absurdly contemptuous of the engineers, whom they regarded as mere mechanics. Deck officers, according to Fisher, were liable to say to engineers "My Ma will never ask your Ma to tea," and if the officers of a British warship were invited to a function ashore, it was tacitly understood that engineers were excluded.

Fisher despised these antiquated prejudices, and grew ever more impatient with the immense gilded structure of English society that underlay them. "Mr. Democracy is not going to stand for it!" One of his earliest extant letters makes fun of an Oxford swell encountered in Hong Kong—"Ar, you belong to the, ar navy, yaas, really?"—and half a century later he was still complaining about "the d—d strain of snobbishness that pervades the feudal relics of the British race." The British social system was not just unfair, but actually ungodly. Fisher remembered seeing the Chartist riots of 1848, when he was a child in London, and being horrified even then at the brutal behavior of the police; sixty years later he and Kitty used to entertain slum children from London at their home in Norfolk—"Just imagine some of these children twelve years old who have never seen a green field in their lives before! It's awful!" Fisher loved to quote the verse "Sworn to no party, of no sect am I / I can't be silent, and I will not lie," but the older he got the more his instincts leaned to the left, and in the end he was often accused of rank socialism.

He never declined honors for himself: as an old man his chest was rigid with stars and medals, and when he was ennobled in 1909 he happily had coronets of varying size embossed upon his writing papers. Nevertheless, in theory at least he disapproved of hereditary titles and antique forms. After the death of his friend King Edward VII he became a republican too, and talked spaciously about kings being as cheap as herrings, of sweeping away thrones and abolishing monarchies—he even called George V and Queen Mary by their scurrilous nicknames: Futile George and Fertile Mary. "God Save the King" was "worn out." The very word "imperial" was sickening. Europe's royal houses were responsible for the carnage of World War I. All the kings were against all the people, and the whole d—d lot should be swept away once and for all, "not even shadows of them to be left!"

Some of this was the farrago of old age. More was personal sensitivity. Jack reduced much of life to matters of personality. If a king (Edward VII) was good to him, he was a royalist, if a king (George V) was hostile, he was a republican. His social conscience was doubtless sensitized by his own status as an outsider. Even as a peer he was never really absorbed into the traditional governing class of England. He seldom dined at fashionable London houses. His closest friends, if not naval people, were politicians, industrialists, journalists and businessmen. Far more than ancient titles he admired the ability to make money, and some of his highest commendations were reserved for those who made lots of it. The career of the tycoon Sir Basil Zaharoff particularly dazzled him: "He is worth 20 millions sterling and has been twice bankrupt and practically rules France and owns Vickers Limited and lives with Clemenceau and some Spanish grandee's wife." More than once Fisher was tempted to leave the navy himself and accept jobs in the shipbuilding and armament industries.

He had a particular prejudice against the British Army, because it represented all he resented most in its combination of privilege, conservatism and inefficiency (besides spending money the navy could use better). During World War I, infuriated by the working of its recruiting system, he suggested the whole process might be handed over to Sir Joseph Lyons, the great Jewish grocer, who would be paid three shillings a head per recruit and make 10 percent profit.

Fisher gravitated naturally toward nonconformists, mavericks and radicals of all kinds. He got on well with the two most notorious liberals of the time, Winston Churchill and Lloyd George, and once suggested naming a new class of battleship after them—His Majesty's Ships *Winston, Churchill, Lloyd* and *George.* Although in his racial views as in all others he was often inconsistent, he was anything but xenophobic. Offhand I can remember, from his correspondence, admiring references to Germans, Frenchmen, Turks, Belgians, Russians, Maltese and Americans, and he was at least half serious in claiming that the British were really the Lost Tribes of Israel: when it was argued that they didn't look much like the other tribes of Israel, he retorted that of course they didn't, or they wouldn't be lost.

Colonial boy that he was, readily though he undoubtedly clobbered Johnny Chinaman at Fatshan Creek, enthusiastically though he sent his armored train in pursuit of Arabi Pasha, he was never much of an imperialist. He was not always keen on Irishmen, but he believed in home rule for Ireland. He sympathized with the Boers in their struggle against the British Empire—he "simply loved" their brilliant leader Louis Botha. He thought it would be ridiculous to defend the Canadians if they were ever attacked by the United States, and said the self-governing British colonies— Australia, New Zealand and Canada—were all as bad as each other in wanting "to grab all they possibly can out of us and give us nothing back." He did not believe in the supposed Russian threat to India, which preoccupied the imperial strategists for half a century, and he never admired glory for glory's sake. What was the good of Captain Scott's expedition to the South Pole? Did the British Navy need *glory?*

When the time came it was an action of Fisher's, more than any other single act of policy, that symbolized the beginning of the end of the imperial era: the retreat of the Pax Britannica was sounded first in 1904, when he ordered the gunboats of empire home.

. . .

As soon as he had the power, Fisher tried to apply to the navy his ideas of social justice and efficiency. He wanted it to be the people's navy, as it had been in Cromwell's day. The army might be an adjunct of the court, but the navy was of the nation—all his life Fisher hardly ever called it the Royal Navy. He made life better for the lower deck, not only by improving pay and conditions (providing knives and forks, for instance) but by giving men a chance to graduate through the ranks of warrant officer to commissioned rank—"they are entitled and they are worthy." He tried hard to make education at Dartmouth, the navy's cadet college, free to all, opening it to the other 39/40ths of the population. He began at last the trend to modernize the officer caste, in theory anyway giving engineer officers equality with executive officers, and even trying unsuccessfully to make them professionally interchangeable, so that an engineer might command a ship, a deck officer attend to a turbine. In the end, he said, "we shall glory in being Engineer-Admirals." He wanted the navy to be "a service of all the talents," and he hoped that all officers, whatever their specialty, could share a partial community of knowledge and a lifelong community of sentiment.

It made him hosts of enemies. "We should view with grave apprehension," announced the *Naval and Military Record* in 1910, "any attempt to officer the fleet at all largely with men of humble birth," and much of fashionable London agreed. "All the dukes and duchesses are banded together against me!" Mothers were appalled at the idea that sons entering the ancestral profession might have to get their hands greasy messing about with machinery, and mixing with men of humble birth. "What!" some toff said in horror to Lord Spencer, a former First Lord of the Admiralty who supported Fisher's schemes. "What! *Are you going to defend our officers going down the coal hole?*" Fisher did not help his own causes by his crass inability to compromise, his vindictiveness and his spite, but at least he made a start in democratizing the British sea service: it was several generations before executive officers genuinely regarded engineers as their equals, and not until 1948, under a socialist government, that education at Dartmouth was made free.

All his life Fisher prided himself on being different. The journalist J. L. Garvin, who knew most of the great men of his day, said he had never met anybody so unlike anyone else, and after his death the London *Times* described him, in terms that could hardly be applied to any other public figure, as a ruthless foe, a wholehearted friend, a dark schemer, an open fighter, a tyrant and a perfect playfellow. Even his enemies thankfully admitted him to be unique (though according to Jack an admiring doctor once told him that he ought to have been born twins).

He made only four public speeches in his life. One was at the Lord Mayor's Banquet of 1907. Two were very short statements in the House of Lords, his only interventions as a peer. The fourth was at the Royal Academy Banquet of 1903. The banquet is held each year on the occasion of the summer exhibition, and when I was once invited I was present half in person, at the banquet of 1992, and half in imagination, at the banquet of 1903. It takes place within the exhibition rooms themselves, all among the pictures and the sculptures, and is a formal, fashionable and extremely picturesque occasion. Such medals and ribbons and sashes of honor! Such a splendor of titles and distinctions! The president of the academy receives his guests with courtly ceremony, now an archbishop, now a cabinet minister, women in tiaras, men in frilled dress shirts, and there are clutches of people looking at pictures, snatches of laughter in corners, huddles around television personalities, politicians holding court, until at eight o'clock a fanfare of trumpets announces dinner. The company festively settles itself in long parallels, and the speakers, toying with their soup at the top table and making desultory conversation with their neighbors, begin surreptitiously to eye their notes.

In Edwardian times the armed forces were always toasted at the banquet, and the toast was answered in alternate years by a representative of the army and the navy. That Fisher should be replying in 1903 was ironic, because at a time of repeated invasion scares he was brazen in his belief that the British Army needed a fundamental shaking-up—"about three more Boer Wars will do the trick." Two table places away from him was seated St. John Brodrick, as secretary of state for war the army's political chief, but that did not in the least disconcert the admiral, and he prepared to make his speech in high spirits and extempore.

It was a measure of Edwardian England that the names of so many of the guests are familiar to us today. There were the *ex officio* dignitaries, presidents of societies, heads of colleges, ambassadors, viscounts, earls, bishops, the chief rabbi, the governor of the Bank of England, the Prince of Wales. But there were also Pinero the playwright, Gilbert of Gilbert and Sullivan, Hubert Parry the composer, Baden-Powell the founder of the Boy Scouts, James Murray the lexicographer, Sir Ernest Cassel the financier, Sir Frederick Treves the surgeon who befriended the Elephant Man, Benjamin Baker the great engineer—and, of course, the Royal Academicians—Alma-Tadema, John Singer Sargent, W. P. Frith, Luke Fildes, George Clausen (whose daughter was presently, as it happens, to be affianced to my uncle Geraint).

Fisher's brief address was highly unconventional. It was rambling, breezy, mischievous and spontaneous. He reminisced a little about his naval career. He talked about changes in naval warfare, and the need for open minds. He told how, when commander in chief in the Mediterranean, he had boarded a destroyer and noticed the motto *Ut Omnes Veniant* above its wheel. " 'Hallo,' I said [to its commander], 'what the deuce is that?' Saluting me, he said: 'Let 'em all come, sir.' " (*Great laughter and cheers.*) But the punch of the speech came at the end. Upon the British Navy, said Fisher, rested the British Empire. "Nothing else is of any use without it, not even the army. We are different from continental nations. No soldier of ours can go anywhere unless a sailor carries him there on his back." The navy knew its responsibilities, he assured the banquet and the nation, the Admiralty was united and progressive, and he concluded with the most famously ringing of all his phrases: "You may sleep quietly in your beds!" (*Loud cheerss.*)

It was quoted for years afterward: for example by P. G. Wodehouse in his 1909 novel *The Swoop! or How Clarence Saved England,* a comical story of invasion in which he called it "Fisher's tip—and Fisher was a smart man." Jack was delighted with his own bravura performance: "I never had a note and had not the faintest idea what words were coming out of my heart! *But they came out all right!*"

Technology

Let us now attend a famous naval occasion of Queen Victoria's reign—not one of the spectacular displays with which the navy advertised its almost metaphysical grandeur, like the Gibraltar jamboree when 2,000 rockets blazed an archway over the emperor of Germany's yacht, or the Spithead review of 173 warships, which celebrated the queen-empress's Diamond Jubilee, but a more private and professional event. We sit on the rough turf above the water at Dunboy, near Castletown, County Cork, in Ireland, on a July day in 1885. Below us is the harbor called Berehaven, sheltered from the wide expanse of Bantry Bay and from the Atlantic beyond by the long hump of Bere Island. This is one of the principal western anchorages of the British fleet, and Castletown and its pubs have been familiar to generations of British sailors. Today the ships of the Channel Fleet (Commander in Chief Admiral Sir Geoffrey Hornby; on special duties, Captain J. A. Fisher) are assembled here on their summer maneuvers, their convoluted shapes filling the anchorage, their smoke rising in parallel plumes into the sky. The scene is set for a technological experiment.

Immediately below us, fixed into the rocks, are the heavy

metal stanchions that support the Berehaven boom—the enormous steel hawser, several feet thick, designed to prevent enemy entrance to Berehaven from the Atlantic. It is said to be the biggest boom ever made, and this morning it is raised and lies heavily along the surface of the narrows from Dunboy to Bere Island. This almost aboriginal method of defense is now to be tested against the very newest weapon of naval warfare, the semisubmerged torpedo ram *Polyphemus,* 2,640 tons.

All eyes are on this peculiar vessel, lying there half awash among the battleships and cruisers. She is all new, and very expensive. Named directly after one of Nelson's ships of the line, and indirectly after the most bloodthirsty of the Cyclops, she is already known to the navy as "One-Eye," and constitutes a class of her own. She has a single mast and funnel and a low gray superstructure. Her hull is bulbous, and culminates in a long underwater ram. Actually within the ram is a torpedo tube, but there are also four broadside tubes, and six twin-barreled machine guns. The deck of *Polyphemus* is armored, she has rudders both at bow and stern, and her 7,000-horsepower engines drive her at the extraordinary speed of eighteen knots, making her potentially one of the most formidable warships afloat. Only an elaborately gilded scroll at her bow softens her iron functionalism.

The Royal Navy of the 1880s is in constant experiment, and symptomatic of its condition is *Polyphemus'*s curious combination of the antique and the futuristic: electrically propelled torpedoes, that is, emerging from the bow spike that has been a naval weapon since the days of the Greek galleys.

Some theorists are convinced that the spike is about to enjoy a renaissance, and think of *Polyphemus* chiefly as a steam ram; others, like Sir Nathaniel Barnaby, who designed the ship, consider her ram only an adjunct to her torpedoes. Whatever her chief function, she is in Berehaven today specifically to test her efficiency as a projectile. She is simply to throw herself at the harbor boom at our feet, and see what happens. There is nothing secret about the trial. Crowds wait on the Bere Island cliffs, scores of sightseeing boats mill around the harbor. A huge Union Jack flies on the principal tower of Dunboy Castle behind us, and even now the admiral's barge is taking up its position just inside the narrows.

The moment comes. A gun fires somewhere. A few ships' whistles blow. Through our binoculars we see the steam hissing from the *Polyphemus*'s funnel. Her officers are crouched on the bridge. Her superstructure seems to shudder, like a dog about to leap. There is a blast of smoke and a flash of flame, and suddenly "One-Eye" is away—her engines echoing around the haven, the foam gathering around her prow, her ensign streaming at the stern—and up she comes toward the narrows, faster and faster, her engines thumping—pounding between the bigger warships, whose crews line the rails to wave and cheer—rocking and bobbing the small boats in her wake—past Admiral Sir Geoffrey Hornby in his barge, Captain Fisher in attendance—past the castle point, rushing into view immediately below us until—*crash!*—with a terrible scraping, clashing and splintering, with fragments of steel flying in the air, and the huge broken hawser whipping out of the water—*crash!*—*Polyphemus* is through the boom, and scudding triumphantly toward the open sea.

As it happened they never built another ship like *Polyphemus,* and the ram never again came into its own as a weapon of war. If I have taken some imaginative liberties in describing that moment at Berehaven, it is because it was the sort of moment that Jack Fisher particularly relished—at once theatrical and technical. By the 1880s he had established himself as a specialist in equipment—matériel, as they called it in naval circles. He had been repeatedly associated with the very latest in warships, from *Warrior* to *Inflexible.* He had commanded HMS *Excellent,* the navy's gunnery school and the center of its most advanced technical thinking, and been the first commander of its torpedo school. As early as 1868 he had privately published a paper about electric gunfire and self-propelled torpedoes, then virtually unknown in Britain, and when twenty years later a seaman was asked in an examination paper to define electricity, he wrote that it was "a suttle and impondrous fluid invented by Captain Fisher."

In those days the Royal Navy's rule of thumb was that revolutionary technical change should be left to foreign competitors—in particular to France, Britain's most obvious rival. The French had produced a brilliant sequence of naval designers, but their industrial capacity was so inferior that it was easy for the British to emulate and overtake their inventions. The first seagoing ironclad was the French *La Gloire,* a totally new kind of vessel. She was built of wood with iron cladding, because there were no foundries in France capable of building a suitable iron hull: but only a year later the British were able to launch the *Warrior,* far more powerful and built of iron throughout.

Through the later decades of the nineteenth century, then, when Britain's industrial power was still unmatched, there came a long series of British warships that were generally built in response to foreign initiatives, but were themselves full of new ideas. They were seldom built as classes, but generally only in ones and twos, like *Polyphemus.* They were sample ships. The navy's officers might still yearn for masts and sails, but its designers were boldly innovative, and its battleships began to look very avant-garde. There were ships with huge single funnels, like factory chimneys, and ships with slender funnels side by side. Some ships had guns sticking out of their prows, some below their bowsprits, and some carried ordnance of eight different sizes—the navy used ninety kinds of ammunition. The little paddle-steamers of Fatshan Creek were now developing into fast torpedo gunboats, and the *Polyphemus* gave notice of even deadlier things to come. That picture of the fleet behind my desk displays a truly astonishing variety of forms, shapes, types, masts, riggings and armaments: it was not until the 1890s that the design of battleships, at least, achieved a kind of equilibrium, and the Royal Navy felt confident enough to build a whole class of ships, the seven *Royal Sovereigns,* to a single design.

Dozens of inventors were at work on hulls, guns and equipment, and British public opinion was intensely interested in every development. The design of warships was regularly discussed in the House of Commons. The newspapers were full of jingo pride or petulant complaint about the navy's equipment. Fisher was very much at home in this atmosphere of change and experiment. I think he actively disliked the past—he dismissed history as a record of discredited ideas—and he seems to have had no nostalgia at all for the sailing navy. The beauty of sail meant nothing to him, and he never altered the view he expressed when, at the age of fourteen, he joined the sailing two-decker *Calcutta*: "*Now sailors all take my advice / Let steamships be your motta / And never go to sea again / In the sailing ship* Calcutta!" The *Warrior*, so overwhelmingly functional, had been just his kind of ship. Charles Dickens, who visited her on her launching slip, had realized at once that she was a portent: the warship as gunmachine. Fisher agreed entirely, and expended much energy in trying to persuade the Royal Navy of this unwelcome development, at a time when the captain of one British warship believed the best way of improving gunnery was to award a pie and a bottle of rum to the first man to hit a target, and the captain of another, told by his engineer officer that the ship was going as fast as it could, ordered him testily to "put some more oil on, then."

Fisher's enemies held it always against him that he was too much concerned with technology as against what used to be called the "sublime part" of the naval profession—the study of strategy and history. This was perhaps an echo of the times, long before, when the navy was divided between Gentlemen, who led men and commanded fleets, and Tarpaulins, who worked ships and fired guns. Fisher was es-

sentially a Tarpaulin, and he was always proud of his technical proficiencies, acquired entirely on the job. "Is this
Lieutenant Fisher," one of the Lords of Admiralty was heard
to inquire, after inspecting his work as a gunnery officer, "as
good a seaman as he is a gunnery officer?" Instantly Jack presented himself. "My Lords, I am Lieutenant Fisher—just as
good a seaman as I am a gunnery man." (At which, we are
told, "they each bowed their heads.")

In 1913 the battleship *Renown* was broken up by the shipbreakers Dorman Long at Blythe on Tyneside, eighteen
years after her launch at Doc Penfro in Wales. Garden furniture was made from her oak and teak, and a shop was opened
on Dover Street, London, just to sell it. It was run by a relative of one of the shipbreakers' families, Mrs. F. M. Denslow,
and years later she wrote to tell me how one morning a man
in a long rough tweed coat said he would like to look around
the stock. Mrs. Denslow, who guessed him to be an expatri-
ate retired to take up farming in England, told him the history of the ship, how it had been a fleet flagship but was
considered a technical failure. The man stayed for a full
hour, looked at everything, thanked Mrs. Denslow for a most
enjoyable visit, and revealed himself to be Admiral of the
Fleet Lord Fisher, who as Third Naval Lord had been responsible for the construction of HMS *Renown,* and whose
very favorite warship she had been.

She was only one of several ships for which he had a close
personal feeling, for if he was not moved by sail, he was intensely excited by everything to do with the modern steam

warship. When he doodled, he drew plans of imaginary battleships, a habit he shared with the kaiser and with Adolf
Hitler. I have one of these doodles in front of me now. The
ship is to be called HMS *Incomparable*, and is drawn with
tremendous gusto in a sort of slapdash detail: guns bristling
all over the place, scribbled amendments in every corner of
the sheet, sometimes crossed out, sometimes heavily under-
lined, and conveying an effervescent impression of spontaneous invention. Fisher was always thinking about new ships,
and defied his own opinion that all enthusiasts were bores by
pouring out his ideas to anyone who would listen, men and
women alike.

He was a genuine visionary when it came to naval technique. Sometimes his ideas were mistaken and inconsistent,
and often they were impracticably ahead of their time, but
his record of intuitive prophecy was astonishing. He was
among the earliest to recognize the significance of the self-
propelled torpedo, the turbine engine, oil fuel, long-range
gunnery and the firing of guns by electricity. He fought for
the adoption of the water-tube boiler, in which the old way
of raising steam was reversed—"the water where the steam
used to be, the steam where the water used to be." He seized
upon the idea of the all-big-gun battleship, which was to set
the pattern of capital ships everywhere. He foresaw refueling
at sea. He thought of oil pipelines under the English Channel
four decades before they were used in the Normandy invasion of 1944. He envisaged a deep-water ship canal across
Scotland, enabling battleships to be transferred swiftly between the North Sea and the Atlantic, and an underground

reservoir containing 15 million tons of fuel oil. He suggested applying the internal combustion engine to a turbine long before it was technically possible—half a century later it powered most of the ships of the Royal Navy. He was an enthusiast for aviation, and prophesied that one day it would put an end to navies as history had always known them. He suggested that ships' decks should be covered with linoleum.

He was also one of the first to realize the potential of the submarine, and in this he ran against the whole instinct of the Royal Navy. In the average British naval mind of his time, as steam was to sail so the submarine was to the surface vessel. It was not just newfangled and ugly. It was ungentlemanly. Old 'Ard 'Art called it "underhand, unfair and damned un-English." Adopting it for the British Navy would only encourage other navies to adopt it too, upsetting the essential balance of maritime power. Many senior officers believed submarines should be internationally outlawed: almost nobody thought they would ever be used to attack merchant ships without warning—even Winston Churchill maintained that no civilized Power could be so caddish. Anyway, they could never be oceangoing vessels, and so were only useful as a means of coastal defense.

Every one of these tenets Fisher dismissed. He too originally conceived of the submarine as a defensive weapon, a new means of denying enemy access to the seas around Britain; but later he also foresaw it as a deep-sea weapon of offense that would one day be used to sink any hostile vessel that came its way, naval or merchant, indiscriminately and without mercy. The time would come when defending

British commerce against enemy submarines would be the Royal Navy's chief purpose. In the meantime, the navy must have a submarine branch of its own, and Fisher was its real father. In his old age he was to be concerned with all kinds of submarine projects—boats with aircraft in hangars, boats with gigantic guns, steam-propelled boats. The M1 submarine had a twelve-inch gun that would be fired with only its muzzle above water, and Fisher rightly called it "the forerunner of the Battleship of the future." He foresaw the time when such huge submersibles would be capable of circumnavigating the globe underwater, and I saw it come true at Groton, Connecticut, in 1953, when I watched the world's first nuclear submarine, USS *Nautilus*, slide down the launchway into the Thames River. I thought of Fisher then, of course, and half-fancied I saw him on the launching stand charming Mamie Eisenhower, and snatching a bud from her bouquet of red roses.

Submarines were in their primitive infancy, though, when he first became interested in them. It was only in 1901 that the Royal Navy received its first boat—built under license from American manufacturers—and Fisher became wildly enthusiastic about them as commander in chief at Portsmouth in 1903. The first flotilla, of five boats, was based there under the command of one of his favorite protégés, Captain Reginald Bacon, and he reveled in the brio of its young officers. As the ultimate Tarpaulins they were disdained by most of the fleet, and nicknamed generically "The Trade," but no doubt that endeared them to Jack all the more, and made him imagine himself one of them. He delighted in having them harass the ships of the Channel Fleet during exercises, popping up at odd times to declare a kill—no matter that sometimes battleship captains resolutely refused to have been sunk, and continued sniffily on their way. He adored the cocky restlessness of them, their liberation from all tradition (they were said to look like unwashed chauffeurs), and at all opportunities showed them off to visiting bigwigs. Once he invited the future George V to go down in a submarine, and he always remembered with relish the Princess of Wales's sole and placid remark as she watched her husband disappear into the murk: "I shall be very disappointed if George doesn't come up again."

Sometimes boats never did come up, or became involved in fearful accidents, and Fisher's grief was intense—he loved his young bloods of the submarine service. When one boat was damaged in a collision, and its commanding lieutenant was taken terribly injured and brain-damaged to the naval hospital at Gillingham in Kent, a weekly visitor to his bedside was Admiral Sir John Fisher. Imagine opening one's befuddled eyes at the nurse's soft voice, to find that legendary figure already settling in the chair beside your bed, propping his stick against your chest of drawers and hanging his cap on your bedhead! "I don't know who you are," the lieutenant once said, so Fisher himself reported, "but you *have* got a funny face!"

In principle the submarine was very much Fisher's weapon. It was *pure ship,* he said, and it epitomized his attitude to naval design, which was rather polypheman. He was for suddenness in weaponry, overwhelmingness, a savage ability to hit first and hit hardest. Most of all he was for speed. If you had a faster ship and a bigger gun, ran his simplistic maxim, no enemy could beat you—simplistic because it ignored a third factor, the ability of your bigger gun to hit its target. Speed became a kind of fetish for him. He drove his ships at maximum speed almost everywhere, and everything under his control had to be done flat-out. He urged shipbuilders to build ships faster, dockyards to hurry repairs, engineers to get more power out of their engines. Throughout his middle years, and even into old age, he seemed to be impelling his service and himself at full speed all the time, foaming and churning through all opposition, glorying in the panache of his young men and the horsepower of his ships. No wonder he had no taste for sail. He loved to feel the shudder of engines beneath his feet, to see the torpedo boats racing recklessly out of harbor, and the submarines surfacing mean and dripping from the deep. For his Christmas present in 1909 King Edward VII sent him a silver model of a submarine. "He thinks I'm mad about them."

I went back to Berehaven recently. It is in the Republic of Ireland now, and the Royal Navy is almost forgotten there. No hatbands or pictures of warships hang in the old sailors' pubs of Castletown, the guns have gone from the island cliffs, and I could find only a few ancients who remembered the days when the British fleet anchored in the haven and its admiral attended matins in the Anglican church beside the water. Dunboy Castle was burnt in the Irish Troubles of the 1920s, and is now a blackened ruin. At the narrows only a few last bits of iron stanchion remain from the greatest of harbor booms.

Nobody I met there knew about the *Polyphemus* and her exploit of 1885, but the ship has been immortalized anyway. She never went into action in fact, but under the transparent alias *Thunder Child* she was almost the only earthly weapon able to resist the onslaught of the Martians in H. G. Wells's *The War of the Worlds*, hurling herself as furiously at the wading space machines of the Thames estuary as ever she fell upon that boom in Ireland, until the heat ray got her in the end.

Piety

One Sunday morning the congregationalist minister at Richmond in Surrey noticed a stranger walking up the aisle, and assuming that he was some visiting farmer, wondered if the sermon would be above his head. He was catastrophically mistaken. It was Jack Fisher who was joining his congregation, and there was never anyone more knowledgeable about sermons, more fiercely critical or more enthusiastically appreciative than this unnerving churchgoer. Chaplains, ministers, vicars, curates and canons around the world quailed at the sight of his strange face glaring intently up at the pulpit as they cautiously navigated their way through the Scriptures; after the service Fisher was only too ready to engage them in dialectic about the redemptive significance of Leviticus or the correct interpretation of a parable. Far more common than the response of the Richmond minister was that of the English chaplain at Lucerne, whom Fisher once reported complacently as being "very meek and nervous to a degree."

Jack's religious zeal was lifelong. His father, writing to him from Ceylon when he was thirteen years old, adjured him:

"Never forget your religion and your prayers, and don't let any bad fellows laugh at you for being better than they are." He faithfully obeyed. His letters to Mrs. Warden at Shanghai are studded with religious sentiments, sometimes getting (to my taste, anyway) uncomfortably close to priggishness. Remembering his father's instructions, he lectures fellow midshipmen who would like to be confirmed but are afraid of being laughed at, and rejoices when someone his moral equal arrives on board: "We had such a nice fellow join us here the other day. . . . He has established himself as my chum. . . . His great fault is he's too good. . . . It's very jolly having a fellow like that who you can talk to, instead of a parcel of noisy wretches who are always fighting one another, etc., etc. . . ."

By the time he is in his twenties, and a married man, the evangelical strain is intense, and his interminable letters to Kitty, mostly written at sea, are heavy with piety. He is very grateful to God, he says, for separating the two of them, "for it has made me feel much nearer to Him." He copies out great slabs of the Bible for her instruction. He complains that the captain of the *Ocean* never comes to Holy Communion— "I see he feels he ought to come and he offers a sort of unpleasant kind of resistance to it, such as coming and asking me what the bell is tolling for, and what the Chaplain is doing, etc. . . ." He thinks Admiral Sir Henry Kellett a most wicked old wretch, because he never goes to church and he once heard him whispering something blackguardly to Mrs. Smith concerning her confinement. He falls "quite in love" with the Anglican bishop of Zanzibar. He is pleased to be dining with Commander Blomfield, "a nephew of the late Bishop of London of that name."

Here he finds some lines in Ecclesiasticus "which I feel to apply so entirely to myself," or opens his prayer book to discover a sentence "almost sent" to him: "Man's goings are of the Lord; how can a man then understand his own way?" He wishes he had known John Keble, and hopes that divine's sacred thoughts will be of help to Kitty. He urges her, if she is unable to get to church, to "go through the Communion Service by yourself and take the Sacrament, as it were, in your heart." Sometimes he is frightfully humble. He fails most miserably in his prayers, he says, and when he sends a check to the vicar of St. Jude's, Southsea, in appreciation of an excellent sermon, he soapily tells the cleric: "You will heap coals of fire on my head if you ever think, speak of, or write to me as even a mediocre example of Christian life"— (which I have to say, during the seventy-nine years of Jack's existence, very few people did).

Fortunately this sanctimony abated. He had read somewhere that the very devout seventeenth-century judge Sir Matthew Hale carefully concealed his religion, for fear that it might incite "impious men to blaspheme the name of God." Perhaps Fisher's religiosity had indeed fired impious men to blasphemy—the captain of the *Ocean,* for instance; certainly in later life, though he attended the Eucharist almost daily, his faith was relatively unobtrusive. The evangelical cringe left his letters, and his biblical references were now more generally employed as arguments for bigger guns, more merciless strategies or the need for revenge. He justi-

fied brutality in general by quoting Matthew 11, verse 12—
"The kingdom of heaven suffereth violence, and the violent
take it by force"—but the Old Testament figured far more
often in these manifestos. It was Jehovah the war god whose
values he generally summoned. "The Sermon on the Mount
don't pay where the Articles of War are concerned!"

His command of secular literature might be limited, his
understanding of history superficial, but there is no denying
his mastery of the Bible. The writer Filson Young thought
his brain was "convoluted and patterned" by it. Like a
doorstep apostasizer (he sometimes thought he would like to
have been a missionary), he had a biblical simile, analogy or
riposte for almost everything. The prophets were his famil-
iars, and all the tales of Israel had their resonances for him,
especially those (as Young said) having reference to Smiting
or Coming Swiftly from Behind. A campaign for the adoption of water-tube boilers might be Absalomic. Opponents of
turbine propulsion were the forces of Baal. He constantly
took as his text Jeremiah 51, verse 56—"The Lord God of
recompenses shall surely requite." Joshua and Elijah, Pilate
and Herod, Korah, Dathan and Abiram, Jephthah and his
oath, Ahab and the bow, the Foolish Virgins, King David,
Jonah—all found themselves hurled about in Fisher's writ-
ings.

His references must sometimes have been abstruse to his
less religious correspondents. Did Winston Churchill really
know what the admiral meant, when he recommended for
some recalcitrant critics "a strong dose of Haman"? How fa-

miliar was George Lambert with the Balaks, sons of Zippor?
Did Edward Goulding entirely understand when Fisher confided in him that "the fate of Rehoboam taking the advice of
the friends of his youth is surely impending?" What *did* the
prophet say to Ahab that was so relevant to Fisher's views
about the distribution of fleets? And had King Edward VII
ever heard of the grapes that Caleb brought to Moses, compared by Fisher to those sold in the South Tyrol at twopence
a pound?

Fisher was a staunch Protestant. He was a grandson of the
rectory, after all. He distrusted the Roman Catholic Church
in a rather unpleasant way, even suspecting it of Jesuitical
activities within the navy itself, and revered the English
martyrs of the Counter Reformation—"Where are monu-
ments to these great heroes?—and Generals you never heard
of all over the place." But he was an idiosyncratic kind of
Protestant, a sort of pragmatic fundamentalist who wor-
shipped in churches and chapels of many denominations. An
example was his attitude toward Jews. Their only weakness,
he once said, was their lack of patriotism and fighting spirit,
and from the start he supported the idea of a Jewish national
home in Palestine. I think he was perfectly serious in declaring the British to be the Lost Tribes of Israel. So passionate
and heartfelt were his references to the story of Israel, so important a part did the Old Testament play in his thinking and
his imagery, that his acceptance of the British Israelite no-
tion—in those days the basis of a thriving cult—does not
seem preposterous. If he did not really believe in it histori-

cally, he may well have embraced it in a visionary way, which is perhaps why he trusted so strongly in strokes of Jehovan destiny.

All his life Fisher did what his father told him, and braved the contumely of the heathen. Everyone knew he was a practicing Christian, whether as mate of a frigate on the China station or Admiral of the Fleet, and in his old age he became so insatiable an attendant at Westminster Abbey that the dean warned him against spiritual indigestion.

He admired all expertise, and none more than the expertise of theologians. He eagerly read the treatises of divines— "Robertson of Brighton, the greatest preacher of the world after Buddha," or "that wonderful Hebrew scholar Dr. Ginsburg." William Inge, the publicity-loving dean of St. Paul's, was a hero of his (splendiferous sermons and phrases that were "too lovely"). He conducted a protracted correspondence with the dean of Wells about biblical translation and the authorship of the collects. When I first began my pursuit of Fisheriana I heard from a lady whose husband had been English chaplain at Naples in the early years of the century. She remembered as if it were yesterday the appearances of the admiral at her husband's services, and the rapid-fire discussions at the luncheon table afterward. Forty years later, when I began to write this book, I heard from her daughter, recalling those doctrinal exchanges of her childhood just as vividly.

Fisher had powerful and sometimes eccentric theological views of his own. For example he thought that Thursday

should be the Christian Sabbath, because on that day the
Ascension happened: while scientific agnostics might try to
explain away Christ's resurrection with theories of trance or
catalepsy, there was no disputing the fact that the apostles
saw Jesus carried up into Heaven—*"Vide* the Collect for the
Sunday after Ascension Day!" Fisher's views on Heaven and
Hell were extreme but I hope tongue in cheek. Hell he described as "the unquenchable fire and the undying worm that
the Almighty so righteously reserves for the blackguards of
this life." Heaven he defined as a place where engineers and
executive officers would all be playing the same kind of harp.
He had strong feelings about the episcopate. He wanted the
Chaplain of the Fleet to be a bishop, so that he could confirm
sailors into the faith, and in 1910 he went so far as to urge
upon the prime minister, Herbert Asquith, his own nomination for a new bishop of Winchester—all the existing bishops
were papists, he said, except John Percival of Hereford.

He loved the Bible with an undying passion, and his
one commitment to art was his adoration for the English
of Cranmer's Bible—the Great Bible of 1539. "All nations
and tongues of Christendom have come to admit reluc-
tantly," he rashly declared, "that no other version of the Book
in the English or any other tongue offers so noble a setting
for the Divine Message." Its cadences were constantly reflected in his own writing, and he despised all attempts to
improve it in later translations. What he would have said of
twentieth-century versions I shudder to imagine: the "diverse excellent learned translators of the Great Bible," as he
saw it, were "holy men who were not hide-bound with a dic-

tionary, and gave us the spirit of the Holy Word and not the Dictionary meaning."

As a pagan myself, believing that kindness is all, I have to say that Fisher's seems to me an equivocal kind of Christianity. As that embittered admiral asked on page 11 of this book, how could Christian gentlemanliness really be reconciled with the snakelike intrigues, the unforgiving vendettas, the invective and the snarl that characterized so much of Fisher's progress through history? He pursued an un-Christian profession, the profession of arms, and he pursued it with an acceptance of its most lethal practices, devoting his talents to the more efficient disposition of violence. He argued of course that the point of power was to make sure that war never happened, but there was no denying that his public God was the God of wrath and vengeance—"the angel of the Lord went out . . . and when they rose early in the morning, behold, they were all dead corpses." He may have been exaggerating for peaceful ends when he talked about boiling prisoners in oil; he was not bluffing when, during World War I, he arranged that U-boat prisoners should be treated with especial harshness *("Thou shalt not kill, but needst not strive / officiously to keep alive . . .")*. Ruthless, Relentless and Remorseless were the watchwords of his professional career; he could hardly argue that they were watchwords of his savior.

Fisher's private God, though, was gentler. In his old age he behaved in a sadly un-Christian way even to his faithful

Kitty, but beyond his fundamentalist views, expressed in such hyperbole, there lay a kindlier conviction. "I have never been good, so I admire it more in other people." The essence of his faith was the idea of service. A man should always be striving, always looking upward, as the apostles looked up to their Lord ascending into the clouds—the imagery of the Ascension was constantly in his mind. My querulous old admiral of page 11 would not think so, but Fisher did have a true gift of understanding, which made his friends lifelong and sometimes even mollified his enemies. He genuinely felt for the men of the lower deck, and "the poor little midshipmen." Grandee though he became, to the end of his life he retained something of the common touch, and he was never patronizing.

After the publication of his two autobiographical volumes, almost at the end of his life, he embarked upon a third book, which was still in crude draft form when he died. It was to be called *Visions*, and perhaps it expressed the real Jacky better than all his hundreds of explosive letters, his rip-roaring reminiscences and his naval memoranda. Its purpose, he said, was to encourage young people never to repress their emotions, and it is a rambling, half-senile production centered upon Nelson's death at Trafalgar—"the most pathetic scene in human (not holy) history." It meanders on through collects and mystic quotations, references to Dean Inge or Jeremy Taylor, thoughts about the importance of conscience, the overrating of logic, the godliness of Abraham Lincoln, miracles, angels, the wiles of the Devil and the religious convictions of Lord Kitchener. It is a mess, but an affectingly aspiring mess, and it ends perhaps unwittingly with a couplet that might well be Jack's own epitaph, had he not already arranged a grander text for himself:

> The hues may be of common earth
> The lustre is of Heavenly Birth.

Intrigue

"My mission is that of the mole—my existence only to be known by upheavals." Fisher knew perhaps that he could never be one of the great fighting admirals, and instead came to recognize that his life's purpose must be to rejuvenate the British Navy before the next war happened—to drag it out of the eighteenth century into the twentieth. To achieve this he had to beat what in the 1960s radicals would learn to call the System—the profound and resolute inertia of an ancient establishment—and he did it partly by intrigue. Rudyard Kipling once wrote that the officers of the Royal Navy struck him as being half simple, half wily, and Fisher fitted the description perfectly.

The British had a small army but a big navy, and much their largest defense costs were for ships and their equipment. As always, there were constant conflicts between the claims of security and economy. The 1870s were to become known to navalists as "the Dark Ages of the Navy," because the Liberal governments of the time had been particularly tightfisted, but in the last decades of the century a series of so-called Navy Scares, well-orchestrated campaigns of artificial panic, led to repeated sudden splurges of expenditure. In the United States a century later, similar arguments, with similarly mixed motives, raged about the demand for more aircraft, newer ships, or Star Wars: and just as behind the scenes in America an immense military-economic complex fought for greater armed forces in the interests of profit, so in Victorian Britain shipbuilders and steelmakers and gunmakers pressed for the expansion of the Royal Navy, in effect simultaneously the navy, the air force and the space agency of the age.

Fisher prided himself on being as conscious of economy as any politician, and he was sometimes blamed by the navy for reducing its building programs, but in general he was of course on the side of growth and modernization. He very soon became aware of the forces behind the scenes that really dictated policies, and he astutely learnt to manipulate them, striking up friendships with politicians, shipbuilders, armament makers and influential men of affairs, and assiduously cultivating the press.

The navy was big news in those days. Everything about it was assiduously reported, pictured and discussed, often very outspokenly, there being no Official Secrets Act to dictate discretion. New ships were glorified in purple prose, or summarily dismissed as a waste of taxpayers' money. The appearance of a new kind of warship, a *Warrior* or an *Inflexible*, commanded long columns of reportage and editorial comment, often to be followed by weeks of correspondence from naval officers serving or retired. When the revolutionary battleship *Devastation* had engine trouble on her first cruise in 1869, a storm of mockery and contumely erupted in the papers; one week in 1906 the lead cartoon of *Punch,* by its celebrated cartoonist Bernard Partridge, concerned improvements in the navy's gunnery. The newspapers employed full-time naval correspondents, and essayists in the Kipling mode were frequently let loose upon naval exercises or launchings—Kipling himself sometimes (and he must have pleased Fisher when in 1898 he described a British battleship cleared for action as being "naked and grim, like a man swimming with a knife between his teeth . . .").

I daresay Fisher first realized the power of the press at Alexandria in 1882. Two civilian guests, Moberly Bell of *The Times* and an artist of the *Illustrated London News,* were present on Lord Charles Beresford's ship in that action, and this ensured that the exploit of the little *Condor* became far better known in England than the services of the *Inflexible,* or even of the armored train. WELL DONE CONDOR, WELL DONE INFLEXIBLE, said the admiral's signals when the bombardment was over, but only the first message got into *The Times,* while nothing could be much more patriotically inspiring than Our Special Artist's depiction of Lord Charles's feat. Two years later Fisher had learnt enough to play an important back-of-the-hand part in the first and most effective of the Navy Scares, the campaign of 1884. This was orchestrated by the brilliantly sensational journalist W. T. Stead, editor of the *Pall Mall Gazette.* He was afforded powerful incitements by various politicians, and lyric support by the Poet Laureate,

Lord Tennyson, who dreadfully warned Lord Northbrook, the First Lord of the Admiralty, that the very fate of England depended upon more money for the navy:

> You, you, that have the ordering of her fleet,
>   If you should only compass her disgrace,
> When all men starve, the wild mob's million feet
>   Will kick you from your place,
>   But then too late, too late.

Much of the technical information for this agitation was provided sub rosa by Jack Fisher, who was then still on sick leave after Alexandria, and the experience had a lasting effect upon him. During the next four decades he seldom missed a chance to influence newspapers in the direction he required, or to ingratiate himself with their correspondents. Temperamentally he was on their side—he greatly admired a scoop of Stead's achieved by illegally boarding HMS *Implacable* up a rope ladder from a small boat—but he was also perfectly conscienceless in exploiting them.

Some of the leading journalists of the day, among them other celebrities like J. L. Garvin and J. A. Spender, were lured into Fisher's web, and a massive correspondence survives to illustrate their often furtive relationships. Fisher was an early master of the leak. His letters are littered with hugely scrawled instructions of confidentiality—"Secret!," "Profoundly Private!"—but Arnold White, one of his most carefully cultivated confidants, said once that if a Fisher letter was headed "Burn and Destroy," it meant "publish as widely as possible but don't give me away." Fisher thought of his tame writers as missionaries of his word, or preaching friars, but he would not hesitate to deceive one at the expense of another, or to feed them all misinformation. "I have not told anyone but you," he assured the naval correspondent Gerald Fiennes about an event in 1912, but actually he told four others too. He skillfully flattered newspapermen, some more sincerely than others, inviting them to his ship or his house, and addressing them as Dear Friend, or Beloved. Some of them, useful of contact but not always gifted of style, probably got their best reviews from Jack—"the finest article I ever read"—"nobody understands but you!" He likened the gratified White to a second Aaron, "Moses being in the background in the shape of a multitude of humble admirers who like myself venture to ask you to say what they feel themselves full of but unable to express."

The most influential of the naval correspondents, and one who became a real friend, was Sir James Thursfield of *The Times,* presently to be father to an admiral himself. Half a century later Thursfield's grandson and I were contemporaries at *The Times,* and Patrick Thursfield lent me a stack of correspondence between Fisher and his grandfather. It is scattered before me now. Fisher's letters are sometimes in bold ink, sometimes in crayon, sometimes in violently scrawled pencil, but their prevailing tone is constant: they are instinct throughout with an air of highly collusive urgency, as though war is about to break out at any moment.

Even now Jack can seem almost criminal in his indiscretions. Here is a note written from the Admiralty in wild pencil in January 1907, when he was First Sea Lord:

> Dear Thursfield. This enclosed is the ultimatum signed by all the Sea Lords & presented yesterday at 4 pm to Lord Tweedmouth. You will see how secret it is. Please return by the next post. Ever yours
>
> J. A. Fisher

He can be fascinatingly tantalizing, too, like all the best manipulators of the press—"Tomorrow I shall probably send you the greatest secret I possess!"—and shamelessly devious. He suggests that an opinion of his might be printed in *The Times* as being "one strongly held by strongly-minded people," and after sending a pseudonymous letter to the editor of the paper, proposes that Thursfield paraphrase its content as his own. He would rather *The Times* did not publish the contents of a circular he is issuing to the fleet, preferring them to "ooze out from one of the home ports." He reports vital goings-on within the Cabinet Defence Committee cheek by jowl with ridiculous tidbits from Admiralty instructions: "Addendum p670, 4. Cuffs of the full dress coat. The Regulations for the cuffs of the Flag Officer's Full Dress Coat are undergoing further consideration."

Sometimes he is urging *The Times* to support a new measure of technical reform. Sometimes he is complaining about a politician's gaffe. How perfectly brilliant was Thursfield's article on the recent maneuvers—"a regular knocker-out!" It would be useful if Thursfield could look in at the Admiralty on Monday evening, when Fisher would have a *bonne bouche* or two for him. "I think it would be as well to say no more about what a certain Cabinet Minister said to me. . . ." He is looking forward to luncheon next Tuesday. He must tell Thursfield sometime what the king said to him about–

About? Very likely about some enemy of Fisher's within the service. Jack's methods of dealing with the press were not so different from his behavior toward his colleagues. Within the navy too he cultivated his friars and deceived his confessors. His generosity was great, but he could bear a grudge for decades. Asked once what he had against a captain whose preferment he had recently blocked, he said he couldn't remember, but he knew there was something. When Fisher retired, he heard from an admiral who had long been an opponent, but who wished to send to the First Sea Lord and Lady Fisher his kind wishes, and those of his wife, on the occasion of Fisher's return to private life after so many honorable years of service—to offer his congratulations on the honors Fisher had received, to express his indebtedness to Fisher for his own advancement in the service, and to express his sincere gratitude for all the First Sea Lord's kindnesses and hospitality in days gone by. Fisher told him to go and hang himself.

Even friends like A. K. Wilson were not immune to Fisher's devices. When Jack was made Director of Naval Ordnance in 1886, Old 'Ard 'Art was appointed to be his Director of Torpedoes, but before he could even move

into his office Fisher demoted him to be *Assistant* Director
of Torpedoes, annexing the senior appointment to himself.
It was, Wilson wryly observed, "as if they had offered
me a situation as a cook and then made me scullery-maid."
Fisher believed in the Solomonic precept: "Treat your
enemy as if he was one day going to be your dearest friend,
and your friend as if your bitterest enemy." George Clarke,
later Lord Sydenham, was a friend in 1904, but by 1906
Fisher was suggesting that he be made governor of some
West Indian island, so that he could die of yellow fever (he
became governor of Bombay instead, but survived until
1933). Lord Selborne, one of Fisher's warmest admirers,
spoke warily about Fisher's "powers of hocus pocus,"
and Frederick Ponsonby said he had "an early Italian
type of mind," by which he meant, I suppose, the stiletto
type.

These tendencies, and an undoubted taste for subterfuge,
made Fisher his most bitter enemies of all—not his reformist
zeal, not his radical tendencies, not even his philandering,
but the suggestion of the underhand that ran through his behavior. This was the serpent trait that Mrs. Churchill hated,
and it was this above all that earned Fisher the inexorable
hostility of George V. Perpetual rumor had it that he placed
spies among the navy's wardrooms, charged with reporting
back to him on the condition of ships and the loyalty of captains, and sometimes he doubtless did. Certainly the members of the Fishpond kept Fisher closely in touch with the
moods and opinions of the fleet and the tactics of his enemies

within it. When the newly commissioned Lieutenant Filson Young, Royal Naval Volunteer Reserve, went to join the Grand Fleet in 1915 he was dismayed to be invited by the First Sea Lord to report directly to him, by private bag, on "anything you do not think quite right." Reginald Bacon, one of his most loyal acolytes, once sent him a series of private letters from the Mediterranean Fleet containing derogatory comments about its commander in chief. Fisher had them printed and circulated, confirming some of the navy's worst suspicions of him and blighting Bacon's career (though he went on nevertheless to write the first and most eulogistic of the Fisher biographies).

The more consequential Fisher became, the profounder his plots. He arranged for friendly questions to be asked in the House of Commons. He conspired with some of the great men of state, men like Arthur Balfour, Winston Churchill and Reginald Brett (Viscount Esher), an *éminence grise* of the court who was Fisher's confidant for years and in the end ruined him. He had the ear of Edward VII, and made subtle professional use of it. "He would write me long letters," Ponsonby recalled, "apparently intended only for me as they were so outspoken, but really for King Edward to read. . . ." Fisher was never a great diner-out—as Ponsonby said, he preferred the back door—and even in his glory days he generally avoided fashionable London society, but once a quarter he would meet for dinner with a remarkably handy trio of friends: Esher, Lord Knollys, the king's principal private secretary, and the Marquis de Soveral, Portuguese minister to the Court of St. James's and one of the most influential men in London. Fisher knew his velvet ways around the mole runs of power.

Of all the many contradictions in Jack's life, the dichotomy of his nature was the most disturbing, and it worried people always. It made him seem like a trick court card. Look at him one way, and he was the mischievous boyish figure whose company everybody enjoyed, infectiously proud of his ship and his navy, kind to his crews, never forgetting old friends, delightful to women and children. Turn him the other way up, and what do we find? A schemer and a man of malice, unforgiving in his rancor, who would balk at nothing to achieve his ends and who ruined more than one promising career— "Anyone who stands in my way I crush!" It was partly a conflict between his private and his professional life, but it ran deeper too, and must surely have reflected some profounder conflict within himself.

He was more of a Manichaean than most of us, I suppose, possessing in his character a quite unusually powerful respect for good and bad. In his old age he became very conscious of it himself, and liked to call it the Rembrandt Effect—"the Good stands out all the more strikingly if there is a deep shadow." Infatuated member of the Fishpond though I am, I cannot bring myself to like this disingenuity. I fear there was always too much calculation to his nature, to his childish charm at Catton Hall, to his engaging adolescent attitudes on the China station, to his friendships with admirals and people of influence. He was going to win, and he used the whole armory of his talents and personality to do it. When I first started thinking about Fisher, some of my informants would allow no good to him at all, and believed his life to have been one long act of premeditated self-promotion.

This book, though, is a game of love. Being neither a disgruntled fellow officer nor the affronted wife of a rival, at a remove of seventy years I think the lovable in Fisher far outweighs the distasteful. I accept that his ambitions were far more for his service and his country than for himself, give or take a peerage, a command or a burst of applause. I am sure his fun was spontaneous, and his eagerness to please not all self-seeking. I know that his gift for friendship was as true as his capacity for enmity: one friend, the MP Alan Burgoyne, actually named a daughter "John" after him, and many of Fisher's shipmates remembered him with affection to the end of their days.

One of them, John Moresby, who became an admiral himself and has a town named after him in Papua New Guinea, watched Jack's progress through the decades with pride, and frequently wrote to express his encouragement, comfort and admiration. It was to this old comrade, by then in his ninetieth year, that the dying Fisher sent one of his very last letters, on July 6, 1920. This is what it said:

My dear old Moresby,
I am dictating a few lines to you to show you I have you in remembrance. I have had a serious setback. They tried

the X-ray treatment on me before leaving London, and
the shock was too great. But I have a very eminent physi-
cian looking after me, and he takes a cheerful view.
Don't you trouble to answer this.
Yours

FISHER

Among the last written words of famous men, "Don't you
trouble to answer this" stands up well enough; though more
characteristic of Manichaean Jack might have been BURN
AND DESTROY!! SACREDLY PRIVATE!!!

Principles of War

I recently sailed on a cruise ship to Devil's Island, the old French penal colony off the coast of French Guiana where Major Alfred Dreyfus spent his tragic years of imprisonment (and where particularly recalcitrant prisoners of France were confined until 1945). We were not allowed to land, allegedly because of a high sea swell. This contention was angrily refuted by some of my fellow passengers, who threatened to sue the shipping company for false advertising, and certainly the conditions did not prevent the Devil's Island customs officials from coming out in their own boat and enjoying a hearty lunch in our dining room.

From the ship's deck the island did not look like much anyway—a low scrubby thing, with a few shacklike buildings here and there, apparently deserted and so close to the mainland that beyond it we could see the French space-launching facility at Cayenne shimmering in the heat haze. It meant something special to me, though, because it plays an illustrative role in Jack Fisher's views about the nature of war. In the last decade of the century, during Dreyfus's imprisonment on the island, Fisher was commander in chief of the North America and West Indies station. His trim little fleet included a battleship, eight cruisers, three sloops and a destroyer, and was based jointly upon Bermuda and Halifax—he had a comfortable Admiralty House in each. It was an agreeable posting, though distant from the centers of consequence, political or professional, and Fisher regarded it as a stepping-stone to more fateful appointments. His flagship was his favorite *Renown*, small, fast and elegant, and he used it as much for pleasure as for warlike preparation, throwing frequent dances on its quarterdeck, and offering excellent dinners prepared by his private French chef, who later set up a restaurant in Paris on the proceeds. ("He really was excellent—but so extravagant!") In Halifax Fisher charmed many a susceptible Canadian; in Bermuda the beautiful American Mrs. Peek was frequently to be seen in his admiral's barge.

However, it happened during these easy years of snow and sunshine that there boiled up one of those perennial disputes with the French that so often seemed likely to end in war. This time it concerned the control of the Upper Nile, which a French expedition was threatening to acquire in a manner totally unacceptable to the British Empire. The Fashoda affair was taken very seriously on both sides of the English Channel. British fleets throughout the world were warned to be ready for action, and for a time Fisher thought that his Nelsonic moment might have arrived. In those days British commanders in chief were free to evolve their own war plans, and Fisher's were characteristically racy. He himself would charge across the Atlantic at *Renown*'s full nineteen knots. Ten of his ships, however, would be left behind to undertake a *coup de main*. They would sail to Devil's Island, cut the cable to France, send a landing party ashore (whatever the state of the swell), and abduct Captain Dreyfus. They would then make for Europe—and, I assume, a rendezvous with Fisher—to land the bewildered officer upon the coast of France, where his arrival would be greeted by an uprising among the populace, chaos in the French war machine and victory for the queen.

I tried to picture this audacious little operation for myself, as I leant over the rail off Île du Diable, but it all seemed too improbable even for my sort of virtual reality. All I saw was the customs launch, taking those officials replete and recumbent back to their duties, all I heard was the reiterated complaint of my fellow passengers in the heat—"I shall write at once, it's a disgrace, the brochure clearly claimed . . ." It is uncertain whether Fisher really meant to implement the plan, but there seems no doubt that he had worked out the dispositions, and when the crisis died away and war never happened after all, he expressed a certain disappointment: "I think we should have made rather a good job of it."

It was a truly Fisherian idea anyway. Surprising, fanciful, individualist, it expressed the sort of attitude that could sweep a woman off her feet, inspire a sublieutenant to daring deeds and induce journalists to acclaim Fisher as the next Nelson. At the same time it was slapdash, ill-considered and risky. I doubt if Fisher had thought out its implications; certainly he never coordinated the scheme with the plans of other admirals, with the Admiralty itself or with the Foreign or Colonial Office.

Admiral though he was now, his warlike instincts had evidently not much matured since the 1870s, when he defined his idea of an attack on an enemy vessel as follows:

1 Make for the enemy at full speed.
2 Fire bow guns at it.
3 Ram it.
4 Fire one broadside at point-blank range.
5 Fire a torpedo on one quarter.
6 Fire the opposite broadside at point-blank range.
7 Fire another torpedo on the other quarter.

Such a tactic, while certainly conforming to Fisher's dictum that war could not be conducted upon homeopathic principles, seemed to presuppose that the enemy would not be fighting back very hard. Most of his bellicose projects were like this—spirited, bold, but lacking in realism. He was a man of war, but more in the theory than in the practice, and so high-flown were his ideas that people could seldom be sure whether he really meant what he said.

This was partly deliberate, and if it made his strategic thinking unconvincing, it carried more weight politically. He believed in the deterrent power of overwhelming force, and in this, hyperbole could play a useful part. The idea of an omnipotent, merciless Royal Navy might well be sufficient in itself to prevent a war, or even to win one. As the American Captain Alfred Mahan had recently been arguing, in a book that every intelligent naval officer had read, it was the mere existence of Nelson's fleet—the "fleet in being," upon whose storm-tossed warships the Grande Armée had never looked—that won the Napoleonic conflicts for Britain.

Fisher was accordingly just the man (so Lord Salisbury, the prime minister, thought) to be sent as Britain's chief naval representative to the International Peace Conference convened in 1899 by the young Czar Nicholas II of Russia. It was to be held at The Hague, in the Netherlands, and its declared purpose was to limit the spread of armaments and temper the frightfulness of war, making it a more civilized means of settling national differences. The British took all such aspirations cynically, but had no wish to offend the Russians; fully restored to health by the pleasures of the North American station, so gregarious and entertaining an admiral as Fisher would help to keep the conference on a friendly level, while not for a moment conceding Britain's God-given if self-declared privilege of supremacy—that is to say, a navy as powerful as those of any two of its potential enemies.

Socially Jack was indeed a great success during the ten weeks of the conference. He was the senior naval officer there, but undoubtedly the merriest. Fifty-eight years old and full of gusto, his vitality was infectious and he happily indulged his hedonism. He stayed at the excellent Palace Hotel on the seafront at Scheveningen, where he could entertain handsomely on the terrace above the sands. He called upon other delegates at their hotels, dined with the representative of Siam, swapped ideas with Captain Mahan, who was his American opposite number, and went for long walks along the beach with General Gross von Schwarzhoff, the German military representative. He gossiped with W. T.

Stead and other likely confidants. He turned up at a banquet at the queen of Holland's palace wearing a shawl and a civilian greatcoat over his uniform, because he had left his uniform cloak behind. He danced into the small hours nearly every morning. He grumbled when he found himself charged five francs "for a tiny bit of beefsteak" and a bottle of beer. He was fun, he was invigorating, he was friendly to all. In a photograph of the assembled British delegates, all top-hatted and nearly all mustached, he looks less like a government representative than a light comedian: he alone wears a white hat, he alone is in spats, his tie is worn more elegantly than any other, and he sits with both hands on his walking stick as though he is about to spring into a soft-shoe shuffle.

It could be said, all the same, that he carried more weight than anybody else at the conference, for his tour of duty in the North Atlantic had ended, and he was about to take up his duties as commander in chief of the Mediterranean Fleet, the single most powerful instrument of war in the world. Everyone at The Hague knew this, and realized that Salisbury's choice of Fisher as chief naval delegate carried messages beyond the mere sociable. When he danced the night away, he danced with a dozen battleships at his back, and when he walked with General von Schwarzhoff along the sands at Scheveningen both men could doubtless hear distant gunfire of the mind.

At official sessions of the conference Fisher behaved with perfect diplomatic propriety. He had no faith in the main purposes of the meeting, though—"the humanizing of war! You might as well talk of humanizing Hell!"—and in private conversations made his own views all too clear. His attitude then was dreadful. "The essence of war is violence. Moderation in war is imbecility. Hit first, hit hard, hit any- where." According to one of the British naval correspon- dents, Harold Begbie, he left his listeners "with blanched faces, with horror in their eyes." If a British fleet ever went to war under his command, he assured everyone, nobody would be immune to its power. Neutral ships supplying an enemy would be sunk without compunction. Captured submarine crews would be put to death. He talked about hitting the enemy in the belly, kicking him when he was down, tortur- ing women and children and boiling prisoners in oil ("if any prisoners are taken"). Captain S. Siegel, the German naval delegate, summed up the import of all this in his official re- port to Berlin. "England is firmly resolved to employ with all cunning and ruthlessness, in case of need, the instrument of war which she possesses in her fleet, according to the princi- ple Might is Right."

It was big talk—Fisher loved to exaggerate—but it was policy too. With his magnificent scowl and his vocabulary of invective, Fisher was the personification of his own warn- ings. The French at that time were building warships which, like some sorts of medieval armor, were specifically designed to look terrible—they called it the fierce-faced school of naval architecture. Fisher's own face, during these discourses at The Hague, fulfilled the same purpose: and just as the merry dancer of the evenings was seen to be the ferocious blood-chiller of the morning after, so it was implied that behind the ornate façade of the Royal Navy was a fighting force modern, ready and implacable.

It was hardly true, but Fisher was already determined to make it so, and his principles of war were to remain atavistic. He believed in unchallengeable strength under the control of a single mind, preferably his own. Luke 14, verse 31, he used to say, was never absent from him—"What king, going to make war against another king, sitteth not down first, and consulteth whether he be able with ten thousand to meet him that cometh against him with twenty thousand?" He stubbornly resisted the creation of a naval war staff. He preferred allies to keep out of the way—they could "come in afterwards and pick up the pieces." The first three general principles of naval war were: (1) Give no quarter. (2) Take no prisoners. (3) Sink everything. There was no time for mercy. In 1901 he suggested, perhaps only half in jest, the introduction of plague germs from Bombay to disaccommodate the French, and during World War I he seriously proposed the shooting of German prisoners in reprisal for zeppelin raids on London.

He was alarmingly predisposed to the preemptive strike. Time and again, as the Germans increased their naval strength in direct and obvious challenge to the British, Fisher suggested attacking them first. The best declaration of war would be the sinking of their fleet. "A Pitt or a Bismarck would not hesitate!" In 1905, when the Germans seemed likely to acquire a coaling station at Mogador in Morocco, Fisher said it should be made a *casus belli*: it did not matter twopence to Britain whether Germany got Mogador or not, but it would give the Royal Navy an excuse to destroy the German fleet and seize the Kiel Canal. "You must be mad!" said Edward VII when Fisher once expressed such an opinion to him, and even Esher thought, in 1906, that Fisher might deliberately precipitate a war with Germany. "The chances are," he wrote, "that we shall take the fatal step too soon, rather than too late." In the same year Kaiser Wilhelm II himself told Alfred Beit, the South African industrialist, that Fisher wanted to provoke war while the German navy was still unprepared: "I don't blame him. It is quite human."

Fisher himself always maintained that he was a man of peace. He wrote in visitors' books: "The supremacy of the British Navy is the best security for the peace of the world," and he doubtless believed it. Nevertheless his reputation as a warmonger was to survive him. "Hit first, hit anywhere." Many people took his word for it, and were afraid that Fisher's deterrent was not really intended as a deterrent at all, but as a weapon of first strike. There were always to be historians to suspect that his ideas, far from preventing World War I, only made it the more inevitable.

Fisher was a great administrator, an innovator, a reformer, a propagandist; but when it came to strategy many agreed with the view of one of his unfriendliest critics, Admiral K. G. B. Dewar, that he displayed "an ardent temperament and a superficial mind, undisciplined by criticism or study." Revisionist historians, on the other hand, have lately concluded that his strategic instincts were a good deal less slapdash than he made them appear—almost nothing about Jack Fisher can be taken at face value. Either way, there was something irresistible about his braggadocio, even merely in the principle. The elements of brutal speed, surprise and insolence that he seemed to express were very seductive, and although, as I stood at the rail of the cruise ship that day, I simply could not envisage his marines grabbing the astonished Captain Dreyfus, I could not help thinking what fun it would have been.

Lord of the Inner Sea

Almost imperceptibly the barge nudges the quay, and instantly the ropemen are ashore. With a salute and a smile of appreciation to the boatswain the admiral disembarks, and followed by his flag lieutenant and a couple of signalmen hastens up the crowded steps. All around are the fortress walls of Malta. The sun is extremely hot, the steps are steep, there is little shade and he is only just on the right side of sixty, but it would never do to show weakness; so he keeps up a steady pace and is gratified to hear Flags and the ratings panting behind him.

A few people look down from their casement windows to see him pass, but without surprise. He is a familiar figure here. Small boys stop to stare, shoppers and deliverymen get out of his way respectfully. A couple of off-duty seamen hastily salute, smartening themselves as they emerge from a side alley. "Afternoon, Admiral!" says a man whose face he vaguely knows, and adds facetiously: "Keeping the weight down, I see." He nods a response, no more. He is not in sociable mode. He is about the navy's business. He is Admiral Sir John Fisher, GCB, fortieth commander in chief of the British Mediterranean Fleet, and he is hastening to the Upper Barracca, the stony promenade high above Grand Harbor, to see his ships coming in.

There is no denying the satisfaction of the moment, when at last, wiping his brow with the big handkerchief from his breast pocket, he reaches the promenade. This is a place full of history. The Knights of St. John built the ramparts of Valletta all around, but by now the glorious harbor is a dramatization of British greatness, and the black-and-white ship of the line *Hibernia,* lying in Dockyard Creek as the Royal Navy's base ship, symbolizes the navy's long connection with the island—she has been part of the Malta scene for nearly a century. Many an imperial hero is commemorated on the Barracca: Admiral Sir Thomas Fremantle, Admiral Sir Henry Hotham, Governor Sir Thomas ("King Tom") Maitland, here a colonel of the First Ceylon Regiment, there a captain of the Fortieth Regiment of Foot (killed at the battle of Ferozeshah in 1845).

Fisher would be less than human if he were not a little puffed up to be heir to such traditions. Commanding the British Fleet in the Mediterranean is one of the supreme duties that can be entrusted to a naval officer, and the arrival of the ships in the Grand Harbor is spectacle enough to stir a dullard. That is one reason why, whenever the fleet returns from exercises, Fisher brings his flagship in first, hurrying up to the Barracca to watch the rest arrive. Another reason is that from this vantage point he can judge for himself the aptitude of his captains. He expects them to come in fast, maneuver smoothly and moor with polished briskness to their respective buoys in mid-harbor.

Here they come now. The lieutenant raises his telescope. The signalmen prepare their flags. Fisher knows his captains can see him clearly, up here on the terrace, and he bears himself at his most commanding. He has old friends and likely enemies down there on the ships, and nobody is going to be in doubt as to who runs this fleet. Out at sea, beyond the harbor entrance, his destroyers and torpedo boats are scudding into Sliema Bay, on the other side of Valletta; below him his flagship *Renown* lies already at her own mooring, swarmed all over by busy seamen. And here now, one after the other into Grand Harbor, come the battleships of the fleet in their white, buff and yellow liveries, ensigns flying, pennants streaming from their mainmasts, mooring boats lowered from their davits even as they enter: *Royal Sovereign* and *Royal Oak, Devastation* and *Illustrious, Ramillies* and *Revenge* and *Empress of India*—the most powerful squadron of capital ships in the world. One by one they sail in, swing around 180 degrees and take up their mooring buoys, bow and stern—some faster than others, some more efficiently, but on the whole up to the standard Fisher expects. "Not bad," he says to Flags. "Not bad, sir," Flags replies, but he knows as well as Fisher that there has been an exception. "Take a signal," says the admiral, and in a matter of moments the signalman is flagging it out across the harbor for all to see.

THE SECOND-IN-COMMAND'S FLAGSHIP IS TO RETURN TO
SEA AND RETURN TO MOORINGS IN A SEAMANLIKE MANNER

One can almost hear the gasp that greets this humiliating message, spreading across the fleet below and focusing upon the battleship *Ramillies,* flying the ensign of the rear admiral. Fisher leaves them to it. Dismissing the lieutenant and his men, he walks back across the Barracca, past the magnificent Baroque Auberge de Castille where the commanding general has his headquarters, past the monstrous opera house designed by Edward Barry of Covent Garden, down busy South Street to the eighteenth-century palazzo that is Admiralty House. The sentries stamp and salute. The steward takes his cap and stick. Loyal, comfortable Lady Fisher is in the drawing room with their daughters Beatrix, Dorothy and Pamela—the Fishcakes of Malta. "Welcome home, dear. Just in time for tea. Sit down and tell us all about it."

The sunny prime of Jack Fisher's life was lived as commander of the Mediterranean Fleet, from the summer of 1899 to the summer of 1902. He was at his very best then. He was, as he turned sixty, fit, confident and sensible. Never again would his life be so straightforward or his success so universally acknowledged. It was, as he said himself, *"the* tip-top appointment" with a fleet at sea, and it was almost certain to be his last. He intended to become First Naval Lord, the head of the service, before the statutory retirement age of sixty-five, and he used his term in the Mediterranean to do in little for his command there what he proposed later to do for the navy

at large: to prepare it, that was, for instant modern war—
"each ship manned, gunned, provisioned and fuelled, ready
to fight within five minutes."

The navy had come a long way since we last inspected its
condition, back in the 1850s. It was still experimenting with
its ships and guns, but the age of sail was distinctly over, and
with it had gone much of the navy's rakish eccentricity. No
major ships had sails now, so the old disciplines of topmast
and yard drill were lost to commanders. New drills had been
devised to compensate—the ritual spreading of awnings,
hoisting of boats, laying out of anchors. Spit and polish was
all the rage, captains spending large sums of money gilding
guns, nuts and hatches, and sometimes throwing ammunition
overboard rather than tarnish their brasswork in gunnery
practice. Paint was so heavily applied that ships' drafts were
increased by the weight of it. "ASPINALL'S Special Outside
Enamel," said an advertisement in *Navy and Army Illustrated,*
"was tried on H.M.S. *Magnificent* of the Channel Squadron,
and with such success that . . . now we are told that it is becoming quite the fashion in the Fleet 'to ASPINALL' the big
guns and turrets."

Still, there was much more professionalism around now.
Some able and imaginative admirals had commanded in
the Mediterranean, and Fisher had taken over a fleet trained
on relatively modern lines. As the Royal Navy's most powerful force, on its most strategically important station, the
Mediterranean Fleet was more than ever an arbiter of world
affairs. The Anglo-Boer War in South Africa, which broke
out soon after Fisher's arrival in Malta, seemed liable at any

time to ignite into a wider conflict. All Europe was delighted by the Afrikaners' brilliant successes, and Britain had never been more derided or unpopular. The jealousies and resentments of many decades had come perilously to the surface of affairs, and made even the British feel that splendid isolation could be an uncomfortable condition.

Fisher was aware that this made him a man of singular importance. His name had become well-known in the European chanceries since his dramatic performance at The Hague: perhaps for the first time since Nelson, a British fleet commander was an international figure. The Mediterranean was, as the propagandists loved to say, the Lifeline of Empire—most of the oceangoing traffic that passed through was on its way, via the British-controlled Suez Canal, to the British colonies of the East. The British considered themselves to have special rights and privileges there, won in battle and safeguarded by force majeure. There were other British authorities of high rank in the Mediterranean. The governorship of Malta was an important appointment, and there were governors too in Gibraltar and Cyprus. In Egypt, Lord Cromer, officially only a consul-general, was really an imperial viceroy. Admirals were in charge of the dockyards at Malta and Gibraltar, there were generals in Egypt and Malta, and besides the ambassadors in the great capitals a network of consuls, some professional, some honorary, many of them men of distinction, sustained British interests around the inner sea.

But among these magnificoes the commander in chief of the Mediterranean Fleet was captain. "The Admiral in command of the Mediterranean" is how the kaiser once addressed Jack Fisher. Cromer might rule a province, the British ambassador in Constantinople might be one of the diplomatic swells of Europe, but the whole British presence depended upon the guns of *Renown, Illustrious* and their sisters. More than that, the balance of world peace might be said to depend upon them: Russian designs on the Dardanelles, Greek rivalries with Turkey, French ambitions, Italian frustrations, German dreams of empire—all were restrained by the mighty force that resided in Grand Harbor, Malta, at the center of the sea.

Fisher particularly kept his eye on France and Russia, Britain's chief potential enemies as the new century opened. He had little faith in the British government's sources of information. Its ambassadors had no more idea of what was going on than infants in arms; the ambassador at Constantinople was charming but effete, the minister at Athens even more charming but couldn't remember his own name. Instead Fisher built up an intelligence network of his own among the consuls in the Mediterranean seaports, among British businesspeople and among friends and acquaintances of all nationalities. His Levantine talent for intrigue was a help here. In his old age he claimed mysteriously to have established a clearinghouse for intelligence in Switzerland, and said he was able to decipher "all the cypher messages passing from the Foreign Embassies, Consulates and Legations through a certain central focus." Certainly by arranging direct telegraphic links with consular agents from the Canary Islands to Perim, he made himself independent of the Admiralty in following the movements of foreign warships. When he met foreign officers, dignitaries or commercial people he pumped them for information—"my dear friend Kiamil Pasha, who may yet be Grand Vizier," or "my faithful friend" the U.S. minister at Constantinople, or "Grech, who owns all the small steamers in the Levant," or Cottrell, manager of the Eastern Telegraph Company at Syra, or Gerald Fitzmaurice, who knew everything there was to know about Turkey, or even "old Gervais at the French Admiralty." The Hungarian governor of Fiume sent Fisher some of the family Tokay. He was "very great friends" with the commander in chief of the Austrian navy.

How carefully he kept his finger upon the pulse of things one can see from the innumerable letters he wrote in his own hand to his superior the First Naval Lord, Admiral Lord Walter Kerr. I have a pile of them in front of me now, courtesy of the Kerr family. The two were not close friends (Kerr was a Catholic convert), and the letters are generally steady and impersonal—not at all in the flamboyant, reckless style that later became Fisher's epistolary hallmark. He suggests for example that before the battleship *Empress of India* goes to Tangier they should find out if there would be political objections to the visit. He reports that the Russian cruiser *Gromoboi* is leaving Piraeus for China, and that the battleship *Petropavlovsk*, recently visiting Malta, has six or eight Maxim guns in her fighting top. He hopes to be able to dodge the attentions of Admiral Bettolo, the Italian Minister of Marine, during the fleet's forthcoming visit to Naples. He hears that the Russian consul in Malta has arranged to cut the cable to Syracuse in case of war, and that large Boer subsidies are going to the French press. He wonders that Disraeli didn't take Lemnos, with its magnificent harbor, rather than Cyprus. He notes the elliptical conning tower in the French battleship *St. Louis,* and sensible new anchor arrangements in the Spanish *Carlos V.* He suggests that dark green might be a good color for torpedo-boat flotillas. He urges the need to get rid of wooden fittings in warships—the Austrian navy even has steel sea chests for midshipmen. He sends a photograph of the Brazilian coast-defense ship *Marshal Deodoro,* recently completed at Toulon. He learns that both the French and German navies are adopting a new "diamond" method of attack, and reports that according to *Le Petit Journal* of Paris war is likely to break out immediately after the Paris Exhibition of 1900. "The Russian Admiral . . . Birileff is a very clever fellow and he makes no disguise of the Russian and French intentions—the Mediterranean is to be the theatre of war . . ."

Like all admirals writing to their superiors, he constantly argues the need for more ships under his command—he wanted twenty battleships, thirty-six cruisers and sixty-two destroyers in all—but in general Fisher's letters from Malta are restrained, if inevitably opiniated. He was a professional of long experience, and he was confidently on top of his job.

Kerr was of the opinion that Fisher exaggerated the French and Russian threats—"as though they are going to fall on him at a moment's notice." This was, of course, part of

Jack's professional philosophy. He firmly believed that Armageddon, when it came, would happen somewhere off the island of Minorca, but anyway, at all times, everywhere, his fleet must be ready for immediate warlike response. It was a new concept for the Royal Navy, and Fisher's arrival at Malta had a revolutionary effect. "It is impossible to exaggerate the new ardour produced in the younger generation of officers," reported Reginald Bacon, who was one of them.

The fleet was still a heterogeneous affair. The oldest of its twelve battleships dated from the days of the early turret ships in the 1870s. Its newest included examples of the first big standardized class, the *Royal Sovereigns*. Some had 12-inch guns, some $13^1/2$-inch, some breech-loading, some muzzle-loading. The very look of these great ships was bewilderingly varied. Some had funnels fore and aft, some side by side. All had grace notes of their own, figureheads, ornamental scrolls at bow or stern, extra bridgework fitted by individual captains, differences of rigging or paintwork or boats. In full ceremonial fig, all flags and parading sailors, these ships looked like instruments of festivity; when they were stripped for action, their rails down, their awnings packed away, their decks cleared, they looked almost stagily ominous. And behind the big ships was the host of supplementary vessels—cruisers with two, three or four funnels, white-painted destroyers, torpedo boats, gunboats, dispatch boats, the torpedo-boat carrier *Vulcan*, which had six boats on its upper deck and enormous cranes to lower them, the ancient ironclad *Rupert*, which could make no more than ten knots, and the spectacular *Polyphemus*, an object of great interest when she was high and dry in the Malta dry dock, *The War of the Worlds* having been a bestseller.

All these ships Fisher set out to weld into a single modern weapon. He might have to put up with lesser anachronisms from the past, too much emphasis on appearance, too devoted an addiction to tradition, but he was determined to impose upon the fleet his own convictions about modernism and the offensive spirit. *Ut Omnes Veniant,* read the motto above the wheel of the destroyer *Boxer,* 265 tons, commander Lieutenant C. J. Twistleton-Eykham-Fiennes, and this was the spirit Jack wanted to instill from top to bottom of his command.

One method was to ignore the age-old hierarchical instincts of the British Navy, and encourage the cooperation of all his officers, senior and junior. He invited them to submit ideas directly to him, and eagerly absorbed them, great or petty. Lieutenant the Honorable Arthur Strutt of the torpedo-gunboat *Speedy* showed him his electric flashlight as an answer to the problems of conning a ship in the dark, and Fisher, who had never seen one before, immediately passed on the suggestion to the Admiralty. Lieutenant Herbert Richmond of the battleship *Canopus* made a proposal about torpedo tactics, and found them tested by the fleet the very next week. The chief naval constructor in Malta, W. H. Gard, became a great friend of Fisher's, and together they discussed all possible aspects of naval architecture: "We've got out an excellent scheme for making the conning tower a real jolly comfortable safe convenient place to navigate the ships and the Fleet from!"

Fisher invited groups of officers to lectures and discussions at Admiralty House, where a ground-floor room with a large plotting table was adapted for the purpose: officers who declined the admiral's invitation to attend were unlikely to find themselves quickly promoted (but as was reported by one lieutenant, later to become an admiral himself, "his smile is irresistible"). Tactics, gunnery, ship design, engines, all were constantly and vehemently discussed. Fisher treated everyone's opinions with equal respect, while at the same time making sure, he said, that the senior officers of the fleet were *"saturated"* with the views of their commander in chief. Bacon said the whole process made him feel "literally born again."

Gunnery practices were greatly intensified during Fisher's time in the Mediterranean, gunnery ranges were extended, there were endless experiments with wireless and torpedoes. And of course new speeds were achieved. In the Mediterranean, Fisher's obsession with speed reached fulfillment. Everything had to be done fast, from mooring the battle fleet to clearing the quarterdeck tables after an al fresco banquet (three and a half minutes were allowed the stewards, never mind how much crockery was broken). Ships' engines were strained to limits previously thought impossible in the admiral's determination to sweep his fleet about the sea; it was said that Fisher transformed a twelve-knot fleet with breakdowns into a fifteen-knot fleet without breakdowns. Haste in all things became endemic to the Mediterranean Fleet. When the navy undertook landing exercises with the British Army garrison in Malta (as Fisher told the tale), and the sailors found themselves repeatedly held up by the military, a rating was overheard saying to a sweating major: "Get a move on, you bloody lobster." In 1946 I stood on a quayside in Trieste to watch a British destroyer tie up, its decks alive with busy seamen, and chanced to hear the comment of an Italian standing beside me. "British sailors," he said to his companion, *"never keep still"*—and I like to think it was Fisher's legacy he was marveling at, twenty commanders in chief later.

Fisher's methods of command, as always, were at once exhilarating and infuriating. Up at four or five in the morning himself, he demanded absolute commitment from all his underlings. An admiral, he once said, had to be like the four beasts in the Book of Revelation, full of eyes behind and before, and he was ready to interfere with anything, regardless of proprieties or hurt feelings. That signal from the Barracca was by no means unique. He was once so rude to Vice Admiral Gerard Noel that Noel sent him a response rather in kind: "I am on my way to see you, *in my frock-coat and my sword."* Sluggish or uncooperative officers found themselves abruptly on the mailboat home, or transferred to the China station. Once, when the fleet was exercising off Salonika, Fisher summoned the venerable *Rupert,* then acting as guardship at Gibraltar, to join his flag at the other end of the Mediterranean. At her arthritic ten knots the ship just about managed the voyage and anchored with the fleet, to be ordered at once to put out her antitorpedo nets. Her unfortunate commander had to admit that he had left them behind. RETURN TO GIBRALTAR FOR NET DEFENCE, said the admiral's signal instantly—and all the way back poor old *Rupert* had to go.

The fleet spent much of its time at sea, sometimes as a whole, sometimes in detached squadrons. No corner of the Mediterranean was unfamiliar to its captains. There were exercises off the coast of Lebanon, with visits to ports in southern Turkey. There were calls at Alexandria, where Lord Cromer obligingly arranged to have the harbor deepened for the British Navy's use. They cruised among the islands of the Ionian Sea and into the Adriatic, where the Austrian navy was based, and among the Balearics, and frequently along the coasts of France and Algeria. Once they sailed through the Dardanelles to pay a courtesy call upon the sultan of Turkey, Abdülhamid II: the sultan decorated Fisher and his wife and distributed several hundred thousand Turkish cigarettes among the ships. In 1900 the fleet conducted joint exercises with the eight battleships and six cruisers of the Channel Fleet, commanded by A. K. Wilson. "All went splendidly," Fisher wrote of them, "40 vessels of all sorts were dashing about at full speed with no lights in every direction. . . ." He was very excited by such war games. "The more I work at them," he wrote to the First Naval Lord in one of his bubbliest letters, "the more lovely they seem to get . . . (as you will probably think I am becoming silly, I had better leave off)."

They were volatile times, and Fisher's slogan "Instant Readiness for War" really did have immediate meaning here. The visit to Abdülhamid was a warning to Russia, the cruises along the coast of France were notice that in the event of war the Royal Navy would once again, as in Napoleonic days, immediately blockade the naval base of Toulon. Fisher claimed afterward to have been secretly thanked by the sultan for preserving the peace in a dangerous period, and it may well have been true. During the three years of his command, the Mediterranean Fleet, fast losing its last nostalgic echoes of the yacht club, undoubtedly exerted a deterrent power throughout Europe. It influenced the diplomatic strategies of all the Powers, and the reputation of its commander, "Admiral commanding the Mediterranean," was borne in mind from Wilhelmstrasse to the Sublime Porte.

In Malta Jack Fisher was a *grandissimo*. Almost everything that happened there was geared to the needs of the fleet, much the biggest employer. On French Creek the great dockyards clanged and steamed. In the huge new Royal Navy Steam Bakery the ovens worked night and day. A hundred pubs catered to the sailors of the fleet, and in the narrow street called the Gut, familiar to every navy man, successive generations of whores welcomed their customers. A soiree at the opera house would have been incomplete without its complement of naval officers. Shops were Suppliers to the Admiralty. Photographers spent their whole careers photographing ships and their crews. Words from the Maltese language had long gone into the naval argot— "spitchered," from *spicca,* meant all done in, "sahha" meant good-bye. The coming and going of the fleet was an everyday part of Maltese life, and everyone knew its ships by name.

Even now, almost a century on, one may still sense the depth of this association. The Royal Navy has long left Malta, the dockyards are civil yards now, the opera house was bombed in World War II, but memories of the fleet pervasively linger. In the premises of Ellis's the photographers there hangs a large portrait of Alfred, Duke of Edinburgh, one of Fisher's predecessors, in his full-dress uniform as commander in chief: he it was who appointed the Ellis family Photographers to the Fleet. There are still pubs with names like the Black Cat or the Rule Britannia, and on the walls of the old Admiralty House are inscribed the names of all the Royal Navy's commanders in chief in the Mediterranean—thirty-nine before Fisher, twenty-six after him.

It is a museum of fine arts now, but in it I can still see Jack, making his officers laugh around the big plotting table downstairs, or giving Kitty and the girls a homecoming kiss before settling down to tea. It was a palace fit indeed for an admiral. Its magnificent double staircase was guarded by lions, and it was heavily pillared, and illuminated by big oriel windows and by a gallery window rather like a warship's stern-walk. All was light and white, with galleries on two floors and a courtyard outside for brandies after dinner. Just across the road, the northern bastion of Valletta's fortifications had been turned into a public garden, and there in all weathers Fisher would go for his daily walks—he preferred flat ground, so that he need not worry about where to put his feet. Often he was alone, deep in thought, but sometimes one

or other of the Fishcakes joined him, and officers with something interesting to say were always welcomed. All among
the palms, olives and oleanders he would walk steadily up
and down, pausing now and then to ponder an idea, empha-
size a point, or look down for a moment to Sliema, where his
destroyers lay, and "One-Eye."

He had social obligations, of course—social agonies he
called them, not altogether convincingly, telling Walter Kerr
that "life would be endurable but for its pleasures." *Ex officio*
he was bound to attend the frequent ceremonials and recep-
tions that sustained the prestige of the Crown in Valletta.
There was a good deal of political and social unrest in Malta
then, often concerned with conditions in the dockyards, but
Fisher had no responsibilities within the colony itself, and
the affairs of the dockyard were handled by its admiral-
superintendent, so he was able to maintain a pose of resplen-
dent benevolence. At Admiralty House, as in foreign ports,
his style was spacious and hospitable (he sent large expense
claims to the Admiralty). His flagship *Renown,* which he had
insisted on bringing with him from Bermuda, was a sort of
ideal British warship, whatever Mrs. Denslow of the Dover
Street shop might say: suavely awninged, immaculately
painted, its fore-topgallant mast heightened to carry his flag
higher than anyone else's, its admiral's quarters like the cabins of a liner and its admiral's barge so splendid that both the
king of England and the emperor of Germany were said to
covet it. Fisher also loved to show off the 1,650-ton dispatch
vessel *Surprise,* which was virtually his private yacht and

which he used for official visits to ports too shallow for his flagship, and jaunts for his wife and family.

In later years Fisher recalled that "a recent C-in-C" in the Mediterranean had paid his private chef £300, and that the chef had his own valet: circumstantial evidence (i.e., the extravagance of M. Augé, his chef on the North America station) suggests that he was referring to himself. His shipboard dances were celebrated, and at them he would forget the dignities of his office, and "caper about all evening," as the future cabinet secretary Captain Maurice Hankey wrote, like a junior midshipman. He put on a wonderful water carnival when the First Lord of the Admiralty visited Malta in 1901; each ship created some electrically illuminated animal or device, and the pièce de résistance was a gigantic representation of Jonah, all in electric bulbs, being repeatedly swallowed and regurgitated by his whale. The fleet itself he liked to present as a grand display, and he once described a new maneuver he had devised as "quite 'Augustus Harris' as a spectacle"—Augustus Harris being then the Cecil B. DeMille of the London stage.

Fisher might be intimidating when he was on the job, but in social life he was entertaining and attentive (it was as commander in chief in Malta that he was threatened with divorce proceedings), the perfect host at balls and parties, a compelling figure as, in his cocked hat, frock coat and gold-striped trousers, he paraded with his excellency the governor, the Roman Catholic archbishop, the grand prior of the Order of St. John, the general officer commanding, the diplomatic corps and the nobles of the Maltese aristocracy at celebratory functions.

It was one time of his life when almost everybody admired what he was doing (though Walter Kerr, at the receiving end of so many and such assertive letters, grew increasingly impatient as time passed). Fisher knew it. "We are going on splendidly," he wrote to Kitty, "but I must take care of the 'foot of pride.' " By the summer of 1902 he was ready to carry his reforming zeal closer to the heart of the navy, and he was not sorry to be appointed Second Naval Lord, the next step toward supreme power at the Admiralty.

His departure from Malta was an emotional occasion. There were farewell balls and banquets, "Auld Lang Syne" was sung, and "Good-bye, Dolly Gray," Jacky danced the Lancers with the elderly chief engineer of the dockyard and almost all the captains of the fleet came to *Renown* to say good-bye. At twelve noon on June 4, 1902, Fisher saw himself out of Grand Harbor with appropriate panache, at sixteen knots in his favorite ship. Mr. Ellis the photographer took some pictures of the occasion, and I have them before me now. The *Renown* herself went first, followed by the *Royal Sovereign*, the *Surprise* and the torpedo gunboats *Hussar* and *Dryad*. Between the moored lines of battleships they pounded at maximum speed, *Renown* herself flying from her topgallant mast, as Beatrix Fisher said, "the largest Admiral's flag that has ever been flown," together with an enormous White Ensign and signal flags fluttering all over the place.

Fisher stood proud and smiling on her bridge, the crews of his ships cheering from decks, bridges, masts and riggings as he passed. The sun shone, the bands played, sightseers waved from pleasure boats, along the ramparts a battalion of soldiers doubled to their positions—half an hour late as usual, Fisher commented. As she left the harbor *Renown* fired a farewell salute to the governor, and the smoke of her guns drifted in the sunshine up the golden walls of the fortress. It was Fisher all over, and one can hardly suppose that even his most resentful opponents failed to enjoy such swagger.

The *Renown* made for Genoa, where Fisher was to disembark for the train journey to London, but somewhere in the Tyrrhenian Sea that evening, in the calm of a Mediterranean twilight, the ship hove to. Presently there arrived alongside the little *Surprise*: and as the battleship lay quietly in that silent sea, Jack Fisher, his loving wife, his daughters and the officers of the flagship dined beneath the stars on its quarterdeck, serenaded by the band. What it was to be a British admiral, in the heyday of the breed!

III

FACE THAT LAUNCHED A
THOUSAND SHIPS

The Great Reformer

It was a case of *Athanasius contra mundum,* declared Jacky
Fisher when he set out to make a new navy, and *mundum*
had better look out, because Athanasius was going to win.
"We must have no tinkering! No pandering to sentiment! No
regard for susceptibilities! We must be ruthless, relentless
and remorseless!"

The year was 1904, and at the age of sixty-three he had
become the senior of the Naval Lords, whose titles he immediately caused to revert to the older and more romantic "Sea
Lords." It was to be the third and apocalyptic installment
of his periods at the Admiralty. He was the professional head
of the service at last, subject only to the civilian First Lord
of the Admiralty. An Order in Council made him, unlike
all his predecessors, solely responsible for the fighting
and seagoing efficiency of the fleet, and he was also specifically charged with reducing its enormous costs. The British
Navy had to be cheaper and more belligerently effective,
and during the next six years Fisher was to take the whole
of it as it were by the scruff of the neck and violently shake
it into modernity. The entire naval profession would
be plunged into change, controversy and sulfuric enmity.

There would be no rest. It was a volcanic experience for everyone.

It was obvious by now that Britain's most likely enemy was Germany. Admiral Alfred von Tirpitz, Fisher's opposite number in Berlin, had forced through the Reichstag two Navy Acts that would make the German navy the second largest in the world. Germany must build a battle fleet so strong, declared the 1900 Act, that a conflict with the greatest sea Power would "involve such dangers for that Power as to imperil its position in the world." It was not in Fisher's character to consider the possibility that Britain's arrogant confidence (and his own, for that matter) might have contributed to Germany's posture. His task was simply to prepare the Royal Navy for victorious war, and in this he became an obsessive. Filson Young thought him monomaniacal about it: "the universe was one storm cloud" for him, and he had no thoughts at all about the purposes of war, only about the British fleet's ability to wage it destructively and decisively.

By the time he had finished with it the navy was no longer an imperial exhibition but essentially a European weapon of war, based upon the North Sea and girded against Germany. Fisher in effect signaled the start of the British Empire's decline: to my mind of all the reforms he thundered through, historically the most resonant were his closing of imperial dockyards around the world—Halifax, Esquimault, Trincomalee, Jamaica—and his recall from the imperial seas of 155 aging warships whose chief purpose had been to display the benevolent superbia of empire. The first of the legions were coming home. "Well, boys," the captain of a gunboat on one such happy commission used to ask his officers in the morning, "where shall we go today?" Never again. Fisher saw to it that the holiday was over. "Because in the days of Noah we did the peace duties of the world at sea, we ... have vessels scattered over the face of the earth according as they settled down after the deluge!" Most of the ships were scrapped, the rest put into reserve in Britain.

Here in brief are the other chief achievements, or part-achievements, associated with the name of Fisher during the era of his reforms. The equipment of the Royal Navy was entirely modernized, and its ships were redistributed. The system of officer entry was reformed, and something was done to break down the preposterous social barriers between engineers and the rest. Lower-deck conditions were improved. Naval shipbuilding was greatly speeded. A new system of naval reserves was devised. Destroyers and submarines were introduced. Turbines and oil-burning engines were adopted, and oil supplies from Persia were ensured. The battle cruiser was invented, and a revolutionary new class of battleship was introduced, instantly changing the nature and the balance of all the world's battle fleets.

In short, by the erratic force of his personality Jack Fisher re-created the greatest sea force the world had ever known, transforming its matériel, ravaging its codes and customs, ruthlessly tearing apart its convictions, splitting it into bitter rivalries, but making it ready for his long-prophesied Armageddon, which certainly did not happen off the coast of

Minorca, but did burst upon the world, just as he said it would, in the late summer of 1914.

That personality was now developing into a climactic ostentation. It was mirrored in Fisher's handwriting, which like most people's had begun small. His letters to Mrs. Warden in Shanghai, written when he was in his teens, were cramped and careful. His voluminous letters to Kitty, as a young husband, were still jammed tightly on the page. His letters to Lord Walter Kerr, from the Mediterranean, were written in a moderate and businesslike script. But as he became more conscious of his fame and authority, he perfected a hand amazingly florid and assertive.

His signature in particular was majestic, especially when, having been ennobled in late middle age, he was able to sign himself simply "Fisher," or better still "Fisher, Admiral of the Fleet." It was written always with a flourish which gave an impression of spontaneity, but I suspect it was really meticulously crafted, and it ended his letters in a symphonic way, like a grand return to the dominant. He liked it so much himself that he had it imprinted, hugely enlarged, on the covers of his memoirs. The writing above it was just as idiosyncratic, and I love peering over his shoulder to see it in action. It is very large too, its letters rounded and its punctuation marks fierce—the whole performance rather fierce, actually. Capital letters figure large ("It's lovely how she throws in promiscuous capitals," Fisher once declared of somebody else's writing). Every now and then he furiously underlines something, often with two or even three muscular strokes of the pen, and he scatters exclamation marks every-where. Rapidly he hurls the thoughts, jokes, quotations and expostulations across the page, and when it is full he turns the paper sideways, and runs up and down the margins, and at the end he adds one of his music-hall farewells, and his enormous signature, and an italicized postscript or two, and a heavily scored adjuration to secrecy, before sitting back in his chair to survey the design (for the effect is as much visual as verbal), and hold it up with a grin for my ad-miration.

With the style of handwriting went a no less remarkable style of prose. Fisher was a self-educated man, and it owed nothing to literary example. It was in the most absolute sense *l'homme lui-même*. He wrote thousands and thousands of let-ters. His letters to Kitty from sea often run to scores of pages, but he was equally adept at the instant four-line note, dashed off aphoristically, or the pithily reasoned letter of policy. All were unmistakably his. One relatively steady letter about weapons and strategy, written to the prime minister in 1904, contained sixteen exclamation marks, seven italicized words and phrases, one passage in capital letters, three proverbs and two biblical references (the first to Satan, the second to David and Goliath).

Fisher's correspondence is like one long heady rush through life. Praise and invective are carried to equal extremes. A woman is the most beautiful creature alive, a friendly newspaper article is incomparable, an officer of the Fishpond is as clever as Archimedes or the greatest sailor since Nelson, Britain's naval position in 1906 is "in every little particular magnificently splendid." On the other hand, enemies are backstairs reptiles, limpets, parasites, jellyfish, poltroons, pestilent pimps, skunks, sneaks, fossils, Adullamites, syndicates of discontent, cabals of mandarins, bits of wood painted to look like iron, psalm-singing fools, rotund little curs, serpents of the lowest type, unmitigated cold-blooded rude brutes, exactly like weasels or full of sawdust. Lord Cromer, despite that harbor channel, is "an anointed scoundrel." Bonar Law the prime minister has no chest and sloping shoulders. The Foreign Office has as much courage as a louse and as much backbone as a slug.

Fisher loved his own epistolary style, and seldom rewrote a letter. "I like putting things down as I think of them, and if I was to read them over twice I should get disgusted with the stuff." He began his letters emotionally—My dear old Mams, My beloved Friend, My faithful Pamela, My Beloved Angel, My very dear, My darling B., My darling Heart, My darling Kitten, My own most darling Kitty. He ended them, famously, with comic valedictions: Yours till charcoal sprouts, Yours till the Angels Smile, Yours till we play Harps, Yours till a cinder, Yours till Hell freezes, Yours till we part at the Pearly Gates ("You'll get in! I shan't!").

The letters are full of calculated indiscretions, and Fisher was not above writing in one sense to one correspondent, in another to the next—or alternatively sending more or less the same letter to them both. In a single letter he would frequently range from petty details of family life or frivolous asides to great affairs of state. The longer he held high office, the more egotistical and repetitious his style, but the energy

of his letter-writing never flagged, and the handwriting
weakened only when death drew near.

One of Fisher's favorite sayings was "Reiteration is the secret
of conviction." There was certainly a hammerlike quality to
his thinking, as he pressed home his ideas and his prejudices
time after time, year after year, and he frequently expressed
himself in quotations. For a man who left school at thirteen,
and whose reading was mostly either technical or biblical, he
amassed an impressive repertoire of Latin tags, perhaps
without knowing their original context. I have counted
twenty-two at least, from elementary one-liners to complex
epigrams, all thrown into the correspondence with great
verve. How did he find them? From anthologies? From
Brewer's Dictionary of Phrase and Fable? He seldom reveals his
sources, only occasionally observing "as the Latin Grammar
says," and once appending gnomically to a saw: *"Found in an
old book."*

The English aphorisms were more often his own, but they
also included lines from some of his favorite poets. His tastes
in English literature were unusual. He claimed seldom
to read a book—"I look at the pages as you look at a picture,
and grasp it that way"—and he once told Winston Churchill
that the three best things in the language were the Bible,
the sermons of F. W. Robertson of Brighton and *The
Competition Wallah*, by G. O. Trevelyan, as serialized in the
Strand Magazine. He seems to have read quite widely, all the
same. His own adult verses (to judge by the only one I have
seen, and forbear from reproducing) were not above false

rhyming, but the poets he quotes include Shakespeare, Swift, Byron, Dryden, Burns, Gay, Pope, Wotton, Goldsmith and Thomson. He considered Tennyson and Browning "damned mystical idiots," but in later years he especially admired the work of Sir William Watson, one of the less immortal of the Edwardians who was to write a posthumous poem about Fisher himself. "Time and the Ocean and some Guiding Star / In High Cabal have made us what we are": this was Jack's favorite Watson quotation (or rather misquotation, because Watson's "Ode on the Day of the Coronation of Edward VII" actually wrote of a "fostering" star) and he sometimes added "copyright" to it, as though he had written it himself.

Other phrases recurred so often in Fisher's talk and writing that they became mantras, to be recited for semimagical or hypnotic effect. Some were Aurelian, some resembled sayings copied from matchbox covers. Here are a few, taken at random from his letters, and from an anthology of them obligingly provided by Fisher in his memoirs.

- Do right and damn the odds.
- Stagnation is the curse of life.
- The Royal Navy always travels first class.
- The best is the cheapest.
- Emotion can sway the world.
- Mad things come off.
- Think in Oceans, Shoot at Sight.
- Any fool can obey orders.
- A decrepit camel can carry the burden of many asses.

• History is a record of exploded ideas.
• Life is Phrases.

All this was an odd mixture of the derivative and the original. Some of the most characteristic Fisherisms were not his at all—"Yours till hell freezes," for instance, which he learnt from Frederick Ponsonby. On the other hand, some of his alleged proverbs, like the one above about the decrepit camel, sound to me decidedly homemade. His style itself was certainly all his own, and was very adaptable. It could be splashy. It could be polemical. It was often effectively urgent. It was fine for knockabout comedy, but it could also be dry, as in a suggested reply to a parliamentary question asking if one of his reforms had been a success and if so, why it had not been introduced earlier: "The answer to the first part of the question is in the affirmative; as regards the second part, it might have been asked the Deity about the Creation."

Not everybody relished the effervescence of everything. Some people thought Fisher no more than a poseur, or a showy Philistine. He went to the theater once a year and seems to have had little interest in art, architecture or music. It outraged him that the actor Henry Irving should be buried in Westminster Abbey when Dr. Barnardo the philanthropist wasn't, and in one of his moments of cheapness he sneered at Balfour the prime minister for playing the piano. Herbert Richmond despised his dismissive attitude to history—"ignorance could go no further." Sophisticates like Violet Asquith were not entertained by his schoolboy humor. "Do you know why an alchemist is like Neptune?" he once asked Admiral of the Fleet Sir Geoffrey Hornby, when he himself was already a full admiral. "Because he is a-seeking what never existed" (and he spelled it out—"Sea-King"—in case Sir Geoffrey did not get the joke).

Still, nobody ever denied his prodigious originality, like it or not.

Besides, he was stylish in life. He liked everything to be the best. His clothes were good, and he wore them well. He had an eye for typography: when he had documents printed they were elegantly typeset in several colors and handsomely bound—he brought his own typographer home with him from the Mediterranean, to ensure continuity of taste. His high-pitched conversation (he tended to drop his final *n*'s, too) was as vivacious as his writing. His appetite for enjoyment made him easy company in all circles, and several of my informants told me that he sometimes made them laugh until they cried. He was not a sporting man, though at one time or another he had a go at tennis, handball and even golf, but an essential part of his personality was his indefatigable walk—steady and regular wherever he was, on his ship, on the Malta ramparts, on a London street, fourteen miles at a stretch in Marienbad or Richmond Park.

There was no machismo to him. On the contrary, he was instinctively sympathetic with frailty, and believed that St. Paul's "charity" should really be translated "sympathy." He was no admirer of blind courage, and did not hide his fear of a bull, when he was once walking in the country with

Esther Meynell. All his life he was concerned about the bullying of midshipmen. If he was not exactly a valetudinarian himself, he was on behalf of others, and his letters are full of gratuitous medical advice. He warns C. P. Scott, editor of the *Manchester Guardian,* about the aftereffects of influenza (so likely to give one pleurisy). He advises Commander Thomas Crease, who is "very seedy," to leave at once for Carlsbad, where there is a marvelous Austrian doctor *absolutely certain* to cure him. He privately arranges for two specialists and a nurse to travel to Scotland to attend the ailing Admiral Sir John Jellicoe, commander in chief of the Grand Fleet. He recommends cod-liver oil for his daughter Dorothy, and confides in Esther Meynell his trust in *Pearson's Shilling Guide to Health.*

Yet he was a naval administrator of the most pitiless force! It was no wonder that as he navigated ever-stormier weathers toward old age, his face became even more complex than it was when we first saw it on *Inflexible.* His hair never receded—he kept that cowlick to the end—but around the eyes and mouth everything was intensified. When he was appointed First Sea Lord in 1904, he was said to resemble a withered Cox's Orange Pippin. Violet Asquith likened his eyes to smoldering charcoal, lighting up at his own jokes. Esther Meynell thought he had a mouth like a prehistoric animal's, and Filson Young said he looked like Paul Kruger, the testudinal leader of the Boers. There are innumerable images of Fisher in his fifties, sixties and seventies, and almost every one seems to project some different aspect of his character. A Spy cartoon published in *Vanity Fair* shows him looking almost cherubic, and is captioned simply "Jacky"—it hangs above my staircase at home, above the toby jug of Lloyd George. A drawing by William Nicholson makes him look bulldoglike or Churchillian. Arthur Cope, in 1903, seems to have tried unsuccessfully to give him a Nelsonic melancholy.

The best-known of the portraits was painted by Hubert Herkomer in 1911: it hangs now in the National Portrait Gallery in London, and there are several copies of it, too. Fisher declared it a masterpiece, and claimed that Herkomer also thought it one—certainly the artist enjoyed painting the picture, and completed it in four sittings with little revision. It shows a Fisher essentially wise, benign and accommodating, which is perhaps why he and his family liked it so much. In his uniform as an Admiral of the Fleet, with his telescope under his arm and the ribbon of the Order of Merit around his neck, he stands, one hand in his pocket, looking straight at the viewer without a trace of arrogance or astringency, only a paternal smile. I find it rather boring.

At another extreme is Jacob Epstein's bust, done in 1916. This shows Fisher almost paranoically congealed in self-esteem. His hair is cut short and bristly. His chest is a molten mass of medals and orders. His head seems to be held in place less by native vigor than by the high and stiffly gilded collar of his full-dress uniform. The sculpture took a week to do, in daily sessions, and Epstein never forgot the old admiral's extraordinary appearance: "his light eyes, with strange colours, were set in a face like parchment ivory. . . ." Fisher, who believed Epstein to be the greatest sculptor in the world, must have liked this image too, because he had a photograph of it reproduced on a poster.

I think the best portrait, though, is a three-quarter-length painting by Augustus John, also done in 1916. John took much pleasure in the company of the admiral, who frequently broke off to take him for a short walk—just the length of a quarterdeck, the artist assumed, up and down the street outside his Chelsea house. He told me thirty-five years later that Fisher had been the best of sitters, and described him in his autobiography as "a superb and lovable old egotist who would strike his flag for nobody, except Lady Fisher." His depiction of Jack's face shows it looking wryly over the viewer's left shoulder, its eyebrows raised in irony, its round eyes alert, its mouth mocking, cynical and affectionate, all at the same time. It is a quirky and highly intelligent figure (and perhaps had an influence, if only subliminal, upon the career of John's son Caspar, who was to become an Admiral of the Fleet himself).

In all these portraits Fisher seems a remarkably timeless man. He does not look old-fashioned even now. In uniform he retains his lifelong ease of manner. In civilian clothes he is dapper, and with his stick and his spats looks remarkably unsailorlike. Whether he was in uniform or in mufti, nobody could fail to notice him, if only because he was so proud of his own appearance. He liked a "robustious Falstaffian figure," he said.

This was the character, then, that fell upon the British Navy in the first decade of the twentieth century. "Anybody who opposes me had better get out of my way," Fisher said as he forced through his reforms, and he meant it. A vast body of traditionalism, prejudice, jealousy, apathy, snobbery, resentment, nostalgia and honest disagreement resisted him, and there were no weapons he would not use to break it down. As always, charm was one of them. Fisher was sustained by his cohort of favorites and admirers, and by powerful political friends. He was generally on good terms with his various First Lords of the Admiralty, his immediate political masters, and he had King Edward VII comfortingly on his side. Providing one agreed with his reforms, it was a pleasant experience to visit him in his official suite of rooms at the Admiralty, so let us do so now.

We let him know we are coming, of course—as he says himself, the Admiralty is more frightened of women than of any enemy fleet—and he lets us know the number of the bus we ought to take. We get off at Trafalgar Square, pass through Robert Adam's exquisite stone screen, decorated with sea horses, on Whitehall, cross the famous courtyard beyond, and climb up a grand old staircase to the First Sea Lord's rooms. What another world from *Inflexible!* The merry but formidable captain has become the genial but monumental Admiral of the Fleet, and the cabin that seemed the cockpit of a fighting machine has become the elegant drawing room from which the affairs of a navy are directed.

It is a lovely room in the best Admiralty manner. Its three big curtainless windows look out on the Mall, up through the trees toward Buckingham Palace, so that there is no mistaking our closeness to the centers of power and the realities of history. The floor glows with a huge red-and-blue carpet, and a cozy fire is burning. Fisher's desk, beside the fireplace, is scrupulously neat, with racks of sharpened pencils and ordered papers, and his chair is hard and highbacked—a working chair. There is a standing desk between the windows, too, with a drawing pad on it, and more pencils. But there are comfortable sofas and armchairs, and a chintzy screen, and a host of naval prints on the walls, and a couple of model warships. Big portraits of the king and queen hang above the mantelpiece, and as he welcomes us Fisher sweeps an arm toward them, as though to introduce us—"my beloved friend King Edward, and the blessed Alexandra."

He sits us down on a sofa, rings for tea, and launches himself into an exuberant flow of reminiscence and anecdote and gossip and inquiry—about the old *Inflexible,* about the foreign minister of Russia, about the weevils in sea biscuits, about the dean of Westminster, about the price of rooms at Marienbad, about the beneficial effects of Horlick's Malted Milk, about that malignant little cad X. and that incomparable genius Y., about last night's performance of *The Mikado* ("my annual treat—how we laughed!")—and suddenly, grabbing us by the hands and pulling us over to the window, he is showing us the scribbled plan of a warship that lies on his window desk. "You see? ten eighteen-inch guns, or twenty-inch, better still, quadruple screws, four torpedo tubes each side—see the citadel here, diamond shaped? See the turtleback hull? No masts! No funnels! Enough fuel to take it around the world! Nothing like it ever! Nothing can catch it, nothing can sink it! I drew it at three o'clock this morning, and all the old fossils will say it's impossible!" And so on, laughing, talking, eating cake, telling stories, until as the evening draws in he sees us to the door again and reminds us that on no account must we forget to change at Marble Arch from a number six bus to a number two, on our way back to St. John's Wood. We shall need fourpence for the fare, but might save a penny by walking as far as Piccadilly.

Charm, however, was most decidedly not enough, and was supported in Fisher's armory of reform by vehemence, conspiracy and unscrupulous brutality. There was almost no branch of the navy that he did not assault. The collection of papers that he called *Naval Necessities* (splendidly printed and expensively bound) covered everything from the training of cooks to the refitting of ships, from chaplains to signaling.

Everything was urgency, black and white, whole hog—*"totus porcus!"* "Whatever you want," he told one of his committees, "you can have. . . . The whole power that is necessary is at your beck and call." If people could not build, work, change or adapt, they must get out of the way. Fisher had warships built faster than ever before, and he made all the venerable cogs of Admiralty whirr faster, too. He stuck on his papers labels emblazoned RUSH, in big black letters on a crimson ground—sometimes he stuck them on people, or so he claimed. One notice in his office said DO IT NOW. Another said: IF YOU HAVE NOTHING IMPORTANT TO SAY PLEASE GO AWAY AND LET ME GET ON WITH MY WORK. He was alleged to have been seen patrolling the corridors of the Admiralty with a placard pinned to his chest, asking for something to do, or something to sign.

If true, it was irony. He was a great delegator—he authorized people to forge his signature on unimportant documents—but he worked like a slave. Always an early riser, as First Sea Lord he habitually got up at four in the morning and walked to the Admiralty from his house at Queen Anne's Gate, generally looking in at Westminster Abbey to say a prayer on his way. After five hours' work, with hardly anyone else around, he went home for a large breakfast, and then worked through until late evening, with a biscuit and a glass of lemonade at lunchtime. This tough schedule, seven days a week, so told upon him during his fiercest concentration of work that at dinner one evening Kitty Fisher dropped a word in the king's ear about it, and a message scribbled on a menu card reached the admiral from along the table: "Admiral Sir John Fisher is to do no work on *Sundays,* nor go near the Admiralty, nor is he to allow *any* of his subordinates to work on Sundays, By Command. Edward R."

He took no notice, and continued to labor for his reforms as though time were running out. Behind him his network of informants and confidants worked away like an engine of its own. More flagrantly than ever now, Fisher courted newspapermen, influential foreigners, politicians, industrialists, entrepreneurs and anyone else who could help him, and in the end he became a more familiar public figure than any sailor since Nelson himself—in the years before World War

I he was "Jacky" not only to the fleet, but to the general public too.

Half the navy and much of London society despised him for this populist instinct, and implacably resisted almost everything he tried to do. During these years of the great reforms the controversies that swirled around him were vicious. Age-old etiquettes of Admiralty were forgotten, and Fisher said himself that he was "vehemently vilified with malignant truculence." He was accused of every kind of chicanery, from socialist subversion to crooked land deals. Sometimes he was blamed for extravagance, sometimes for parsimony, often for disloyalty to the navy or the empire. "He may be a very clever fellow," said Admiral Sir Frederick Richards, *"but he abolished Jamaica."* He had set an evil example of noisy, blatant, publicity-hunting self-advertisement, thought Admiral (retd.) C. C. Penrose Fitzgerald. All his old enemies revived their grudges, and were never to relax them: an ancient who wrote to me furiously in 1951, excoriating the name of Fisher, turned out to have been assistant paymaster on the *Surprise* during Fisher's Mediterranean command half a century before, and had evidently brooded over some slight ever after. Even much of the press was hostile— since Fisher served under both Liberal and Conservative governments, he was a useful political cockshy.

"I've been through hell," Fisher declared, but he remained irrepressible anyway. "All those who get in my way," he announced, "come to a nasty end. They all die of worms in the stomach or some other horrible complaint." He once chalked on a hesitant colleague's door, during an especially explosive

period of change, the words REMEMBER LOT'S WIFE—no looking back. He accused his opponents of being in a trance, or a
state of locomotor ataxia. One day they would find their
wives widows, their children fatherless and their homes
dunghills. He said he would bite them, if he got the chance.

Sometimes his boisterous excess of high spirits, whether expressed in encouragement or in malice, disguised the essential seriousness of his purposes. Even his devoted disciple
Arnold White thought he was too flippant sometimes. But he
was anything but a joker. He was dealing with matters of life
and death, tremendous matters of history, and more clearly
than most of his critics he foresaw the dreadful times that
were to come. In everything he did he had in mind the titanic
clash of the warships that was so soon, he was convinced, to
dictate the progress of the world. "To get a fighting Navy we
must be ruthless, relentless and remorseless in our Reforms.
Parasites . . . must be extirpated, like cancer—clean cut!"

I have in my hand a program he had produced, in 1907,
for a visit by colonial premiers and parliamentarians to
Portsmouth Dockyard, the largest naval dockyard in Europe,
at that time in a frenzy of construction under Jacky's inspiration. This was to be, as it were, a public exhibition of the
Fleet That Jack Built, and he stage-managed it himself in
theatrical style. The program was produced to his precise
instructions, I do not doubt, probably designed by his typographer from the Mediterranean, and it is a luxurious object
(it cost me £93 in 1993). It is bound in red leather, gilt-edged
and elaborately embossed with the Admiralty cipher and the

royal crest. Its endpapers are of watered silk, its photographs are faced with India paper and there is a folding map at the back. It is like a very rich family souvenir, of a coming-of-age perhaps.

Inside it is pure Fisher. Here is a photograph of the Royal Navy's latest and most revolutionary battleship, built at unprecedented speed—"From Laying Of Keel Plate To Going To Sea, A Year And A Day." Here is a destroyer "Going 36 Knots," and here are submarines "In The Act of Diving." The distinguished visitors would tour the gunnery school at Whale Island, would see another battleship under construction and inspect submarines and destroyers in dry dock. A mock attack from the sea by a squadron of vessels would be followed by the landing of a naval brigade, and the delegates would then go out in tugs to watch submarines diving and torpedo practice. Lunch would be served—no speeches!— and tea would be provided on the train going back to London that evening. It all went off very well, too. A flotilla of destroyers, firing torpedoes with dummy heads, steamed up the harbor at spectacular speed—faster than any warships before or since, so someone who was there assured me—and two of the young parliamentarians were so excited that they climbed into the control top of a battleship and threw their hats to the jetty below.

What a great day it sounds, with the irresistible First Sea Lord to jolly them all along! At the back of my festive program, though, there is a somber appendix to remind us what Fisher was really about. It is a list of the warships of the Channel Fleet on station at Portsmouth that day: 12 battleships, 17 cruisers, 24 destroyers, with a total of 1,127 major guns—in themselves enough to blow most of the world's navies apart. "*This one thing I do,*" ran one of Fisher's favorite Pauline texts, "*forgetting those things which are behind, and reaching forth unto those things which are before, I press towards the mark.*"

His Beloved Master

One day in the 1900s Fisher, having taken the train into East Anglia, stood in his shirtsleeves unpacking his belongings at Sandringham, the favorite country home of King Edward VII. He had put his suitcase on his bed and had a boot in each hand when there was a fumbling at the doorknob. "Come in, come in," called Fisher a little testily, and who should enter the room but His Majesty himself, smoking a very large cigar. They sat down together for a chat, the admiral in his braces, the king with his cigar, and before long it was very nearly dinnertime. "Sir," said Fisher, "you'll be angry if I'm late for dinner, and no doubt Your Majesty has two or three gentlemen to dress you, but I have no one." The king gave him a sweet smile and left.

I like to imagine them there, one on each side of the fireplace in a room which I take to be rather like a bedroom in one of today's very up-market country-house hotels: two elderly, solidly built men, both remarkably un-English of appearance, looking more like a couple of cosmopolitan entrepreneurs than a king of England and his principal naval aide-de-camp. I can smell the mingled fragrances of pomade, cigar smoke, polish, boot leather and whiskey (I take it the king had one before coming up). I can hear the contrasting timbres of their conversation, one voice dartingly tenor, the other lubriciously bass. Fisher remembered the occasion always, and described it affectionately in his memoirs.

It was only one of a score of such minutiae by which the old admiral cherished the memory of his times with Edward VII. If there sounds something a little smarmy to the relationship, at least to a republican ear like mine, there is no doubt that Fisher loved his king. Perhaps the sentiment was not returned in altogether equal measure, but Edward was certainly entertained by Fisher, enjoyed his company, admired many of his policies and was extremely helpful in getting them adopted. Unfriendly or less favored admirals often resented Fisher's privileged place at the heart of the court, and thought it a last impertinence in the elevation of the arriviste: but it was more professional opportunism than social climbing, and genuine friendship too.

It was an odd association in some ways. Fisher was eight months older than Edward, but infinitely less worldly, and while he was a roué manqué, so to speak, Edward was the real thing. The king's mistresses really were mistresses, and a flirtation with him might well take you upstairs to the bedroom. He was a voluptuary, and the friends of his youth had all too often been louche, prank-loving and high-living, not at all Jack's sort. Edward was a famous sportsman, and it is hard to suppose that he shared Fisher's preoccupation with sermons and biblical references. He was also not merely a king, but the descendant of a long line of German princelings, those unshakable upholders of conservative principle—hardly the man to sympathize with Fisher's outspoken radicalism.

Fisher had no illusions about the king, either. Edward was no saint, of course, but he was also "not in any way a clever man." He could not grasp details. He might well be incapable of reciting the three times table that got Jack into the navy. He was an absurd stickler for correct dress and convention. He could be very unpleasant, and rather childish—Fisher was only half amused when the king, having seen some Spanish admirals conveyed in a magnificent antique pulling-barge, rowed by sailors in crimson and gold sashes, pettishly demanded one like it for himself.

In other ways the mutual appeal was not surprising. Both men were above all originals, aping nobody, and they both *enjoyed* everything, as Fisher said. They were amused by the same jokes and attitudes. Edward was evidently intrigued by Fisher's persistent strain of innocence—the admiral had been all around the world, said the king, but had never really been in it. Fisher for his part enjoyed walking the courtier's tightrope between respect and familiarity. When the king, at a jovial dinner table, once remarked that sailors had girls in every port, Fisher sang down the table, "Wouldn't you love to be a sailor, sir?" There was a moment of frigid doubt, while the guests held their breath, until the king decided that it was jester's license rather than lèse-majesté, and led the company in laughter. "Pretty dull, sir, this," Fisher said to the king at a luncheon party, "hadn't I better give them a song?"—and up he stood, there and then, and presented a ditty beginning "We live in Trafalgar Square, with four lions to guard us," and ending "What's good e-nough for Nelson is good e-nough for us." At Balmoral once, Fisher launched into so violent an exposition of an argument that the king expostulated, "Will you leave off shaking your fist in my face?" In another exchange he was provoked into shouting, "Look here, am I the king, or are you?"

Once the king told Fisher that he was too single-minded—having only one idea at a time would ruin him in the end. Fisher disagreed. After all, he had entered the navy "penniless, friendless and forlorn," and there he was spending a fortnight at Balmoral with the king of England.

"The King sent for me yesterday," Fisher once recorded, "—a wet afternoon and he wanted someone to talk to." Fisher was always fun to talk to, but he was also by then one of the most powerful men in Britain, and his relationship with Edward was not all frivolity. By 1904 he was not only the king's ADC, he was the professional head of his navy. He constantly solicited help from Edward, but he also freely offered advice. This was sometimes idiosyncratic. For example he urged the king to pay a visit to the sultan of Turkey, and he warned him about the dangers to his kingdom of an alliance between the Germans and the Americans—"the only one thing that England has to fear." Nevertheless Esher assured Fisher that the king would always back him. He would always say to himself, "Jack Fisher's view is so-and-so, and he is sure to be right."

Sometimes Fisher accompanied his monarch on voyages abroad, and one such occasion provides a perfect microcosm of the association between the king and the admiral. It was a visit in 1908 to Reval, now Tallinn, the Russian naval base in Estonia on the Baltic. There the king was to meet the czar, his nephew by marriage, in an encounter at once familial and diplomatic, and Fisher's role was doubtless partly to provide social emollience, but partly to represent the naval power of Great Britain.

The British party arrived at Reval in the royal yacht *Victoria and Albert,* after a passage through the Kiel Canal during which they were escorted by trotting cavalry all the way. The Russians met them in their own two royal yachts, *Standart* and *Polar Star,* attended by what was left of the Russian navy, most of it having lately been sunk by the Japanese. Nobody went ashore (they might have been blown up by anarchists), but the royal parties entertained each other on their respective yachts, and a Russian choir sang folk songs across the water from the deck of a nearby vessel.

Fisher distinguished himself by his merriment, and in particular by his renewed intimacy with the Grand Duchess Olga. At dinner on the *Victoria and Albert* they laughed so loudly together that the king called down the table to remind Fisher that he was not in the midshipmen's mess ("my dear Duchess thought I should be sent to Siberia or something"), and later the two of them improvised a hilarious dance step of their own, encircled by the two admiring monarchs, their wives, their ministers, their generals, admirals, aides and advisers. Finally Jacky, in full flow by then, was easily prevailed upon to dance a hornpipe on deck. Sometimes in his frock coat, sometimes in yachting gear (an admiral's uniform jacket, white trousers and white shoes) he looked extremely smart, and he was never more full of bounce. "All our gentlemen," the grand duchess wrote to him later, "were delighted with you, as you brought such an amount of frolic and jollity into their midst . . . I haven't laughed so much for ages!"

Everybody knew, though, that this was also Fisher the First Sea Lord of the British Admiralty, just as they knew that the genial Edward was meeting Nicholas not merely as an uncle and a colleague, but as the head of a Great Power at a peculiarly inflammatory moment of European history. The Russian Empire had been a supposed threat to the British for generations—the Bear of the political cartoonists, which had been Britain's last major opponent in war, which had lately been fighting her ally Japan, and which was imagined to be prowling always around the frontiers of British India, waiting for the moment to pounce. By 1908 the rivalries between the two empires had been more or less settled: the purpose of the Reval meeting was to make sure that in another European war they would be allies rather than enemies, and to reassure the nervous czar that he would not be alone if Germany attacked his territories.

This was the start of the Triple Entente between Britain, Russia and France. Left-wing politicians in England expressed themselves horrified at the spectacle of the king of England living it up with so bloodthirsty an autocrat as the czar of Russia, and there was an outcry when it was learnt that Edward, without consulting the Admiralty, had made

Nicholas an honorary Admiral of the Fleet—it was said that Fisher had rushed him into it. However, at least the czar returned the compliment by making Edward an honorary admiral in the Russian fleet, and the general feeling was that the meeting had been a diplomatic triumph. Six years later the British and the Russians were indeed allies in war against the kaiser's Germany.

Jack's part at Reval was by no means insignificant. He was often at the king's side—he generally joined him for breakfast—and his gift for easy converse was invaluable. It was said that in the course of all the socializing the shy and sensitive czarina was once seen all alone in tears, but even she was cheered up by Fisher's joie de vivre, and was actually heard to laugh—"they told me she had not laughed for two years." He seems to have invigorated everyone else, too. "They couldn't get over it," the Grand Duchess Olga reported of the Russian courtiers, "and spoke about you and your dancing, anecdotes, etc., without end. I told them even if they tried their very hardest, they would never reach anywhere like your level."

The time would come when Fisher would feel sympathy for the Russian Revolution, in which so many of the Reval participants were to die, but for the moment he disregarded the objections of the Left, and thought the king's diplomacy surpassed itself. "Every blessed Russian of note he got quietly into his spider web and captured." But then he would accept no outside criticism of Edward, who might not be brainy, but who always did the right thing. He was greatly distressed when gossip reached the king's ears implying that Fisher took vulgar advantage of their friendship, and was grateful to the day of his death for Edward's professional support. This was insidiously described by Sir Sydney Lee, Edward's official biographer, as being no more than a "conditional eagerness," but even so without it Fisher's grand reforms might never have gone through.

He certainly made all possible use of his friendship with the king. Edward was generally on his side in his naval squabbles, often argued his case for him, and once advised him to come back to London from the Continent because, he said, "the mice were playing." In 1905 it seemed likely that Fisher would have to retire, at the compulsory age of sixty-five, without completing his revolution at the Admiralty. A royal promotion to the rank of Admiral of the Fleet offered him five more years of active service; at the same time Edward, consulting nobody in the matter, made him one of the twenty-four members of the Order of Merit which he had himself lately invented. Lord Goschen, a former First Lord of the Admiralty, once said that the king was in Fisher's pocket—Jack had charmed him there. Both men were conscious of the fact. "I am the only friend you have," the king once said to Fisher. "Yes, sir," Jack replied, "but you have backed the winner."

When Edward died in 1910 Fisher was bereft. He had lost, he said, his beloved master and his dearest friend. "No one can know—*can ever know*—what he did for me." At the funeral Fisher, as the king's principal naval ADC, walked alone immediately behind the coffin, looking far more than ritually inconsolable, splendid in his cocked hat, but with all his strut gone. Perhaps he never did quite get over the loss, and he never ceased to bless the royal memory. "What a splendour he was in the world! He went at his zenith like Elijah and Nelson and Moses." Around the tree that Edward had planted at Kilverstone, Fisher's home in Norfolk, forget-me-nots were lovingly embedded.

In the *Dictionary of National Biography*, Fisher recorded in his memoirs, there was a marginal heading in the entry for King Edward VII, reading HIS FAITH IN LORD FISHER. It was, Jack touchingly claimed, "the only personal marginal note!" (but, though I hate to say so, it wasn't).

Dreadnought

If you should ever thumb your way through one of the illustrated histories of capital ships, there will come a
moment when naval architecture seems suddenly to change
gear. The book is likely to end a chapter there, or start a
new one. As at regattas, the weirdly wonderful ships have
been sailing by: peculiar *Devastation* and dowagerlike *Royal
Sovereign*, grotesque French fierce-faced ironclads, Italian
marvels with four funnels and gigantic turrets, the American
Vermont class, which had towering latticework masts like
scaffolding, the Russian *Novgorod*, which was as circular as a
saucer.

Comes the year 1906, and there suddenly before you is a
modern fighting machine, a warship that would hardly look
anomalous even today. Long, low and workmanlike, with
two elliptical funnels and a tripod mast between them, the
ship is altogether without nostalgia—no grand scroll around
the prow, no admiral's stern-walk—and has to it an air of
menacing simplicity. It looks swift and very powerful. It is
the British battleship *Dreadnought*, 17,000 tons, the ship that
has impressed John Fisher's name upon history, and which

gave him the motto for his barony: "Fear God and Dread Nought."

If it looks startling even now, it is hard to imagine the drama of its impact upon the Edwardian world. The battleship then was the king of weapons. It was like an armored division in itself, a squadron of bombers, a whole missile system, a nuclear device. The spectacle of one of these great ships on display, astream with flags and flaunting its guns, was an unforgettable exhibition of national prestige. Armored battleships of iron or steel had been constructed since *Warrior* in the 1860s, and they had grown larger, more terrible and more numerous in every decade. The power of nations was measured in the number of battleships they possessed, and the apparent German desire to have as many as the British was interpreted as a threat to the peace of all Europe.

The arrival of the *Dreadnought* abruptly made every single one of them out-of-date: it was a ship so revolutionary that for a brief space—the gap between those chapters in the naval histories—it could sink with impunity anything else on the face of the waters.

The *Dreadnought* was the most sensational of Fisher's innovations. He claimed her as his own, was immensely proud of her, and liked to say that as she was precisely the same length as Westminster Abbey she was bound to be all right. This was the All-Big-Gun Battleship—ten 12-inch guns in five turrets, unencumbered by lesser calibers, as against the four major guns and varied lesser artillery of previous designs. It was the first big warship to be driven by turbines, making it much the fastest battleship ever built. Because it was more powerful than several battleships of the old kind, it also made financial sense. *Dreadnought* was a wonder of the age, more marvelous in her time even than the *Inflexible* or *Warrior* in theirs. When the colonial premiers went down to Portsmouth that day they were doubtless impressed by the submergence of the submarines, the frenzy of the destroyers, the lunch urbanely without speeches: but it was above all the *Dreadnought,* moored alongside the South Railway Jetty, that they really went to see, and it was from her control top that those spirited young MPs threw their hats.

It was certainly Fisher's energy and conviction that led to the building of the *Dreadnought*—she was the culmination of a thousand doodles. He was not, however, by any means her only begetter, as he was later inclined to imply. The idea of a ship built around a uniform big-gun armament had been current for some years, and both the Japanese and the Americans had already considered building one. The Italian designer Vittorio Cuniberti, his design for such a vessel having been turned down by the Italian government, had actually published it in London under the title "An Ideal Battleship for the British Navy." Fisher himself had begun to contemplate the idea when he was commander in chief in the Mediterranean, and discussed it with his friend W. H. Gard, the chief constructor at Malta. Four years later, when Fisher was First Sea Lord and Gard was at Portsmouth Dockyard, they put it into practice. Together with the naval architect J. H. Narberth they hammered out a series of alternative designs that were presented to a specially convened design committee—its members all Fisher's men, its chairman Fisher himself. *Dreadnought* was laid down on October 2 (my birthday), 1905, was launched on February 10, 1906, and put to sea for the first time on October 3—a year and a day, as that sumptuous program for the colonial premiers boasted, after the first steel plates were laid in Portsmouth Dockyard.

This was a recognizably Fisherian performance. As a former dockyard superintendent himself, Jack haunted the slipway, generally in civilian clothes. Portsmouth was already the most productive shipyard in the world, but it had never worked so hard before. British battleships generally took three years to build, and the 3,000 men who made the *Dreadnought* worked an eleven-and-a-half-hour day six days a week to cut the time so drastically. Fisher made sure that everything not secret about the ship was loudly publicized. Scarcely a day passed without something about *Dreadnought* in the papers, and Fisher would probably have made a musical about it, if he could: to his enemies, who thought all this extremely vulgar, Fisher retorted, as if indeed in song, that if they hadn't dramatized the project they would never have paralyzed the opposition. To meet the magical deadline of a year and a day, much of the ship was quietly prefabricated. The progress of the construction was photographed, week by week, and one can see that on the day work officially began the girders and iron sections had already been massed around the slipway: four of the gun turrets already existed, too, and had been appropriated from other battleships under construction.

Naturally King Edward VII launched the ship, dressed as
an Admiral of the Fleet. The ceremonies were slightly sub-
dued because the court was in mourning for his father-in-
law, the king of Denmark, but there was no mistaking the
epochal significance of the occasion. Australian wine was
symbolically used to christen the vessel. The mallet used by
the king to break the last chock was made of timber from
Nelson's *Victory*. The naval attachés of the world were in be-
mused attendance. When they came to sing the Sailors'
Hymn—"For Those in Peril on the Sea"—Fisher had so
arranged things that he had to share a hymn sheet with his
monarch, side by side at the apex of everything: and he
arranged too that the first captain of the *Dreadnought* was to
be Reginald Bacon, not only a member of the design committee but one of his most fervent acolytes.

A year later, when the battleship had completed her secret
trials in the Mediterranean and the West Indies, the king and
queen came down to Cowes for the regatta, and were invited
to go to sea aboard her. Fisher went too, of course, and it was
one of his proudest moments. Out through the assembled
fleet the magnificent vessel steamed, the royal party on its
bridge, cheered all the way by the crews of the other warships at their moorings. After a demonstration of the battleship's maneuverability, Edward and Alexandra were treated
to a gunnery display, and long afterward I heard from the
widow of the gunnery lieutenant responsible for it. He had
been summoned before Fisher the previous day, and told
that if *Dreadnought*'s guns once missed their target he would
never get a promotion again. He took the threat with ex-

treme seriousness, as well he might, and spent almost the whole night anxiously checking everything in the gun turrets. It was actually not a very demanding exercise—the target was stationary—but nevertheless the lieutenant was perturbed when after the shoot he was again ordered into Fisher's presence. The First Sea Lord looked extremely severe and immediately hurried him along to the king himself, who there and then, smoking a large cigar, with smiles and congratulations all around, awarded him the medal of a Member of the Royal Victorian Order (for personal services to the monarch).

For some years the *Dreadnought,* as flagship of the Home Fleet, was the Royal Navy's chief showpiece, dominating reviews and regattas, but for all his pride in her she was never really the apple of Fisher's eye. He had begun to think that the battleship type, even in so revolutionary a kind, was obsolescent. He thought the British Navy should pin its faith in submarines and destroyers, for security in home waters, together with big, very fast, lightly armored but heavily gunned cruisers to deal with ocean raiders. The latter he called battle cruisers, and he imagined them operating not in squadrons, as battleships would, but in ones and twos, with destroyer escorts. They would be able to outrange and outsail anything else, so their lightness of armor did not matter. They would be the ultimate expression of Fisher's belief that speed was all, and they could be fewer and cheaper than battleships.

This revolutionary strategic concept had been overruled by his own committee, who insisted that battleships should still be built, but Fisher went ahead with battle cruisers too. They were his real delight. He called them his New Testament ships. They were the path to glory! They were the armadillos of the sea, whose tongues could lick up all the ants. Millions of tortoises could not catch a hare, so the Almighty arranged the greyhound. The first three battle cruisers, unlike the *Dreadnought,* were built very secretly. They had tremendous names—*Invincible, Inflexible, Indomitable*—and when all three of them appeared more or less simultaneously in 1908 they excited the world almost as terrifically as *Dreadnought* herself had done.

The gentlest pacifist must surely have been moved by the sight of one of the first battle cruisers at sea. They were the fastest big warships ever built, and according to Fisher's maxims, were habitually driven fast. *Indomitable,* crossing the Atlantic with the Prince of Wales on board, steamed at more than twenty-five knots for three consecutive days, an unexampled performance, and must have given a thrill to the passengers of any transatlantic liner she passed on the way—her low silhouette the very epitome of violent energy, smoke streaming almost horizontally from her funnels, the Royal Standard billowing and a great bow wave. They were beautifully balanced ships: the arrangement of their three funnels, two close together forward, one separately aft, gave them a hunched, forceful look that heightened their impression of urgent intolerance. Some connoisseurs thought them the most splendid-looking warships ever built, and the whole line of the British battle cruisers (there were fifteen in all) gave back to the Royal Navy some of its Nelsonic romance. No wonder Fisher adored them—when he doodled an imaginary greatest of them all, he called it *Rhadamanthus,* after the son of Zeus.

Almost the first thing I heard about Jack Fisher was that he had brought the Royal Navy close to ruin by building the *Dreadnought,* and possibly started the Great War too. Until his time the British had pursued their proven policy of allowing other Powers to set the pace of naval design, relying on their own industrial superiority to catch up and surpass them—a sort of leapfrogging. The building of the *Dreadnought,* it was argued, which made every other capital ship obsolete, meant that Britain's vast preponderance in battleships had been thrown away at a stroke. Now all the Powers were starting from scratch. At the same time, Liberals thought the theatrical introduction of such a superweapon a jingo provocation to the world. Admiral Richards, who disliked almost everything about Fisher, declared that the whole British fleet had been "morally scrapped." Lloyd George, more usually sympathetic, called the building of the *Dreadnought* a wanton and profligate ostentation.

The building programs of all other navies were thrown into disarray or abeyance, and for months no other Power launched a single battleship. Nothing less powerful was worth building. All the capital ships that came later acquired the generic name of Dreadnoughts, and the real gauge of a navy's strength was no longer the number of its battleships as a whole, but the number of its Dreadnoughts. By the second decade of the twentieth century Germany's shipyards could build as fast as Britain's, and it was true that the *Dreadnought* embarked Europe upon a new and more dangerous kind of arms race; but the Royal Navy's head start meant that when, in 1914, the British and German fleets squared up against one another for war, the British had twenty-nine Dreadnoughts, the Germans only eighteen. Fisher felt his initiative justified. The *Dreadnought* type was bound to have been discovered anyway, he said, like the planet Neptune, "but we recognized the perturbations before all others." Besides, as he loved to point out, if only in hindsight, the size of the new ships obliged the Germans to widen the Kiel Canal, costing them a great deal of money and delaying (or so he loved to say) the start of the war.

Dreadnought had her design faults. Her steering was never perfect. Her control top, mounted on the mainmast between the two funnels, could be blinded by soot and smoke, and sometimes the mast itself got so hot that nobody could get up there. Her conning tower, despite Fisher's claim from Malta to have devised such a jolly comfortable safe convenient one, proved impracticable. Nevertheless she was a seminal invention, and a historical artifact of fateful meaning. When the Italian futurist poet Filippo Marinetti needed an utterly modern, bold and virile simile for his country, it was to a Dreadnought that he likened the whole Italian peninsula, "with a squadron of torpedo-boat islands." It was no coincidence either that one of the most famous hoaxes of the twentieth century centered upon *Dreadnought's* illustrious name. In 1910 a group of Bloomsbury pacifists, led by the notorious hoaxer Horace Cole and including Duncan Grant the artist and the twenty-eight-year-old Virginia Stephen (later to become Virginia Woolf), determined to play a truly monumental trick upon the Establishment. They blackened their faces, assumed an exotic variety of robes, took the train to Weymouth and presented themselves as the emperor of Abyssinia and his court upon the quarterdeck of HMS *Dreadnought,* the ultimate symbol of warlike circumstance. They had sent a telegram to announce their coming, ostensibly from the Foreign Office, and they were received with respect. The guard gave them a royal salute. The band, not knowing the Abyssinian national anthem, played Zanzibar's as the next best thing. They were shown around the ship by Captain Herbert Richmond, one of the cleverest officers in the navy, later to become Master of Downing College, Cambridge, and left after sunset in the admiral's barge.

I have never heard what Fisher thought of this effrontery (some of *Dreadnought's* officers went to London and threatened Duncan Grant with unpleasant things) but I hope he would have been amused by it. It was a compliment of a kind. The ship was his most famous creation, and in honoring it, if only backhandedly, Bloomsbury was honoring him.

In all, 181 Dreadnoughts, battleships and battle cruisers, were built for the navies of the world during the following nine decades; the last of the battleships to be laid down, the British *Vanguard,* had 15-inch guns built to Fisher's own or-

ders thirty years before. *Dreadnought* herself was broken up in
Scotland in 1923, but now and then around the world I have
seen the shade of her. Her only contemporary to survive is
the USS *Texas,* launched in 1912, which lies forever in a museum basin near Houston, and walking the clanking decks
of this old stalwart, clambering to her armored bridge, I easily summoned ghosts of Fisher's masterpiece: Edward and
Alexandra holding their ears against the gun blast, the astonished lieutenant getting his MVO, the soot-blackened emperor graciously inspecting the honor guard, those MPs
fooling about in the main top, and most vividly of all Jacky
himself everywhere in the ship, looking into gun turrets, inspecting engines, swaggering on the quarterdeck, talking,
showing off to visitors, dancing hornpipes, boasting to reporters, flirting with ladies-in-waiting, incorrigible, insuffer-
able and gloriously conceited—while all around, unknowing,
the Texan tourists sauntered.

Then only a few years ago I was sitting on a balcony in
Honolulu, having my breakfast, when I saw sliding out of
Pearl Harbor along the coast a truly colossal warship. Its
nine huge guns were all elevated, giving it a prickly and
pugnacious look, and it disappeared into the Pacific at a
spanking pace. I knew just what it was. It was one of the four
Iowa-class battleships, 45,000 tons, built for the United States
Navy during World War II, rescued from mothballing at the
time of Vietnam, and by then half a century old. It was a living Dreadnought, a naval coelacanth! I stood with my coffee
to watch it go, saluting it sentimentally in my mind as one of
the very last of Fisher's ships.

"Who are you, Jacky Fisher?"

The second-in-command whom Fisher insulted with his signal from the Barracca on page 134 was none other than Rear Admiral Lord Charles William de la Poer Beresford, of *Condor* and the Alexandria bombardment. He was the third son of the marquis of Waterford, and he bore upon his buttocks a large tattoo of a hunting scene. In many other ways, too, he was the very antithesis of our Jacky, and fate was to lock the two men in a long and disastrous rivalry.

With Fisher in mind I once made a pilgrimage to the Beresford family home, Curraghmore, in Ireland's County Waterford. It is a far cry indeed from Wavendon in the Sri Lankan heights, from the modest parsonage of Fisher's paternal grandfather, or the boiled rice lodging house on Bond Street. One enters through a great demesne, surrounded by ten miles of stone walling, and the road winds among dense woodlands to a glade in the heart of it. There stands a palace. In front is a graveled forecourt, like a parade ground, with clipped chestnut trees on either side, and handsome stable blocks. The house is a massive classical building fronted by a medieval tower, and on its façade, beneath a pair of real antlers, there sits, gigantically holding its cross, a sculpted stag of St. Hubert, patron saint of hunters—the emblem of the de la Poers, who united themselves with the Beresfords by marriage in the eighteenth century.

Here young Charles Beresford—Charlie B., as he would be known all his life—spent much of his boyhood in spectacularly fortunate circumstances. Those stables housed a 100 horses when he was a boy, the estate employed 600 people and the house was full of treasures. Charlie and his four brothers were archetypal of their kind, class and place. They were always said to have the charm of the Irish, or the luck of the Irish, but in those days that really meant the charm and luck of the Anglo-Irish Ascendancy—the family was vehemently opposed to Irish independence.

The brothers were avid horsemen—they hunted six days a week at Curraghmore—and the annual horse race between them became a great social event in Ireland. One brother was to become manager of the royal stud, one became a rancher in Canada, one was permanently injured in a hunting accident and one was to win a Victoria Cross when he jumped his horse over the barricades that denied the British Empire access to the king of the Zulus. Charlie himself was so reckless a rider that in the hunting field at one time or another he fractured his pelvis, his right leg, his right hand, his right foot, five ribs and both collarbones, and three times broke his nose. When Buffalo Bill brought his Wild West show to London, Charlie Beresford rode around the arena in the Deadwood coach, pursued by screaming Indians.

Among the brothers Charlie evidently had the most natural talent for self-advancement. He was a charming fellow.

Almost everyone felt the appeal of his personality, and he became a popular member of the society that surrounded the future Edward VII (whose mother, Victoria, on the other hand, disapproved of him, and called him one of the "independent, haughty, fault-finding set"). Having joined the navy as a boy, he became an extremely royal sailor. He was an officer on the frigate *Galatea* when Prince Alfred, Duke of Edinburgh, took her on a cruise around the world. He commanded one of the royal yachts. He was an aide to the Prince of Wales when he made a visit to India. His sailors admired him, and were proud of his aristocratic flair. His brother officers were amused by his pranks and foibles—he insisted on Irish stewards and barge crews for his ships, and he was prodigal with Old Irish Stories ("which it was best," recalled a midshipman in later years, "to greet with loud laughter"). He was accompanied everywhere by his grossly overfed and ill-behaved bulldog bitch, Kora.

Beresford was no fool. He was a capable seaman and a successful yachtsman, adoring all the appurtenances of sail. He did much to form a naval intelligence department, he had progressive ideas about gunnery and he was an early advocate of a proper naval staff. He was also a successful politician. In 1874 he was elected to the House of Commons as Conservative member for East Marylebone, and intermittently for thirty years he successfully combined his parliamentary duties with his naval career (it was Beresford's intervention, in 1875, that postponed for another eight years the abolition of flogging in the British Navy). I have a picture of him before me now (one of Mr. Ellis's), standing beneath the guns of his flagship at Malta waiting for the guests to arrive at a ball: potted foliage and bunting surround him, ornamental lights hang from the awning above, and he stands there in his dress suit, legs slightly apart, immaculately gloved hands hanging, like an extremely worldly Santa Claus.

While Fisher, then, with infinite contrivance forced his way up the naval ladder, Beresford easily ascended, hastened by the advantages of privilege and the luck of the Anglo-Irish. He was five years younger than Fisher, but by the time of the Alexandria bombardment he was already the better known of the two. He was a much taller man than Jack, more heavily built, easier to understand, more obviously handsome, and the rivalry between them came to acquire an almost allegorical meaning—the one so powerful of origin, the other so modest, the one Tory to the backbone, the other innately liberal. While Beresford was still yearning for the grace and glory of the sailing navy, Fisher was already thinking of his ships simply as mechanisms.

I can see that both men felt disadvantaged in the presence of the other. Fisher was doubtless put out by Beresford's patrician bearing and privilege; Beresford must have been made ill at ease by Fisher's tangled and unpredictable intelligence, and by his misty origins. For years, nevertheless, they kept their instincts in check. Fisher magnanimously said that Beresford ought to have been made a Commander of the Order of St. Michael and St. George for his conduct at Alexandria (he only got the Khedive's Medal), and when

Fisher was invalided home Beresford tenderly cabled him—
"Old fellow, so concerned to hear you are ill." At first on the
Malta station, too, with Fisher as commander in chief and
Beresford his second-in-command, they worked well enough
together. Fisher respected Beresford's seamanship; Beresford
recognized Fisher's intellect. Beresford was a first-rate officer afloat, reported Fisher to the First Sea Lord, also a most
chivalrous being and a thorough gentleman who never bore
malice. "My dear Sir John," wrote Beresford when Fisher had
won one of his battles with higher authority, "bravo, and
again bravo! The Fleet, the Country and the Empire will
owe you a lasting debt of gratitude."

It was an awkward situation, all the same. Fisher was the
senior officer, but Beresford was still the better-known man.
His exploit in the *Condor* was not forgotten, and since then he
had played a famously dashing part in Lord Kitchener's
reconquest of the Sudan. He had also paid a well-publicized
official visit to China on behalf of the combined chambers
of commerce, calling on the way home upon the emperor
of Japan and the president of the United States, and giving
a short address to the New York Stock Exchange. He was
an active politician still. Fisher was the C in C, but Beresford
it was who brought out fellow parliamentarians to review
the Mediterranean situation, or invited as guests aboard
his flagship delegates from the Navy League. Jack seems
to have tried hard to accommodate this difficult second-
in-command—"I honestly believe he means well," he wrote
once, and in another letter he said, not without affection: "He
really is a *curiosity.*" But Beresford was undeniably annoying.

Once he distributed to the fleet a booklet glorifying *Ramillies* and himself, ending with his successes at a local regatta and what the dog Kora had been up to.

Beresford was at least as adept in press relations as Fisher was himself—he too had leaked documents to W. T. Stead, and he had once been offered a job by the *New York Herald*. Throughout his time in the Mediterranean he got maximum publicity at home. Not only did he maintain a full-time secretary in London, but he had an indefatigable agent in his wife, Mina, herself the daughter of an MP. Fisher described this woman as "poisonous," and other reports are equally unflattering: she was very stout, she was preposterously rouged and according to the Irish writer Shane Leslie she wore false *eyebrows*. Charlie B. seems to have been fond of her, though, and liked to call her "Dot" or "my Little Painted Frigate," and she was evidently a great success as a publicist. Beresford was always in the papers, all his life. A railway engine was named for him. There was a statue of him at the London Hippodrome. He was invited to open the Toronto Industrial Exhibition. At Malta, Fisher was sent a cutting from one of the London newspapers which must have been particularly galling to the commander in chief: "A naval officer with Lord Charles Beresford says that that Admiral is practically revolutionizing the conduct of the Mediterranean Squadron."

Gradually Fisher's tolerance became irritation, and his letters to Lord Walter Kerr show it. Beresford might be a thorough gentleman, but he was also a "deuced impulsive beggar and his tongue is a little member which no man can tame!" He had disappointed Fisher very much by his exaggerations and want of truth. He gave orders off his own bat as if he were the C in C himself. He was like a rubber ball, "squeeze him at one place & he bulges out at another." If the slightest chance arose, Fisher declared in one of his more intemperate moments, he would court-martial Charlie B.

One can imagine the tension, the two senior officers of the fleet ever more obvious in their antipathy, the whispers and nudges when they met at social functions, the wardroom jokes about Kitty and the Painted Frigate, and the whole affair coming to a head in that brazenly insulting signal from the Barracca. Within the decade, when both men had returned to higher duties in Britain, Fisher's feud with Beresford had transcended mere service rivalry and become a national scandal.

Of all the Conservatives who opposed Fisher's revolutionary reforms, Beresford was the most influential, and the most skillful at projecting professional differences into the public arena. He fought against most of Fisher's projects, from the redistribution of the fleets to the development of submarines (which he mocked as "Fisher's toys"). He had his own supporters within the Admiralty, who fed him inside information, and he became a kind of catalyst for all the hostile cliques that Fisher variously categorized as fossils, syndicates of discontent or duchesses. In 1909, when Fisher was First Sea Lord, Beresford became commander in chief of the Channel Fleet, by then the most important seagoing command, and this gave him even more opportunity to express his opposition. "Lest I should be exalted above all measure," Fisher cried with St. Paul, "there was given me a thorn in the flesh."

Fortunately for Jack, Beresford had long before fallen out with King Edward (over the sensitive matter of a love letter), but he still had behind him most of fashionable London, and Fisher himself thought the real vehemence of Beresford's campaigns arose from his vision of a People's Navy, all its ranks open to everyone, all its branches of equal importance. The toxic Lady Charles, he believed, was leading a society conspiracy against him—the Claridges Conspiracy, he called it, or the Knife and Forks campaign. This was not paranoia. The dispute peeled back a layer from the ornamental surface of Edwardian England, to reveal some unpleasant things below. Many a London dinner table spat its abuse at the Mulatto, the Asiatic, the Singhalese, the Siamese, the Half-Caste or the Yellow Peril, or sneered at the new officers Fisher had dragged out of the engine rooms, or told malicious stories about his passion for the waltz, or even turned up its nose, I daresay, at dear Kitty. When one of Fisher's allies, Admiral Sir Francis Bridgeman, paid a social call at the Beresford house on Grosvenor Street, he was ushered by mistake into a drawing room full of plotting admirals, presided over by Lord Charles himself: an embarrassed silence fell upon them all as they hastily hid their faces, poked the fire, turned their backs or pretended to pick things up off the floor. At a royal levee in 1908 Beresford himself offered society's ultimate snub, widely reported and relished. Fisher was standing against a wall talking to Winston Churchill and

David Lloyd George when Beresford passed by, having just made his bow to the king. He shook hands with Churchill and Lloyd George, but when Jack held out his hand Beresford ostentatiously declined it, for all *l'haut monde* to see.

On the other side, Fisher used all his contacts, from the court to Fleet Street, to discredit Charlie B. His letters at this period are almost obsessively concerned with the feud. He called Beresford the leader of the Blue Funk School, or commander in chief of the Yellow Admirals. "Convict him of one lie—he only tells another." Fisher's judgment was warped by it all. In one of his worst decisions he declined to support the inventor Arthur Pollen, who had offered the Admiralty a decisively superior system of gunnery control, probably in part because Pollen was backed by Beresford (he was a Catholic, too, and so doubly suspect). Even Fisher's fondest confidants must have been exasperated by such asides as this to Thursfield: "It may interest you to hear that the mother of Beresford's secretary's wife on September 8 told Captain Moore's wife that Beresford had settled to resign next January!" It was understandable that when Fisher reduced the importance of Beresford's Channel Fleet by transferring many of its ships to a newly formed Home Fleet, many people thought he was doing it in spite.

The enmity had its purely technical aspects. Beresford constantly complained about his treatment as the Channel Fleet commander—in effect the supreme commander at sea, if it came to war. He was denied ships, he was kept in the dark about plans, he was not consulted about the distribution of fleets. He frequently appealed above Fisher's head to the First Lord of the Admiralty, or publicly complained in a way that Fisher thought downright insubordinate, even mutinous—Jack's maxim about any bloody fool obeying orders did not apply when it came to his own subordinates. Sometimes Beresford was unconvincingly conciliatory. "There is not the slightest chance of any friction between you and me," he once told Fisher. "When the friction begins, I am off." More often he was pugnacious. "You dare to threaten me, Jacky Fisher?" he cried in a revealing exchange, towering above his superior officer. *"Who are you?"*

Fisher unsuccessfully urged the cabinet to sanction disciplinary action against Beresford, but in the end managed to ease him out of his command by abolishing it, the Channel Fleet being absorbed into the Home Fleet in 1909. Charlie B. never held another post, and two years later he retired from the navy. It was a Pyrrhic victory for Fisher, though. Sympathetic crowds cheered Beresford ashore when he hauled down his flag at Portsmouth for the last time, and he was now even more free to pursue the vendetta by political means. He persuaded Herbert Asquith, the prime minister, that there should be a public inquiry into the whole management of the Admiralty—really an inquiry into Fisher's own administration. This sorry process halfheartedly vindicated Jack, but also humiliated him. He had expected a resounding rebuke for Beresford, and when the committee of inquiry published its milk-and-water report he dismissed its members as a pack of politically intimidated cowards. Disillusioned by the result, exhausted by the fury of his seven years at the Admiralty, embittered by the squabble itself, almost inevitably he retired too, on January 25, 1910. He was succeeded by—who else?—Old 'Ard 'Art.

A group of Fisher's opponents held a dinner party to celebrate the event, and Beresford sent them a telegram. Their toast should be, he said, "To the death of fraud, espionage, intimidation, corruption, tyranny, self-interest, which have been a nightmare over the finest service in the world for four years."

This wretched dispute, between the two best-known British naval officers of the day, had a profound effect upon the navy, and upon Jack's reputation. Nearly all his reforms went through, but at a cost which was vastly increased by Beresford's opposition. The feud split and soured the navy; without it Fisher might have been able to achieve his revolution with far less of the malice and vengefulness that were to pursue his memory long after his death. It brought out the worst in him, but with reason.

Beresford, like Fisher, became a baron, and thereafter his wife invariably referred to him as "the Baron"—"what is the Baron saying?" or "Would the Baron like more tea?" For him it was the end of the road. He was not recalled to service when World War I broke out. Instead, as a vociferous backbench Member of Parliament, in his last years he became increasingly a buffoon. The asinine streak in him, latent all his life beneath the charm and real ability, became apparent to everyone. He grew so incoherent, according to Winston Churchill (his distant cousin by marriage), that when he got up to speak he didn't know what he was going to say, when he was speaking he didn't know what he was saying, and when he sat down again he didn't know what he had said.

He wrote a polemical book about the Admiralty dispute, called *The Betrayal,* but he was not really the sort to bear grudges, and in his garrulous autobiography was generous about Fisher's achievements in the Mediterranean, and even about some of his Admiralty reforms. Fisher on the other hand fumed about Beresford for the rest of his life, and never forgave officers who had sided with him. "[Beresford] was here the other day," he wrote unsympathetically from Naples in 1914, "on his way to Egypt, for some complaint. I forget the name. It's what ladies get after having a baby." However, in his old age, so he claimed, he found resentment "fading away," and he removed all mention of the quarrel from his memoirs when he learnt of Beresford's death in 1919.

By then he could afford to be magnanimous. His own career did not after all come to an end with his retirement in 1910, and while Beresford died at seventy-three as an admiral, Fisher outlived him for a year, to die at seventy-nine as an Admiral of the Fleet. But then in this protracted struggle with the penniless Mulatto, the marquis's son from Curraghmore was really fighting above his weight.

Concerning Abroad

I think Geneva a most over-rated place," wrote Jack Fisher one day to his wife after a couple of days in the city. "It doesn't compare with Portsmouth in shops, nor is there any view equal to the sunset at Portsmouth, looking up at the old hulks in the harbour." True to his times and his nation, for years he tended to the view that Abroad was fairly bloody. Amsterdam was smelly and detestable. Everything in Rome was a disappointment except St. Peter's ("and I am not sure about that"). The Acropolis was nothing to rave about. Sancta Sophia was unimpressive. The Parisians were the dirtiest and most immoral people he had ever seen. As for the Americans, who seemed to be everywhere in Europe then, they made the whole place nauseating—"such ugly brutes they all are, both men and women."

He was to change his views radically; before he died, Fisher was an enthusiastic cosmopolitan, spending as much of his time as possible on the Continent, and so enthralled by America that he frequently declared his intention, in moments of pique, to go away and die there.

. . .

I have followed Jack's progress all around Europe, and find his presence vivid everywhere. He began his career as a boulevardier in search of health. Diverse remedies proving ineffective for his endemic dysentry, he accepted the advice of "a lovely partner I used to waltz with," and took the cure at the Austro-Hungarian spa of Marienbad, 2,000 feet up in the Bohemian hills. Thereafter he went there regularly for seventeen years, from 1886 to 1913, and it gave him a taste not only for the alkaline water so famously effective for diseases of the intestines (i.e., all too often, the consequences of overeating), but also for the leisured life of international fashion which found its happy epitome there.

There were times, between postings, when he lived a more or less nomadic life, trundling around the resorts and spas of Europe sometimes with Kitty or one or another of his daughters, more often alone. He was not, it seems, a very accomplished or even a very bold traveler. He spoke no foreign language properly (he found himself in peculiar difficulties once because he thought *chiesa* was the Italian for cheese—"anyhow, it is in German"), and deprived of the privileges of rank, with no flag lieutenants to make the arrangements, or coxswains to bring him alongside, he seems to have muddled through with cheerful unpretension. There was no throwing of weight about, and since he was never in uniform few people guessed who or what he was— he was politely asked to leave when, as an admiral, he poked his nose through the portals of the French Ministry of Marine. He and his daughter Dorothy were "in an awful state" at Cologne once, when they thought they had lost their luggage, and when they spotted it at Mainz he was so relieved that he ran out to the platform and threw his arms around it. His bags were nearly left behind, too, when he was crossing Germany in 1889; he was saved from ignominy only by a kindly German fellow traveler who advised him to jump over a barrier and get hold of them for himself. *"Great sensation!"*

Jack was a thrifty traveler. He traveled second-class, sometimes without a sleeper, and he was not ashamed to seek out cheap lodgings. At the Grand Hotel National in Lucerne he occupied, so he reported almost smugly, a small room on the street side, high up and away from the lake ("but the manager and all the servants are most polite to me all the same"). In 1895 he was delighted to find that three weeks in Marienbad with Dorothy would cost only £24, not counting railway tickets and opera glasses. Still, although he talked a lot about his lack of private means, my guess is that most Continental hotel receptionists, eyeing the grandly great-coated figure on the other side of the desk, took his request for inexpensive accommodation as a sign of eccentricity rather than of hard times.

He loved hotels, and got on well with hoteliers—he claimed to have got the manager of the Ritz in London his appointment, and said he wished he had taken the job himself. He particularly admired the manager of the hotel at Lucerne, who was only about thirty, looked a regular Napoleon and "rules the 1,000 in his hotel with the iron hand in the silken glove." Many of the hotels he frequented are still extant, and I have visited lots of them myself in pursuit of his shade. By the nature of things they are mostly florid and opulent, in the manner of the Belle Epoque. Some are spa hotels, some seaside resorts, some big-city hotels, and the livelier they were, the more he liked them. He thought the ancient Hotel Pellegrino at Bologna "the most awful hole I was ever in," but was very happy to find himself in the Excelsior beside the sea at Naples, which had only just been built. He loved the Palace at Scheveningen because it was always on the move—"such a rush always going on. Band plays at breakfast and at lunch and at dinner!!! Huge boxes arrive continuously, and the portier runs about like a wild animal!" The Continental in Paris also suited him. "I never saw anything so large or magnificent—immense sitting and reading and writing rooms, and open and covered courtyards and cool places in verandahs to sit about and do nothing" (but the breakfast was terrible).

I meet him all over the place. He greets the doorman in pidgin German as he leaves the grand old Meranerhof for a stroll along the river at Meran. He eats his lunch beside the Grand Canal, with a bottle of wine on the terrace of the Europa, or a book under the awnings of the Monaco. ("This place Venice is IDEAL! *Noise*-less, *dust*-less, *motor*-less, *dog*-less . . . and only *one* perambulator.") He takes his brisk daily exercise up the hill from the Savoy-Western in Carlsbad. He astonishes the bourgeoisie around the fire at the Grand in Bad Ragaz. He is at Mannheim one year, at Bad Nauheim another, and here in front of me now is a picture postcard from his hotel at Florence, with a smudged arrow on the front to mark his room (he never learned my own technique of using a pinhole instead).

I have often seen him, stick in hand, binoculars around his neck, greatcoat unbuttoned, taking spring outings on the paddle-steamer *Unterwalden* on Lake Lucerne. The *Unterwalden*, launched in 1902, is still in the fleet of the Vierwaldstättersee Steamship Company, and regularly passes the garden of the Beau Rivage Hotel at Weggis, where I frequently spend a few days doing nothing myself. She is just as he would have known her, with the gilded ornamentation of her prow as on one of his older warships, the polished woodwork of her salons, the elegant rake of her funnel, the splash of her paddle and the captain swanky on his high white bridge. Sometimes I can make out Fisher having coffee among the tourists in the dining room aft, as the ship sails by, but more often I fancy he has made friends with the captain, and is up there in the wheelhouse telling tales of the sea.

If it were not for the vibration of the reciprocating engines, he might be writing letters. He used to like to say, employing one of his favorite Pope quotations, that he went abroad "the world forgetting, by the world forgot" (a favorite quotation of Gibbon's too, who applied it in a rather different spirit to the kingdom of Ethiopia, and one that I frequently use myself in moments of self-pity). It was anything but true. Some of his most effective intrigues were conducted from the mainland of Europe, and he never for a moment forgot the affairs of the world. Wherever he went he wrote countless letters home, some of them personal letters to Kitty or his family, most of them letters concerning the state of the British Navy—to naval colleagues, to politicians, to journalists, to anyone he had enmeshed within his schemes of reform and agitation. He read the papers assiduously, and fell like a hawk upon any relevant item of news, instantly pouring out his opinions on it sometimes to only one, but sometimes to three or four correspondents. I have some such letters on my desk, and pungently evocative they are of Jack's peripatetic days, for they are often written on hotel stationery, and their now yellowing leaves, covered with the admiral's tremendous scrawl, are engraved with pompous pictures of Kurhaus or Grand Imperial, with Venetian flags or lakeside scenes, together with Telegraphic Addresses and extremely short telephone numbers.

Fisher's most striking change of heart, when it came to foreign parts, concerned America. His first contact with Americans, as a boy on the China coast, had been happy enough. During his second battle, at Tientsin in 1859, American ships had given the British a helping hand, and Commodore Josiah Tattnall of the United States Navy had uttered the famous phrase "Blood is thicker than water"—actually a quotation from Walter Scott, but for years to be a text of the Anglo-American "special relationship." Later Fisher developed a sour anti-American prejudice, relieved only by the attractions of American dancing partners. As late as 1908 he was still thinking that Britain might one day have to go to war against a United States allied with Germany. However, in 1910 his son Cecil married Jane Morgan of

Philadelphia. Jack went over for the wedding, spent six days in America and never looked back. It was his only visit, but for the rest of his life he was an admirer of things American, and he became a passionate advocate of an Anglo-American federation—"the language English. The literature English, the traditions English . . . we shall be d——d fools if we don't exploit this for the peace of the world and the dominance of our race."

America before World War I was just his kind of country. "All is so splendidly big—they talk in Millions." The hospitality was terrific, the flattery delightful. Customs officials eased his way. Millionaires entertained him. Politicians buttered him up. He told a luncheon party that a damned fine old hen had hatched the American eagle (a phrase he had lifted, as it happens, from an American admiral)—*"and you should have heard them cheer!"* He had a tête-à-tête with the future President Wilson ("like a highly cultivated Abraham Lincoln"). He made friends with Charles Schwab, "the great Schwab" of Bethlehem Steel. He marveled at the new Pennsylvania Station in New York, whose waiting room was big enough to contain St. Peter's, Rome. He acquired a taste for pork and beans, recommended to him by Hiram Maxim, the inventor of the machine gun. He decided that when the time came his biographer should be an American, preferably a woman.

Fisher made good use of America, too. He hired an American contractor to build a new naval college at Osborne in the Isle of Wight, no British builder being able to do it fast enough, and he imported American submarines and motor launches for the Royal Navy. His RUSH stickers at the Admiralty came from the United States. When Beatrix and her husband found themselves trapped in Germany at the start of World War I, he enlisted the help of Schwab and Woodrow Wilson to get them out. And in retrospect he loved to tell the tale that when, in 1882, the news of his improvised armored train at Alexandria was reported in the world's press, an American contractor very soon offered to build a better one 20 percent cheaper.

But of all Abroad, Marienbad was best—"my beloved Marienbad," his Pool of Bethesda, whose atmosphere worked upon him like champagne, and whose food, beer, parks, woods, spring water and company all conspired to make him feel his best. *"I just simply love it!"*

When I first went to Marienbad it was hard to imagine the place having such an effect upon anyone. It was dingy with Communism then, shabby in the aftermath of war, empty of foreigners and largely given over to the communal recreation of trade unionists. By now, as I write this book, it is fast returning to its old character. The hotels are reopening one by one, the parks and gardens are lovely again, and the tourists and valetudinarians once more come in their thousands. Fisher would recognize it all, and would be touched by one addition since his time—a handsome bronze plaque in memory of his friend King Edward VII, another familiar of the spa, mounted on a wall of the now-secularized English Church.

There is a photograph of Jack taking the waters outside

the Colonnade, the elegant glass-roofed construction that houses the main springs of the spa. It was the custom then, as it is now, to promenade with a small china pot of the curative water, sipping periodically through its spout. It is hard to look dignified holding such a piece of crockery, still less swanky, and it was predictable that Fisher would prefer to use an open glass, as it might be of lemonade. Holding this, Fisher is at large upon the esplanade, talking very hard and gesticulating, wearing a greatcoat, spats and a trilby hat, with two very English gentlemen at each shoulder. The scene is like the set of a period movie. There are ladies in feathered hats, and men in bowlers with beards and walrus whiskers, and a general suggestion of decorous Hapsburgism. Only Fisher is speaking, and he is speaking like modern man— rather discordantly I fancy, like an actor insufficiently attuned to the style of the piece.

He became very well known at Marienbad. He never stayed at one of the grand hotels, ranked elaborately around the parks and gardens, but sometimes in lesser hostelries and sometimes in furnished rooms. He knew restaurateurs and even maids by name. He went for long walks in the woods, and sometimes rented a bicycle. Occasionally Kitty went to Marienbad too, but she seems to have found it rather dull, perhaps because Jack was always off hobnobbing with grandees. More often Fisher reported faithfully to her at home: that he had seen the Grants and Colonel Eyre, that a favorite cake of the year before now had currants and walnuts in it, that Stern's restaurant had put in electric light, that the Mädchens at the old Dianahof had welcomed him most cordially and charged him five and a half pence for breakfast, and that in short Marienbad was still like paradise—"only Eve is absent."

In later years something ominous must have entered the atmosphere, as Europe moved unmistakably toward conflict. Many of the powermakers frequented Marienbad. "Is it peace or war?" one London newspaper captioned a picture of Edward VII talking earnestly to his prime minister, Henry Campbell-Bannerman, beside the Colonnade; in fact the two were discussing the relative merits of boiled or baked haddock, but it was a true indication of Marienbad's importance. Fisher made many consequential acquaintances there, and at least once he was in the spa at the same time as von Tirpitz: but each was surrounded by his own claque, and although perhaps they eyed each other warily across the promenade, they never met

Anyway, it was the company of beloved King Edward that Fisher coveted most. Edward was the star of Marienbad. He went there to lose weight, but as usual managed to enjoy himself, and to give pleasure. He presided over everything from the Hotel Weimar, still standing today in a preeminent position above the Colonnade, though dowdily reincarnated as the Kavkaz Spa Hotel; after he left each year, items of furniture from his room were sold at double their value. He handsomely entertained his fellow princes and their chancellors, he set the fashions of the year—on his arrival each summer, magazine artists from Vienna would follow him around, sketching his clothes. Fisher sometimes stayed close to the Weimar, at the far less expensive Grünnen Kreuz, and he basked in the king's favors. How cock-a-hoop he must have been when Edward, finding Jack deliberately excluded from a luncheon party, ostentatiously excused himself to write a note of regret to the admiral! Sometimes the king, emerging from the Weimar to the bows, curtsies and doffed hats of the citizenry, would pick up Fisher in his car, and off they would go into the woods around, rumbling through the dappled shade, smoking their cigars side by side behind the chauffeur: two interesting old gentlemen gossiping and arguing far from home, and frequently subsiding into laughter.

Fisher never forgot Marienbad, and it was many years before Marienbad entirely forgot him. On my own first visit I asked if there was anyone about who might remember British visitors from before World War I. It was possible, said the Stalinist louts who ran the town then. A woman sufficiently old and capitalist might be the caretaker at the civic museum, a few doors from the old Weimar, whose villa it had once been and who now lived in its basement. They summoned her from below, and she came, wiping her hands on her apron. "Here she is," they said, "ask her what you want." I wished I had never brought the old lady into this harsh limelight, but I inquired nevertheless if she had by any chance come across, in former times, Admiral Sir John Fisher of the Royal Navy?

Her answer was immediate, short and convincing. "Jacky Fisher!" she said in the silvery English of fin de siècle. "What a face that man had!"

The Immortal Memory

Of course I search for the best in every element of Fisher's face, when we look each other eye to eye. I like nearly all of what I see, but one quality I do miss. Humor is there, and courage, and resolution, and merriment, and mischief, and competence, and a touch of arrogance, and a suggestion of the conspiratorial, and a strong hint of the sensual: but there is no poetry. Fisher is quite clearly not going to die young of consumption, or defy the world with a doomed love affair on a Mediterranean island. Violins do not attend his person, only brass bands or harmoniums.

This is poignant, because if there is one character in history that Fisher wished to resemble, it was that flaming romantic Horatio Nelson. In this he was doing what the navy did. When Fisher joined the service it had a Nelson fixation. Everyone was compared with Nelson, everything was referred back to his glorious era, his tactics were still considered the best tactics. His famous Trafalgar signals— "England expects that every man will do his duty," "Engage the enemy more closely"—were considered the ultimate texts of British naval behavior. In the wardrooms his

Immortal Memory was regularly toasted, and his flagship was a sort of holy relic: the *Victory* was forty years old even at the time of Trafalgar, but half a century later she was still afloat at Portsmouth, manned, ready for sea and the flagship of the commander in chief. From our distance of time and knowledge it all looks a debilitating myth, keeping the navy in a condition of sentimental self-congratulation: but although Jack Fisher was antipathetic to nostalgia, nobody subscribed to it more ardently than he did. He read Southey's *Nelson,* he said, when he was "about 12 years old," he honored the Immortal Memory until the day he died, and he unquestionably loved to be called (as his more besotted devotees sometimes called him) a Second Nelson.

A series of coincidences seemed to bind him to Lord Nelson, and if they did not quite fit his requirements, he adjusted them until they did. He frequently told the story that Emma Hamilton had worked as a maid next door to his grandfather's on New Bond Street, and claimed that old Mr. Lambe remembered seeing her scrubbing the adjacent front steps. He boasted that one of his maternal great-grandfathers had fought at Trafalgar, and of course that he himself had been nominated for the navy by Nelson's own niece and the last survivor of his captains. His first ship, and his last, was *Victory*—as a cadet on his first day in the navy, as professional head of the service when he flew his flag in her as the custom was half a century later. He arranged to assume office as First Naval Lord on Trafalgar Day, 1904 (though actually he turned up a day early), and had the most famous ship of his creation launched on Trafalgar Day, 1906. Among his few possessions was a small collection of Nelson portraits and an original Nelson letter. I suppose it was only coincidence, but it may have reflected unconscious urges, that the last and most intimate of his women friends was born Nina Poore, but had become by marriage the Duchess of Hamilton—no Emma indeed, and certainly no scrubber of doorsteps, but linked at least nominally with his idol.

He published a pamphlet entitled *Nelson: a sketch by one who served under the last of Nelson's captains* (referring I suppose to Admiral Parker at Plymouth). One of his favorite quotations was the alleged logbook report of Nelson's death, in which having been told of his victory at Trafalgar, Nelson "then died of his wound": the "then," which Fisher generally wrote in capital letters, was unfortunately apocryphal—but never mind, as Jack put it, "Having done his job, [Nelson] went to Heaven in glory like Elijah with his chariots and horses of fire!" He was thrilled to visit Emma Hamilton's boudoir in the Palazzo Sessa in Naples, looking down to Capri, with its painted ceiling "just as Nelson looked on it": when the duke of Capri-Colta offered to sell him the house for £4,000 he said that if he had the cash he would have bought it then and there, "but as my private income . . . is only £302.6.8. . . . I bowed my regrets to the Duke."

"I have been," Fisher claimed of himself, "a humble, and I endeavoured to be an unostentatious, follower of our Immortal Hero." Humble possibly, unostentatious never. He flaunted his devotion. Above the guns of his favorite flagship, *Renown,* Nelson's "England Expects" message was gigantically inscribed. When he presided over the foundation of a junior cadet college at Osborne, he caused a large portrait of Nelson to be displayed in the gym, with the announcement THERE IS NOTHING THE NAVY CANNOT DO. In his memoirs he reprinted a cartoon from the *Daily Express,* Trafalgar Day, 1904, which must have given him particular pleasure. It showed the unostentatious follower striding cocked-hatted into the Admiralty to take up office as First Naval Lord, while high above him Nelson had climbed off his plinth and is clinging to his column in Trafalgar Square. "I was on my way down to lend a hand myself," he says, "but if Jacky Fisher's taking on the job there's no need for me to be nervous, I'll get back on my pedestal."

Actually no two admirals could be much less alike than Nelson and Fisher. Both had their considerable vanities, both their religious faith, both were thoughtful toward their men, both could be quarrelsome and both were considered by their contemporaries to have something juvenile to them— "the great child," said *The Times* of Fisher; "in many points a great man, in others a baby," said Lord Minto of Nelson. There the natural resemblances end.

Nelson was an almost archetypal Englishman, tracing his descent back through generations of Norfolk parsons, farmers and merchants, and growing up himself in the fen country. Fisher hardly seemed like an Englishman at all, and never set eyes on England until he was six years old. Nelson was, by all accounts, grave and gentle: Fisher was flamboyantly extrovert. Fisher was stocky and robust, with a swagger to his step, Nelson frail and slight. Nelson was unfaithful to his wife, but staunch in the one tremendous love affair of his life. Fisher was more or less loyal to his Kitty, but scattered his affections apparently platonically among dozens of other women. Nelson was famous for the sensitive gift for friendship that made his captains a band of brothers, Fisher was notorious for his antagonisms. Nelson was a gentleman among gentlemen, Fisher an infinitely complex outsider. Nelson was virtually humorless, Fisher went through life laughing. Nelson spent a lifetime in action, fighting three great naval battles and countless skirmishes, at sea for years at a time blockading enemy coasts or pursuing enemy convoys. Fisher saw no combat after the bombardment of Alexandria, and never commanded a ship or fleet in a battle at sea. Nelson died in the cockpit of his flagship off Cape Trafalgar, aged forty-seven, Fisher died in his bed in St. James's Square, London, aged seventy-nine.

So I find something poignant in the devotion of the one man for the other. Nothing can raise Fisher to the Nelsonically romantic level to which he evidently aspired. Try as I may, when I look at his picture, I cannot imagine him enacted by Laurence Olivier, with Vivien Leigh beside him in his bed. Yet he really thought he *was* like Nelson— not physically of course, but temperamentally. His letters and memoirs are spattered with references to Nelsonic qualities—audacity, imagination, tenderness, insubordination— which he fancied in himself. Nelson himself described the so-called Nelson Touch, the tactic that won at Trafalgar, as "new, singular and simple," and Fisher too thought of his ideas as essentially straightforward. Fisher believed in favoritism—and was not the Band of Brothers really a band of favorites? Fisher stood not just for victory, but for annihilation: Nelson's response, when he was told that fifteen ships had been taken at Trafalgar, was to regret that they hadn't got the rest. Nelson's conceit ("It was during this period that perhaps my personal courage was more conspicuous than at any other period") doubtless encouraged Jack in his incorrigible self-satisfaction, just as Nelson's clerical background must have encouraged him to take pride in the late rector of Wavendon, and all those reverend gentlemen of Bodmin. He used to say that Nelson's temperament "yearned for enthusiasm and passion and emotion": and that was, of course, pure self-description.

It seems to me, though, that Nelson was organically ruthless, as against ad hoc—professionally and in private life. He was not merely faithless, but heartless toward his wife: "opened by mistake by Lord Nelson," was written on one of her letters, returned to her from far away, "but unread." This cruelty was beyond Fisher. In his last years he did go off to live with another woman, another Hamilton at that, but he was never sufficiently Nelsonian to dismiss Kitty from his life. She was probably as dull to him in his greatness as poor Lady Nelson was to England's champion, but he wrote to her affectionately to the end, and hastened from his lover's company to be at his wife's deathbed.

"Ruthless, Relentless and Remorseless," Jack Fisher constantly proclaimed himself to be, and he certainly had no compunction in sacking people, humiliating them, slandering them and plotting behind their backs. He was not,

however, as reckless with their lives as he was with their rep-
utations. As we shall later see, when once in all his career he
was in a position to put his Nelsonic precepts into practice—
to risk all on a single throw, to sacrifice men and ships in the
cause of an overwhelming victory—Fisher faltered. He was
not absolute enough. He would like to have been a cavalier,
but he was more of a Roundhead really, and he lacked the
gift that more than any other other he admired in the
Immortal Hero: the ability, as he himself expressed it, to
"sweep the world with his heart."

Perhaps it was Fisher's tragedy that he was never to command a fleet in action. Perhaps in battle on the bridge of his
own flagship, with the ships of a terrible enemy visible
through the haze and gunsmoke, he would indeed have behaved as Nelson behaved, died as Nelson died: and as I bent
over him in the cockpit then, pressing the water to his lips,
and kissing his forehead with a tear, perhaps I might have
seen in his face not only the harshness I am glad not to find
there, but something of the poetry I miss.

A Love Match

One of the two MPs who were so frolicsome on the battleship at Portsmouth on page 172, during the visit of the colonial premiers, was the young Winston Churchill (the other was F. E. Smith, the future Lord Birkenhead). Churchill was thirty-three in 1907, and his larking about that day was an early manifestation of a taste for naval matters that was to play a fateful part in two world wars. His background was military—direct descendant of the Duke of Marlborough, former cavalry officer, war correspondent with the British armies in the Boer War—but twice in his career he was to become First Lord of the Admiralty. If his interest in the navy was not first fired by Fisher, it was certainly stoked by him, and the two men enjoyed an affectionate, stormy and tragic relationship which was to last until the admiral died—even longer, for the controversy that eventually attended them rages intermittently still.

A well-known photograph illustrates their association in its happier periods. They are emerging from a government office, side by side, in the Establishment livery of the day. Fisher is in his square-crowned bowler, his open greatcoat,

his spats, with a furled umbrella and his usual assertive handkerchief in his top pocket: Churchill is wearing a gray top
hat and a tailcoat, has a stick in his hand and a watch chain
drooping from his waistcoat. The admiral is looking even
more than usually Oriental, almost Mongol, the politician's face is rosy and chubby. Stepping into the street with
imperial assertion, Fisher is evidently saying something at
once caustic and amusing, while Churchill, from his slightly
taller height, is looking down at him with deferential ex-
pectancy—very much the younger man waiting upon the
older, the neophyte with the old professional.

So long as this was the relationship, Churchill and Fisher
made a formidable and fascinating pair. They were both out-
siders, in their different ways. Churchill was half-American,
Fisher was the Yellow Peril. Churchill was as devoted to the
arts and ambitions of politics as Fisher was to the world of
the fleet. Although the sailor was almost twice the age of the
statesman, for a decade the two worked together, sometimes
covertly, sometimes officially, in a partnership that was to
leave its mark upon history. If you and I had been passing
in the street that day when Churchill and Fisher emerged
from the Committee of Imperial Defence, we might well
have thought what a wonderfully entertaining pair of fellows
they seemed to be, off to a good champagne lunch no doubt;
but between them they were to build fleets, sacrifice ships,
achieve victories, perpetrate disasters, topple a government
and cause the deaths of thousands of men from several nations.

· · ·

We stand now upon the waterfront at Naples. It is 1912, well after dark on a summer night, and there, in and out of the shadows, walking up and down the quay in earnest conversation, those same two figures appear—in white suits now, as of yachtsmen or gentlemen of Mediterranean leisure, but still projecting the same relationship, the younger man earnestly listening, the older interspersing long periods of passionate monologue with burbling laughter. The noise of the city fades above them. The last tramcar clangs its bell. The last hawker packs up his tray and goes. It is two in the morning when they return at last to the gangplank of the Admiralty yacht *Enchantress,* moored in the Porto Grande, Churchill with a laughing farewell to board the ship, Fisher to stump away up the steps to the Excelsior above the harbor.

When he was obliged to leave the Admiralty in 1910, Fisher took Kitty off to Europe, planning to spend some time wandering around the Continent, staying in modest hotels, reading no London papers and so "realizing the delights of that blessed state where the wicked cease from troubling and the weary are at rest." With luck, he thought, in a year or two circumstances might change at home and he would be recalled to office. He was in his seventieth year, but still vivid with gusto, vision and hope. In the event nothing turned out as he had planned. Kitty preferred to go home, the modest hotels seem to have evolved into rather opulent ones, and far from absenting himself from affairs in England, Fisher was as deep as ever in political machination. He kept up a tireless correspondence with all his old confidants, the admirals

of the Fishpond, the friendly naval journalists, Reginald
Esher—who, having been one of King Edward's most influential advisers, was soon to be close to the ear of King
George. Most significant of all, Fisher exchanged a torrential
flow of letters with Winston Churchill: now, though still in
his thirties, First Lord of the Admiralty.

For three years a secret liaison was maintained between
the two men—Churchill, of course, had his own First Sea
Lord at home, Fisher's good friend Sir Francis Bridgeman.
Letters were sent by special messenger because the French
were said to open Fisher's mail: DAMN THEIR EYES, Jack
wrote for their benefit on one letter, but perhaps he really
rather enjoyed the cloak-and-dagger aspect of it all—
Churchill once defined him as Secret, Silent, Saturnine and
Sinister, and he used to fasten his long letters theatrically
with a silk ribbon or a pearl pin. They were conscientious
letters of advice about every aspect of naval administration,
and not least its economics: the design of new battleships, the
appointment of admirals, the future of aviation, the education of young officers. They put Fisher, in effect, back at the
center of power, profoundly influencing naval policy. Once
he made an undercover visit to Reigate in Surrey, where
Churchill had assembled half the cabinet to meet him: "I had
four nights without sleep," Fisher reported. "When I wasn't
talking I was writing. My brain was buzzing like a hive
of bees." Once there was a secret meeting at Plymouth, on
board the *Enchantress,* and Fisher and Churchill wandered
together at night around Portsmouth Dockyard, where the
new battle cruiser *Lion* was on the stocks. And in May 1912

the *Enchantress* came cruising in the Mediterranean, carrying Asquith the prime minister, Churchill, and several other members of the government. The official intent of the cruise was to investigate strategic problems, to visit the Mediterranean Fleet, to inspect naval establishments and to give the prime minister and his family a bit of a holiday.

When the yacht put into Naples, however, ostensibly because of bad weather, who should be there to meet it, and stay a few days on board, but Admiral Lord Fisher. "That old rascal Fisher arrived on board directly we got here," reported David Beatty, the First Lord's naval secretary, "never stopped talking and has been cossetted with Winston ever since." Fisher himself wrote exuberantly of the occasion the day after *Enchantress* sailed: "Winston came ashore with me at 2am last night to have last words with me! I thought to myself what a story dear old Stead would have made out of that episode of the early morning hours!"

I have made an inadequate tale of it myself, but I have long been haunted by that glimpse of the two men on the quay at Naples in the small hours. Such destinies hung upon the dialogue! Churchill's immediate purpose in Naples was to persuade Fisher to come home and preside over a commission on oil fuel for the Royal Navy. This task, which Jack accepted, was historically momentous in itself. It led to the conversion of the Royal Navy to the use of oil rather than coal, a wildly daring step for a Power with no oil resources of its own; it also resulted in the purchase by the British Admiralty of a majority share in the oil fields of Iran, the first great Western investment in Middle East oil and the beginning of immense geopolitical troubles. But the long clandestine correspondence that reached its climax that night also implanted in Churchill's mind Fisher's conception of war: the sweeping use of amphibious power, aggressively bypassing or leapfrogging the obvious centers of conflict, or taking them from behind. Out of that balmy Neapolitan night one hears the familiar voice: *Big risks bring big success—The first of all necessities is speed!—Plunge is the watchword of Progress!!—Hit first, hit hardest!!!*

"Fell desperately in love with Winston Churchill," wrote Jack Fisher when they first met, at Biarritz in 1907. "You are the only man in the world I really love," Churchill told Fisher, at least by Jack's account. Indeed they sometimes seemed, for all the differences in their ages, like a couple of lovers. Edward VII called them "the chatterers," so fond were they of closeting themselves away in lively talk, and Violet Asquith said they could neither live with nor without each other—"they can't resist each other for long at close range." In those days emotional relationships between men were not so often stigmatized as homosexual, but it was surely obvious to all that a distinctly sensual, if not actually erotic current ran through their friendship; it is almost possible to imagine the two of them, as they left the office of the Committee of Imperial Defence in that photograph, holding not their respective stick and umbrella, but each other's hands.

They were, as Violet Asquith saw, "sparks from the same fire." Fisher was impulsive and generous in his affections, and believed passionately in the power of emotion.

Churchill, too, was quick to laughter or to tears. Both were radicals, to a degree that horrified conventional society. Both were romantics, and both were engaged in marriages that were to prove lifelong. Besides, there was physically something compatible to them, in their vigor, their somewhat rotund sense of force, their engaging smiles and their individualist tastes. Their common magnetism, which acted so potently upon other people, whether in a positive or a negative direction, worked all the more powerfully on each other, and seems to have kept them in a permanent condition of heightened susceptibility. Here is how Churchill persuaded the old admiral to come home from Europe to head the oil commission: "It is little enough I can offer you. But yr gifts, your force, yr hopes, belong to the Navy, with or without return; as yr most sincere admirer, and as the head of the naval service, I claim them now . . ."

No wonder he agreed. Fisher loved Churchill because he was a man for the Big Things, and was a Great Fighter. "He is brave, which is everything!" He loved his conversation, too, perhaps because Churchill was so eager a recipient of all his own ideas. Churchill for his part said he admired Fisher because he "painted with a big brush," and was violent. He was bewitched by Fisher's cascading flow of ideas, anecdotes, reminiscences and schoolboy jokes. "He told me wonderful stories of the Navy and of his plans—all about Dreadnoughts, all about submarines, all about the new education scheme for every branch of the Navy, all about big guns, and splendid Admirals and foolish miserable ones and

Nelson and the Bible . . ." Being with Fisher, he said, was like breathing ozone.

Their correspondence was mostly technical, Fisher forcefully and cogently passing on opinions about the running of the navy, from petty suggestions of administration to visionary prophecies of strategy and weaponry. Tenderness, though, repeatedly crept in. Sometimes Churchill called Fisher "Bunty," perhaps after the heroine of a current stage comedy, *Bunty Pulls the Strings*, or perhaps simply because it was a slang word for anyone short and fat. Once on the back of an official note Churchill scribbled:

> Your
> "Troubles"
> Tell me them
> please.

Almost at the end of his life Fisher wrote of Churchill, "I have a very weak spot for him in my heart," and in his memoirs, recalling a dream in which Churchill was apparently having a bad time, he said that he "would not hurt him for the world—even in a dream."

They had their lovers' quarrels. In 1912 Churchill made some appointments within the navy that infuriated Fisher. Admirals Sir Hedworth Meux ("Sir Hedworth Pussy"), Sir Berkeley Milne ("Sir Berkeley Mean") and Sir Reginald Custance ("only a quill-driver") were all on his blacklist, and when Churchill as First Lord gave them important jobs Fisher accused him of treachery. "I fear this must be my last communication with you in any matter at all." "I'VE DONE WITH HIM," he wrote, remarkably as a girl might write to a classmate after a squabble with her boyfriend. "I can't say yet," he told Thursfield in similar genre a little later, "whether Winston & I are going to be friends . . . of course you know we were *very very* intimate before." Churchill wryly observed that evidently hell did sometimes freeze, but tactfully smoothed out their differences, inspiring the admiral to one of his Terentian tags: *amantium irae amoris integratio est* ("lovers' quarrels make love whole again.").

One reason for the tiff was Fisher's suspicion that Churchill had been swayed by his wife, Clementine. The one man Churchill loved and the one woman he married never did like each other. Clementine thought Jack a baleful influence upon her young husband, and in later years was to call him a malevolent engine and a fiend. I am sure Fisher was jealous of Mrs. Churchill in return, and during World War I, when he was once again First Sea Lord to Churchill's First Lord of the Admiralty, he was alleged to have displayed an unbalanced fit of malice toward her. Churchill was in France at the time, on a visit to Sir John French, the British Army commander there, and Clementine, asked by her husband to "look after the old boy," had entertained Fisher to a perfectly agreeable lunch at her house. It was only after the meal, so she claimed, that she was buttonholed by the admiral with a truly malignant suggestion: she was not to suppose that Winston was really in Paris to see the generals; he was there to see his mistress. "Be quiet, you silly old man," she retorted, at least in retrospect, "and get out."

Clementine Churchill was still telling the story in her extreme old age, and in 1979 her daughter Mary Soames was still characterizing Jack Fisher as "the terrifying old man." Fisher's supposed behavior sounds out of character, though, and an alternative version of the matter suggests that Mrs. Churchill had misunderstood a little joke: apparently wags at the Admiralty habitually quipped, whenever Churchill crossed the Channel to visit General French, that he was "seeing his French mistress." Whatever the truth of it, the unpleasant anecdote stresses the overwrought emotions which, especially in wartime, characterized the Churchill-Fisher axis. It was all too hot for comfort. There were many people who foresaw that if ever the two men were to work in tandem the mixture would be dangerous: when it came about, as we shall presently see, tragedy indeed resulted. Long afterward, when all was over, and Fisher was in his grave, Churchill wrote of the old admiral less than wholeheartedly: under Clementine's influence perhaps he called him harsh, capricious, vindictive, "gnawed by hatreds arising often from spite," and suggesting that only "on the whole" were his vendettas and maneuvers inspired by public zeal.

These were hardly terms of devotion, and by and large history remembers Churchill and Fisher more as antagonists than collaborators. But as we shall also see, before the end Churchill was to make one grand lover's gesture, reassuring Jack that those long happy hours talking and laughing in the heyday of their friendship were not entirely illusory.

Among the Great

Now here is a memorable image to conjure: Admiral of the Fleet the First Baron Fisher, Royal Navy, OM, GCB, as viceroy of the Indian Empire! Lordly indeed, gilded from head to foot, His Excellency accepts the obeisance of maharajahs at his palace in Calcutta, beneath the tasseled punkahs. Majestically he parades in the high jeweled howdah of his elephant, his recondite face beneath its white plumed hat looking condescendingly down, half haughty, half self-amused, upon the wondering multitudes below. Never has the viceregal barge sailed with such splendor, with Fisher's favorite coxswain at the tiller, up the Hooghly to the viceroy's country palace at Barrackpore. Never has the garden party for the King's Birthday been presided over by so merry a host. Can you not see our Jacky basking in the adulation of the great ladies of the Raj, waltzing with subalterns' wives on lawns of buffalo grass, or sending acidulously biblical messages to snooty seniors of the Indian Civil Service? The massive creaking machinery of government would soon have been revitalized, under Fisher's viceroyalty, and heaven knows what intrigues would have been fostered, what bitter rivalries excited, what rash imperial projects germinated, under the deodars of Simla.

Of course Fisher never was the king's satrap in his Indian Empire, but he did at one time imagine himself in the job, and dropped a hint that he would be available. For all his radical views, he had a taste for consequence, and was transparently pleased to be associated with the great, or to sit in seats of authority.

We have a curious glimpse of Fisher's first brush with great power. In 1869, when he was a lieutenant of twenty-eight, he went to Germany as one of the British representatives at a portentous ceremony: the inauguration by Wilhelm I, king of Prussia, of a new naval base for the North German Confederation. "I look forward with cheerful confidence," said the king in his opening speech, "to the further development and the future of our young German navy": and he was right, because the fishing village of Heppens on Jade Bay, where the new base was established, was to become Wilhelmshaven, home to the formidable High Seas Fleet. Fisher was chosen for the assignment because he was a specialist in torpedoes, presumably in the hope that there was something worth spying on at Heppens. As a very junior delegate he was put up at a village inn (the honorific sentry box placed outside did not warrant a sentry in it), but he did attend the grand ceremonial luncheon, and sat indeed two places away from the king of Prussia himself.

As usual, Jack seems to have been especially indulged—he was probably the youngest man at the table. The king asked chaffingly why he was there: was it because he was the only British officer who knew anything about torpedoes? Otto von Bismarck, the prime minister, grumbled to him in an undertone when the village burgomaster's speech went on and on. Telegrams kept arriving from Berlin, Fisher remembered, and Bismarck would interrupt his eating to walk heavily around the table and discuss them with the king. Graf von Roon, the Prussian war minister, seemed to Fisher very debonair; Graf von Moltke, the chief of the general staff, was like "an old image, taciturn and inscrutable." But what makes the occasion unforgettable in my own mind is this: that while Jack was dressed in his smartest lieutenant's uniform, wearing the ribbons of the Crimean and China campaigns, the Prussian princes, ministers and generals, like so many Teutonic knights, wore at the luncheon table their long heavy greatcoats, and on their heads were spiked helmets.

He thought it "so medieval," but perhaps it was really the presence of power, rather than its imposing appearance, that most affected him. He was no less struck by the court of the sultan Abdülhamid II of Turkey, "Abdul the Damned"— Fisher had first visited Turkey as a junior captain in the Mediterranean Fleet in 1879. The Turks had just been defeated in war by the Russians, but had been saved from worse ignominy by the arrival of British warships in the original manifestation of militant jingoism ("We've got the ships, we've got the men, we've got the money too"). Ten officers of the fleet were gratefully invited to dine with the sultan at the Yildiz Kiosk, his retreat high above the Bosporus. Pages, black eunuchs, gold-encrusted chamberlains and Albanian guards greeted them, and they ate off plates of solid gold, but Fisher was touched by the despot, describing him as "a little man with a hook nose, very black beard and whiskers cut close." His Sublimity looked delicate and careworn, Jack thought (as well he might look, for he was still embroiled in a nightmare mesh of political and diplomatic skulduggery). He talked very low and softly, and had "a most sweet smile when he spoke."

Fisher encountered several other great men in his youth. Twice he met W. E. Gladstone, one of Abdülhamid's most implacable critics, and he enjoyed those encounters, too. Gladstone, after all, "hated waste but loved splendour," Jack's feelings entirely, and if he once said that fashions in warships were as fickle as in ladies' hats, that was long before the time of *Dreadnought* and the battle cruisers. Fisher first met the Grand Old Man at a London party in 1881, and was introduced as the captain of the Royal Navy's most powerful battleship, with its 80-ton guns. "Portentous weapons," Gladstone solemnly said. "I really wonder the human mind can bear such a responsibility." "Oh, sir," replied Fisher breezily, "the common vulgar mind doesn't feel that sort of thing"—and the statesman's features, we are told, "relaxed into a grim smile." At their second meeting Fisher sat next to Gladstone at a dinner table, and by his own account they got on handsomely, talking about China, missionaries, why Abraham didn't like pigs, how much handsomer bishops used to be, Daniel O'Connell and the possibility of recording the human voice. When the party ended and Mrs. Gladstone called to her husband to come to the waiting brougham, he said he was going to walk home with the young captain: it was midnight, and so we see the pair of them strolling slowly down a bright and bustling Piccadilly, the grave old statesman, the cocky young officer, disregarding the traffic as deep in talk they proceed leisurely toward Carlton Gardens.

We see Fisher's shining face, too, cheering Giuseppe Garibaldi, when the Italian champion (an old sailor himself) came on board the *Warrior* in 1861. He was given an exuberant welcome, the whole ship's company marching around the deck for him, preceded by a band playing the Garibaldi hymn while the general's staff excitedly sang the words ("To arms! To arms! / The tombs are uncovered, the dead come from far, / The ghosts of our martyrs are rising to war . . ."). The great moment came when Lieutenant Fisher, the gunnery officer, was called on to show off the ship's fighting capacity. "We went to general quarters and commenced firing away like fun . . . first we supposed the enemy on one bow and then on the other; in fact the enemy was everywhere in the course of ten minutes." Garibaldi was delighted. He told Fisher it was almost the finest thing he had seen in England. "I don't wonder a bit," wrote Jack, "at people being so enthusiastic about him, for he has such a noble face and at the same time such a very simple manner . . ."

Most of the great men of his youthful acquaintance, it appears, had noble faces, quiet voices, sweet smiles, or were particularly attentive to unimportant young officers; and when he was a great man himself, perhaps he remembered the impact of these early brushes with consequence, and cultivated the same effect.

Later in life Fisher became much more intimately acquainted with the rulers of the world. He joked with Queen Victoria, hobnobbed with Edward VII, discussed the affairs of Europe with the Emperor Franz Josef at Marienbad, socialized with the czar, amused the kings of Spain and Portugal, was entertained by Woodrow Wilson, became the familiar of British prime ministers and foreign secretaries and the confidant of great industrialists. When he met Abdülhamid a second time, it was as commander in chief of the British Mediterranean Fleet, and he was given a diamond star worth 500 guineas. In the end he was a great man himself, as the professional head of the British Admiralty. To be First Sea Lord was not quite like being viceroy of India, but it certainly rivaled an archbishopric, say, or a Lord Chief Justiceship.

The Admiralty in those days was far more than a mere service department. It was one of the most influential organizations in Europe—a very ancient and peculiar corporation, as *The Times* once called it. It was an idiosyncratic world of its own, immensely important to the social and economic structure of the nation, and handling about a fifth of the British government's total expenditure. As well as being the chief industrial patron in Britain, it designed and made for itself an astonishing variety of things, torpedoes to chamber pots, and entire towns like Portsmouth, Chatham and Plymouth were in effect its fiefs. It had its own intricate hierarchy, honoring traditions all its own, and bound by lifelong friendships and enmities. It spoke its own stately language, surviving even into modern times: "Their Lordships desire to express their gratitude for all the benefits thus bestowed upon the Royal Navy" is how the Admiralty thanked the Chinese dockworkers of Hong Kong, when the dockyard there was closed in 1959. Its political chiefs were always noblemen—until 1908 no First Lord of the Admiralty had ever sat in the House of Commons.

The Admiralty possessed vast tracts of land, it was the patron of church livings, it administered dockyards, barracks and Admiralty Houses around the world, it employed scientists, surgeons, clergymen, architects, accountants, archivists. It governed the island colony of Ascension, in the South Atlantic, which was rated as a ship, commanded by a captain of the Royal Navy and borne on the books of the admiral-superintendent, Gibraltar. Samuel Pepys had once been its secretary. Christopher Wren had designed its naval college. It had its pantheon of demigods: Anson, Howe, St. Vincent, Rodney, Nelson himself, whose effigy on top of his column in Trafalgar Square, within sight of the Admiralty offices, might well be considered the central icon of the kingdom.

When Fisher, at the age of sixty-three, became the professional head of this extraordinary organism, he himself entered the ranks of the ruling elite. He was famous already (there was a racehorse named after him). Now he was among the elders of the state. He was never rich, he was simple always in many of his ways, but still he lived as a great man should. He never did retire to a village cottage somewhere, as he often threatened: for the rest of his life his homes were far from cottagelike. As First Sea Lord he had a handsome official house at Queen Anne's Gate, and for some years he and Kitty leased a red-brick Georgian house at Ham Common, near Richmond Park, south of London. It had a magnificent cedar tree in the garden, claimed by Fisher to have been planted by Father Abraham himself, and there they entertained statesmen, royalty and fellow admirals in a fine enough style, and Fisher took friends walking in the park, or called upon his neighbor Lord Dysart to discuss their common British Israelite convictions, or showed off his latest American inamorata—"£40,000 a year, and she won't marry! . . . All her frocks are from Poiret! She startles Ham Common . . . !" When Esther Meynell visited the house, Jack showed her with particular pride his bedroom wallpaper, blowsy red roses clambering over green trelliswork. She thought it hideous—"the sailor being rural"—but hadn't the heart to say so.

Langham House is still there, looking benevolently across the common, and although it is now divided into apartments, and the great cedar has gone, and new housing has taken over most of the garden behind, there is enough left to evoke its old atmosphere of insiders' gossip and China tea upon the lawn. "You come to Richmond underground station," Fisher would tell his guests, "and there you will find a Motor Bus 71 *A* that brings you in about a quarter of an hour to the 'Hand and Flower' Ham Common & our house is only two minutes walk from there." In 1992 the inhabitants of the first-floor apartment of the house wrote to me, hearing I was interested in Fisher, and told me that sometimes to that day they felt his energy in its rooms.

Fisher became a baron in 1910, when he left the Admiralty, and Langham House might have seemed inadequate for his eminence. Fortunately Time, the Ocean and some Fostering Star had come to his rescue, for there had come into the possession of the Fisher family a properly baronial home. Among Fisher's friends in industry was the gunmaker Josiah Vavasseur, technical director of one of Europe's greatest arms manufacturers, William Armstrong Ltd. Vavasseur, who was married but childless, became so fond of the Fisher family, and especially of Fisher's son Cecil, that he adopted the boy as his heir, asking only that he should add the name Vavasseur to his own, and adopt the Vavasseur arms. In 1908 Vavasseur died, and there fell into the hands of Cecil Fisher, now retired from his career in India, the mansion of Kilverstone Hall, beside the Little Ouse river near Thetford in Norfolk, with the 3,000 acres of its estate. Its telephone number, like mine today, was 2222.

The house fell equally, one might think, into the hands of his father, for Fisher immediately made Kilverstone Hall his home. He could never have afforded to keep up such an establishment himself, but Cecil's American bride was rich, and there was room for all. It was a house fit for a peer and a Lord of Admiralty. The original medieval manor had been greatly enlarged by Vavasseur, and it looked across park and meadow very spaciously. Nightingales sang there, there was a dovecote and a fine rose garden. It was also in famous shooting country; Cecil and his guests (including Old 'Ard 'Art) once shot 1,100 pheasants in a single day.

For a time Fisher, coming to Kilverstone after the ferocious turmoil of his reforming years, gloried in it all. On the gateposts at Kilverstone appeared the mailed fist and trident that surmounted his baronial crest, and the bedrooms of the house were named after his ships, with a period portrait of Jack in each. In the garden at Kilverstone was mounted the figurehead of *Calcutta,* his first seagoing ship, and the avenue of yews that led to it became known as the Admiral's Walk. After a lifetime spent in cities or at sea, Fisher manfully adjusted to the life of a country gentleman. He chopped wood, cut ivy, cured hams, grew roses—"So Jacky is growing roses, is he?" said the British naval attaché in Rome. "Well, those roses will damned well have to grow." He took visitors around the estate. He entertained a host of weekend guests. He even aspired briefly to play golf, on the private course of a neighbor across the river. Fisher was not really a countryman, though; in his heart he thought the London parks as good as any rural prospect, and he never stayed away from the capital for long.

I went to Kilverstone recently. No Fishers were there, though it still belongs to the family, and the old house looked forlorn. Until lately the estate had been used as a wildlife park, specializing in the breeding of miniature horses, but the enterprise had come to an end. The meadows by the river were empty, except for a few white deer wandering. The rose gardens were overgrown. I could see no sign of the golf course across the river. There had been a fire among the outbuildings, and the jumble of offices and stables seemed to be awaiting either demolition or reconstruction. I found no forget-me-nots.

The trident and mailed fist still supervised the gateway, however, and modestly beneath a tree in the graveyard of the little church next door, not at all seigneurial, I found Jack sleeping with his Kitty, all at peace. On his lichened tombstone are the noble words "Seest thou a man diligent in his business? he shall stand before Kings, he shall not stand before mean men": and on the footstone he is described in properly Fisherian typography as "Organizer of the Navy that WON the Great War."[7]

Practice of War

So he was. "Resurrected!" he is said to have been heard muttering to himself as he left Westminster Abbey one day in 1914. "Resurrected! Resurrected! *Again!*" As he had prophesied, war with Germany had come on a bank-holiday weekend in the late summer of that year, and within four months he was recalled to the Admiralty as First Sea Lord once more, with Winston Churchill as his political chief. It was a triumph for the aged admiral. He had obstinately refused to countenance a naval war staff, he thought he could handle his young friend Winston, he considered the British Army merely a projectile to be fired by the navy, and he had supreme confidence in himself as the one man in the kingdom qualified to win the war.

He was seventy-three, and had lately suffered a nasty bout of pleurisy, but his bounce seemed undiminished. It was to meet the challenge of 1914 that he had set out to create a New Model Navy, and in most ways he had succeeded. The British fleet now was vastly different from the fleet Fisher had himself commanded in the Mediterranean only a decade before. Most of its matériel was modern, its gunnery had been transformed, it had made a start with aviation, its submarine service was well established, it communicated by radio, the last nostalgic echoes of sailing days were all but silenced. The *Dreadnought* gamble had not, after all, weakened Britain vis-à-vis her great enemy; if the climax of the naval war was to be, as most people supposed, a head-on clash between the battle fleets, numerically the British advantage would be clear.

Thanks largely to Fisher, whether as First Sea Lord between 1904 and 1910 or as unofficial adviser to Churchill between 1911 and 1914, the great mass of British battleships and battle cruisers, with its attendant squadrons of smaller vessels, was concentrated in the North Sea, facing the German High Seas Fleet in its bases on the Jade—where the quondam Heppens, with its village inn and loquacious burgomaster, was now one of the world's principal naval ports. At the heroically remote haven of Scapa Flow in Orkney, in Cromarty Firth on the Scottish mainland, there lay in readiness the greatest fleet of warships ever assembled, around a mighty nucleus of twenty-four capital ships. Their commander, Sir John Jellicoe—"the only man who could lose the war in an afternoon," as Churchill said—had been handpicked by Fisher, and the roster of his captains was packed with members of the Fishpond. Fisher even claimed to have realized before anyone else the strategic value of Scapa Flow itself, and to have ordered its first survey.

"Alone I did it," he said: and contemplating the great gray mass of the Grand Fleet, line after line, humming with power, straining for battle, even one of Fisher's critics, Admiral Sir Robert Arbuthnot, felt obliged to say that everything that was best and most modern to be seen there was due to Jacky Fisher.

Like everyone else he imagined a clash of the North Sea battle fleets as another Trafalgar, with Jellicoe its triumphant Nelson, but he dreamed of racier initiatives. The conventional wisdom was that without a "fleet in being," an overwhelming mass of heavy ships always ready in home waters, Britain would be vulnerable to attack from the sea, or even invasion. Fisher believed in submarines, aircraft and independently acting battle cruisers. Above all he believed in the power of amphibious warfare, the British specialty, swift, sudden, hitting first, hitting hardest. His own few battles had all been amphibious operations, and he had always been interested in the techniques of landing armies on hostile coasts. So he conceived, if only in a vague and delusory way, a strategic obsession known as the Baltic Project.

You may remember that during The Hague peace conference, back in 1899, Fisher had made friends with the German military delegate, General von Schwarzhoff ("a greater than Moltke!"). I don't know what von Schwarzhoff looked like (he was to be killed in China later that year) but I prefer to imagine him tall and gaunt, because I like the picture of the two officers, a German Quixote, a British Sancho, pacing the Dutch sands in the summer sun. They were talking fantastically, too. "I had done him a very good turn indeed," wrote Fisher later, "so he opened his heart to me." They were discussing the prospects of a future European war, and the

German put into Fisher's mind the idea that a British army could easily be landed on the Baltic coast of Pomerania, less than 100 miles north of Berlin, and from there could strike directly at the heart of Germany—"14 miles of sandy beach impossible of defence against a battle-fleet sweeping with devastating shells the flat country for miles, like a mower's scythe."

For years Fisher mulled over this proposition. He talked about it often. The kaiser, asked once what he would do if it ever happened, said he would send the Prussian police to arrest the British army, but Fisher preferred to remember the example of Frederick the Great, who allegedly took to carrying a phial of poison in his pocket after he heard the Russians had landed on the Baltic coast of Germany. In later years Fisher conceived the operation combined with other daring enterprises—seizing the islands of Borkum or Heligoland, blocking the Kiel Canal, landing a force in Schleswig-Holstein, falling upon the Jade bases—and it was a Russian rather than a British army that he eventually imagined hurled from his ships upon the Pomeranian shore. One of my correspondents in 1951, a former colonel of artillery, remembered Jacky instructing a military liaison officer in the early days of World War I: "Take all your fellows out of Aldershot or wherever you keep 'em and send them down to Southampton, as they stand—I'll find the ships, and I'll land the lot on the Baltic coast and we'll finish this war in three weeks."

The landing place he had in mind was on the wide sweep of the Oderbucht, east of the peninsula of Peenemünde, where, in another war, the Germans developed their rockets and flying bombs. It is a glorious stretch of sand, backed by gentle bluffs and overlooked by discreet pleasure palaces. The Dukes of Mecklenburg built the first of all German salt-water resorts at Heiligendamm; in the villas of Heringsdorf the Berlin bourgeoisie spent its summer holidays; out of sight in the east is the port of Swinemünde. In this gentle but quintessentially German place Fisher proposed to deposit the brutal paraphernalia of an amphibious landing; I was there a year or two ago, and since he himself never set foot in Pomerania, I imagined it happening for him.

Filling the horizon I saw the fleet that Fisher had commissioned for the operation, ships of strange silhouette in their scores or hundreds, overlooked by tethered airships and buzzing seaplanes. Now and then three immense battle cruisers, *Furious, Courageous* and *Glorious,* let off a salvo from their 15- and 18-inch guns, raising huge clouds of dust and earth behind the beach bluffs, shaking the villas of Heringsdorf and echoing all around the bay. Queer flat monitors, very low in the water, sailed close inshore to fire their 12-inch artillery. A host of destroyers and minesweepers swarmed among the troopships farther out. And chugging noisily toward the beaches, guided by picketboats with midshipmen in command, came the armored landing barges, the first of their kind and nicknamed "beetles": seamen manned the machine guns in their prows, and huddled helmeted in the holds behind, with the imperial eagle flying on regimental ensigns here and there, and a glint of bayonets, I could see the gray-coated infantry of the czar.

Rifles and machine guns spat from the bluffs; howitzer shells spouted among the ships; the great guns thundered from the sea; whistles blew, sirens hooted, men shouted, signal lights flashed, the seaplanes roared above; and when the first landing craft grounded, their ramps fell and the soldiers stumbled bent-backed onto the sands, I saw that one and all had snow on their boots.

For of course it never happened. It was an expedition in the direct line of imagination from the abduction of Dreyfus from Devil's Island. It was, however, not all fancy. When Fisher returned to the Admiralty in 1914 he appears to have convinced both Churchill and Lloyd George, the Chancellor of the Exchequer, that the Baltic Project might work, and with their backing embarked upon a program of ship-building supposedly for its execution. *Courageous, Furious* and *Glorious* were no figments of my fancy; they did exist, with low drafts suitable for Baltic waters, with enormous guns for bombardment—ships so astonishing that the navy called them *Outrageous, Spurious* and *Uproarious*. The monitors were built too, and so were the landing craft. The Baltic Project was never adopted as government war policy, and perhaps Fisher himself was never entirely serious about it—it has been argued that it was all bluff or blind, masking his real ambitions to develop a navy essentially of battle cruisers, submarines and small craft; yet such was his dynamism, and such the inspiration of the late General von Schwarzhoff, that a fleet really was built to implement it. Fisher claimed in retrospect to have made all the arrangements for the operation "with my own hands alone, to preserve secrecy," one reason why the truth about the project is still unclear; he once wrote a rather groveling letter to his old acquaintance the czar ("With humble duty to Your Imperial Majesty") proposing a joint Pomeranian expedition, but decided not to send it.

Around this chimerical purpose, anyway, Fisher seems to have organized the task of waging a general war at sea. His immediate predecessor had been Prince Louis of Battenberg, who had been forced out of office largely because of his German origins. Churchill enthusiastically welcomed his old friend and mentor back to Whitehall. Fisher restored romance to the Admiralty, he said. All Jack's histrionic and tumultuous methods were revived, and everything was organized to his style once more—even the carpet in his office had to be replaced by something better ("Lord Fisher can only think on a Turkey carpet"). The mantras and gimmicks were employed again, the invigorating slogans, the stickers, the hyperbolic threats, the charm, the subterfuge. A card in his office, probably picked up in America, said unpleasantly

CALL ON A BUSINESS MAN IN BUSINESS HOURS ONLY ON BUSINESS. TRANSACT YOUR BUSINESS AND GO ABOUT YOUR BUSINESS, IN ORDER TO GIVE HIM TIME TO FINISH HIS BUSINESS, AND YOU TIME TO MIND YOUR OWN BUSINESS.

He had no time for red tape or bureaucratic obfuscation— "Find the exact damned ass who did it," he used to say, and I long ago adopted the phrase myself. Shipyards were galvanized into new frenzies of construction. Designers were bombarded with ideas. Industrialists were cajoled or goaded into unprecedented productivity. As always, Fisher usually began work before dawn, attended Holy Communion at Westminster Abbey at eight, worked all day and went to bed soon after eight in the evening. Once he claimed to have worked for twenty-two hours out of the previous twenty-four. Churchill said he made the Admiralty quiver like one of his great ships at its highest speed, and the director of military operations thought an interview with Fisher in 1915 was like being run over by a bus.

As everybody recognized, after sixty years in the navy and three previous appointments as a Lord of Admiralty, he knew his business. As he used to say, "When you have been a kitchen maid nobody can teach you how to boil potatoes." Dozens of accounts, wry or admiring, record his dynamic energy in those first months back at the Admiralty, and several were sent to me by participants. No British yards can produce the necessary submarines? Get on to my beloved friend Charles Schwab, head of Bethlehem Steel in the United States—in six months he'll have half a dozen boats crossing the Atlantic under their own power. There is a shortage of gunboats? Sir Alfred Yarrow will produce them—or if he doesn't, he will be sent to the Tower of London. (Yarrow: Will you come and look at me through the bars? Fisher: No.) Cancel those battleships, make them battle cruisers instead. Convert the *Royal Sovereigns* to oil fuel. Build fifty airships, and train midshipmen to man them. If the superintendent of contracts fails to speed up building times he will have to commit hara-kiri. Gentlemen, I invite you to build submarines for the Royal Navy, knowing that your companies have never built such vessels before. If you succeed no reward will be too high for you, but if you fail I shall make your wives widows and your homes dunghills. I expect your answers this afternoon.

During Fisher's first wartime months more than 600 new ships were ordered for the Royal Navy. Expense was no object now. "Isn't it fun being back?" he wrote to Esher.

For a time it was undoubtedly fun. The British public welcomed Fisher as a savior, because in the first months of the war the Royal Navy, their paragon of services, their criterion of everything most reliably and dashingly British, had dismally failed them. In the North Sea three cruisers had been torpedoed by a single German submarine. In the Atlantic, one of the newest Dreadnoughts had been sunk by a mine. Bold German surface raiders had been storming around the oceans sinking British merchantmen. In the Mediterranean, Admiral Sir Berkeley Milne had allowed the powerful German warships *Goeben* and *Breslau* to escape his vastly superior forces and slip away to Turkey, where they were instrumental in bringing the Turks into the war on the enemy's side (from then on Berkeley Mean became, in Fisher's vocabulary, Berkeley Goeben, and the battered gray silhouette of the *Goeben* still gave me a disagreeable frisson on his behalf when I saw her lying at Istanbul forty years later: by then she was renamed *Yavuz,* and she survived until 1971 to be the last of all the European Dreadnoughts). German

battle cruisers actually had the impertinence to bombard
the coasts of Yorkshire and Lincolnshire. The smashing
Trafalgar that everyone hoped for had not happened, and
the two battle fleets remained immured in their respective
bases on either side of the North Sea. It was not at all what
the nation expected of Nelson's heirs; but the return of Jacky
Fisher, it was confidently believed, would change everything.

And at first it did, because within a week of his return to
office Fisher was able to use the Royal Navy as the nation
wanted it, Nelsonically. Off Cape Coronel, on the west coast
of South America, a squadron of five German cruisers under
the command of Admiral Maximilian von Spee humiliat-
ingly sank two British cruisers without loss to itself. Fisher,
backed by Churchill, responded instantly and furiously.
Within an hour of receiving the news he ordered the dispatch of two battle cruisers to the South Atlantic. *Invincible*
and *Inflexible* were to sail from Cromarty Firth at once, that
same day, via Devonport. *Inflexible* needed some minor repairs, and the dockyard superintendent at Devonport wired
the Admiralty to say that the work could not be done in less
than five days. Back came a response from Whitehall: the
ships must sail in three days, and the superintendent himself
would be held responsible for seeing to it. When the time
was up, the *Inflexible* left with some of the dockyard workmen
still on board.

In command of the squadron was a man Fisher anathema-
tized as a pedantic ass—Admiral Sir Doveton Sturdee, who
had made the mistake of being a Beresford supporter. Fisher

had inherited him as his chief of staff at the Admiralty, and was delighted to get rid of him by throwing him helter-skelter into this adventure. It was fortunate for Sturdee that his distinctly leisurely progress across the ocean, with a protracted stop for coaling in the Cape Verde Islands, turned out to be all for the best. Hardly had he arrived in the sheltered harbor of Port Stanley, in the British Falkland Islands, than the Germans arrived too, intending to destroy the navy's facilities there. They had a shock indeed when they saw, protruding above the harbor mole, the tripod masts that told them two of Fisher's New Testament ships were already there.

The battle was the last to be fought in the old manner, gun against gun, without the intervention of aircraft, submarines, mines or torpedoes. Its conclusion was foregone. The Germans were hopelessly outgunned and outpaced. The battle cruisers did exactly what Fisher had intended them to do—armadillos licking up ants. Four of the German cruisers were sunk with the loss of almost all their crews, including Von Spee himself; the fifth escaped but was routed out later in a Chilean creek. The British ships were hardly scratched. Coronel was avenged: more important, the world's oceans were freed of German surface squadrons. *Invincible* and *Inflexible* returned in glorious vindication. Fisher was exalted. The nation was in his debt for the exploit, telegraphed the Public Orator of Oxford University, gratifyingly in Latin—HOC TIBI PISCATOR PATRIA DEBET OPUS. "This was your show and your luck," Churchill told him. "Your *flair* was quite true." Fisher thought so too, but never forgave the pedantic ass Sturdee for letting one of the German ships get away, even for a month or two.

It was Fisher's most dazzling and gratifying coup, in fact the most absolute British victory of the entire war. It seemed to justify all his principles. The battle cruisers had proved themselves in exactly the role he had designed them for, they had hit first and hit hardest, they had thought in oceans and sunk at sight, they had proved that moderation in war was imbecility, they had demonstrated that the Royal Navy had not lost its élan. The battle of the Falkland Islands really did end a phase of the naval war, in that the Germans never again seriously tried to harass British commerce with surface ships.

But Fisher was not to experience such an epiphany again. The Great War turned out to be above all a murderous slogging match: on land, armies against armies in stagnant grapple, at sea perpetual blockade and an endless contest between submarines and surface ships. Only once did the North Sea battle fleets come face-to-face, and then inconclusively. Fisher's battle cruisers never had another chance to display themselves in their proper function, and his visions of overwhelming amphibious landings on enemy shores found only a tragic fulfillment on the shores of Turkey—a kind of nightmare incarnation of the Baltic Project. Besides, he was getting old. In the end the ordeal for which he had prepared with such epic resolution was to prove too much for Jacky; as he would say himself, when it came to the practice of war his trumpet sounded an uncertain call.

IV

SORROWS OF YOUR
CHANGING FACE

Hubris and Humiliation

The only sad representation of Fisher's face is Jacob Epstein's bust of 1916. Fisher was a man with a genius for enjoyment, yet the sculpture, portraying an admiral in the full panoply of authority, plastered with medals and ribbons, shows a face that is not only cynical, defiant and almost ludicrously egotistical, but unmistakably tinged with sadness. The closing pages of any book about Jacky Fisher, especially such a fond work as this, must have their sorrows too.

They set in at a meeting of the War Council in January 1915. A footnote in Fisher's memoirs says of this occasion that it might "one day furnish material for the greatest historical picture of the war." In the event nobody painted it, so I will set the scene now. The meeting is presided over by Herbert Asquith, the prime minister, smooth, silvery, cultivated. Among the others at the table are the fearful-looking Lord Kitchener, secretary of state for war, Winston Churchill at his most excited, Maurice Hankey, the council's secretary, Old 'Ard 'Art and the aged Fisher, his face apparently contorted in anger.

We cannot hear what is being said, but the atmosphere is clearly inflamed. Churchill speaks passionately. Fisher interrupts. Asquith, calming them with a gesture, seems to announce some final decision, whereupon the First Sea Lord, furiously pushing his chair back, storms toward the door. Before he can get there Kitchener springs from the table to catch him by the arm, and for a moment or two, while the room is hushed and the others look around in anxious embarrassment, the mighty field marshal and the stocky Admiral of the Fleet converse in undertones beside the window. The room waits; the tension is palpable; and then like a child guided back to the nursery table after a tantrum, Jack allows himself to be seated once more among the councillors.

What was happening was this: Fisher was being persuaded, against his better judgment, to give his support to a naval attack upon the Dardanelles, the strait that separates the Mediterranean from the Sea of Marmara, the Bosporus and the Black Sea, with the intention of getting through to Constantinople and knocking Turkey out of the war. One might have thought this was just Fisher's style, and to some extent it was his own idea: he had said himself that if he could not have the Baltic Project, he wanted an attack on Germany's other flank, to bring the Balkan states into the war on the Allied side. Churchill, though, was the prime begetter of the Dardanelles venture, and Fisher found himself swept along in the wake of a temperament just as ardent as his own, a physique much younger and an intellect more formidable.

Both Fisher and Churchill had convinced themselves that as partners at the Admiralty each would be able to control the other. "He was old and weak," Churchill recalled in retrospect, "and I thought I should be able to keep things in my own hands." Despite many reservations the navy itself, whose officers profoundly distrusted Churchill, welcomed Fisher back to office for exactly the opposite reason: that at least he would keep the bumptious politician in order. There were always those, however, who foresaw trouble. It was one thing for the venerable admiral to offer the young statesman his advice, *de haut en bas,* quite another to accept him as a political master. The association was emotional enough in any circumstances: in the heat of war it became overwrought.

After only a few months back at the Admiralty, Fisher's age began at last to tell, too. On the one hand his familiar ebullient egotism was becoming ever more of a pose, almost a caricature; on the other, his strength was failing him. Churchill recalled seeing him once so worked up that "it seemed that every nerve and blood-vessel in his body would be ruptured." The euphoria of his Falklands triumph faded, and by January 1915 Herbert Richmond thought he seemed old, worn-out and nervous. Sometimes he went home for a siesta in the afternoon now, and Maurice Hankey once found him fast asleep at his desk in the middle of the day.

He worked as passionately as ever, but could not keep up the pace. He was at his best in the early morning, but Churchill came fully to life at night, and so the very timetable of Admiralty conspired to set them at odds: we see the vigorous forty-year-old arriving fresh for the night's work just as the exhausted septuagenarian buttons his coat for the weary walk home. For once in his life Fisher recognized a personality more forceful than his own, and something querulous crept into his responses. No longer was Churchill the grateful pupil: now he was the boss, and every argument he seemed to win—"He is always *convincing* me!" Churchill thought of Fisher essentially as a naval constructor, and more and more he acted as though the disposition of the Royal Navy was his responsibility, and his alone. Filson Young, visiting the Admiralty in April 1915, felt uncomfortable at seeing Fisher obliged to accept the authority of this overbearing junior.

Perhaps, too, Churchill was beginning to see through Fisher's postures of aggression. As the months passed, the old admiral's eagerness for instant and annihilating action seemed to fade. He dreaded the loss of ships, and even more of men. He never ceased to demand offensive attitudes, "kicking the Germans before they kick us," and claimed still to be working for a Baltic invasion, but gradually his pronouncements became more cautious. "The *big thing* of the war is to keep our Big Fleet in big preponderance, intact and ever ready to cope with the German Big Fleet!" Or: "Being already in possession of all that a powerful fleet can give a country, we should continue quietly to enjoy the advantage without dissipating our strength in operations that cannot improve the position." He was not, it seemed, a man of risks after all, not the reckless fire-eater that he had always appeared: he believed in keeping the odds unmistakably in one's own favor (*vide* Luke 14, verse 31!). The only battles he wanted were ones like the slaughter at the Falkland Islands, which was really no contest at all.

All this was a far cry from the landing craft storming the Pomeranian shore, and it meant that when, in November 1914, the idea of the Dardanelles operation was first mooted, Fisher's support was less wholehearted than might have been expected. The idea of forcing the Dardanelles had long fascinated the Royal Navy. A squadron had done it in 1807, and in 1887 the two *Sans Pareil* battleships had been designed specifically with a view to doing it again. In peacetime Fisher had twice sailed with British squadrons through the straits of Constantinople, once as a young captain, once as a commander in chief, and he knew the potential dangers as well as anyone at the Admiralty. As long before as 1906 he had argued that the straits could no longer be forced by the navy alone, but that an army would simultaneously have to be landed on the Gallipoli peninsula, and this was apparently still his view in 1914.

But now he was old, he was tired, he was out-arguable, and when Churchill proposed to send a fleet through the straits unsupported by an army, he seems at first to have acquiesced. Once more the Royal Navy would be exerting its superbia in the East, as it had under his command fifteen years before, and this romantic idea perhaps seduced his imagination. The British admiral in the eastern Mediterranean thought the plan feasible, and the War Council formally approved a naval expedition to the Dardanelles "with Constantinople as its objective." Fifteen old battleships were assigned to the operation, and Fisher agreed to send also the magnificent brand-new *Queen Elizabeth*, the most powerful warship afloat—she could calibrate her guns in action.

Almost from the beginning, nevertheless, he had his doubts. He still thought his ships should be supported by landings on Gallipoli. He regretted the offer of the *Queen Elizabeth*. On January 18, 1915, he and Churchill together had an interview with Asquith, Churchill to press for the start of the operation, Fisher to oppose it. Asquith decided in favor—"almost with a gesture," according to Churchill—and the three men went on to the meeting of the War Council upon which we have already eavesdropped: where Fisher, deciding to resign rather than support the plan, was persuaded to change his mind by Kitchener, and thus, returning brooding to his seat, sealed his own destiny.

In retrospect he claimed to have been consistently and overtly against the Dardanelles operation, but this was untrue. He did not speak out against it at that fateful meeting, only got up to leave, and there were times during its execution when he was all enthusiasm. "My God, I'll go through tomorrow!" he cried, already assuming the glory of it, when the news from the East seemed to show that the ships were indeed going to succeed. Once he offered to go out and take command himself. "We are sure to win," he told Churchill. "Do try and remember that *we are the lost ten tribes of Israel!*"

But the ships did not go through. Bombarding the defending forts achieved little, and the British were unable to clear the straits of mines. Three of Fisher's beloved ships were sunk, and when in April 1915 it was decided, as he had al-

ways wished, that there should be a landing at Gallipoli,
it too soon went sour, its soldiers pinned tragically down
on the coast in a cruel pastiche of that fanciful assault on
Pomerania—with the very same landing craft, in fact, that
would have been used there. Scores of ships and immense
stocks of matériel were sent to the Mediterranean in support
of these stagnant operations, and Jacky began to lose his balance. His relationship with Churchill was now more charged
than ever. The loss of his ships and sailors profoundly de-
pressed him. Sometimes he seemed resolute still, sometimes
despondent, and if he really knew his own mind by now, he
certainly made his feelings unclear to others. He quarreled
with Churchill, he made it up again. He insisted on the withdrawal of the *Queen Elizabeth*. Eight times he threatened to resign, only to change his mind. He claimed that the operation
was fatally weakening the navy's resources for its real task, its
Big Task, the containment of the High Seas Fleet in the
North Sea. "Damn the Dardanelles! They will be our grave!"

But he apparently fretted about his Baltic Project, too, and
saw Churchill's attitude as a betrayal of it. It was Churchill,
after all, who had written, only a few months before, that the
Baltic was "the only theatre in which naval action can appre-
ciably shorten the war . . . the Russians [must] be let loose on
Berlin." Now the monitors and landing craft were being sent
to the Dardanelles instead, together with an ever-growing
armada of other vessels. "I really don't think I can stand it!"
Fisher cried. Churchill, no longer the neophyte, did his best
to calm and appease him, knowing well that Fisher's resignation would discredit the operation and fatally weaken his

own position. Filson Young was struck by Churchill's molli-
fying approach to the old man—gentle, sympathetic, diplomatic and soothing. "I honestly believe that Winston loves
me," wrote Fisher during the very worst of their differences.

On May 14, 1915, the War Council once more determined to
persevere with the operation, despite the terrible cost, agree-
ing that yet more ships should be sent to the Mediterranean.
In the evening Churchill called at Fisher's office to cheer
him up, and apparently to reassure him that the reinforce-
ments agreed to that morning would be the end of it. "We
have settled everything, and you must go home and have a
good night's rest." Fisher went to bed; Churchill returned to
work; and during the night the First Lord of the Admiralty
wrote four minutes to his First Sea Lord ordering that,
despite what had been said the evening before, yet more
submarines and monitors should be sent to the Dardanelles.
They were very long and characteristic minutes, dashed
off brilliantly in the night with a peremptory air of fait ac-
compli. Reading them now reminds me of an occasion when
Churchill's son Randolph and I, as reporters, shared a char-
tered aircraft to fly us to a later Mediterranean conflict, the
Algerian war of the 1960s. Halfway there, Randolph suddenly ordered the pilot to make for Malta instead, for reasons entirely of his own convenience. It was my last
Churchillian straw, up with which I would not put; Fisher's
came on the morning of May 15, 1915.

We do not know how much real difference there was between the proposals of the day before and the figures of the

next morning, but when soon after dawn Fisher woke up at Queen Anne's Gate to find the minutes awaiting him, he cracked. For the ninth time he sent the prime minister his resignation, and declared that he was "off to Scotland so as to avoid all questionings." He did not go north that day, but he did entirely disappear from his home and his office, telling nobody where he was and appointing nobody to stand in for him. He ran away from the job, in fact, pulling down the blinds at Queen Anne's Gate behind him. He doubtless went to pray in Westminster Abbey—and what a subject he might have provided then for the narrative painter, vehemently hunched there in his pew, his face ablaze, the prayers tumbling from his lips, while vergers cast him curious glances, and visitors frankly stare! He called at the Treasury to tell Lloyd George he was leaving—"His curiously Oriental features," the Welshman recalled, "were more than ever those of a graven image in an Eastern temple, with a sinister frown." Finally he walked up Whitehall to the Charing Cross Hotel, only a few yards from the Admiralty, where he took a room and immured himself. (I asked the manager recently if there was any record of his registration that day—I would love to know what room he had—but the archives of the period were long age destroyed, and I can only surmise, knowing Jack's thrifty traveling habits, that he asked for one at the back, over the tracks.) Telephones rang across London. Couriers scoured Whitehall. Kilverstone was contacted, Continental trains were checked—he might be making for France. When at last he was found, a messenger arrived at the hotel with a note from the prime minister, ordering him in the king's name to return to his post.

It was no good, though. In the afternoon Fisher went to 10 Downing Street and told Asquith he was determined to resign. He was impervious to a passionate appeal from Churchill. "The only thing to think of now," wrote the First Lord, "is what is best for the country and for the brave men who are fighting. . . . In every way I have tried to work in the closest sympathy with you. The men you wanted in the places you wanted them, the ships you designed, every proposal you have formally made for naval action, I have agreed to. . . . It will be a very great grief to me to part from you." Fisher's reply was adamant, and largely in capital letters: "YOU ARE BENT ON FORCING THE DARDANELLES AND NOTHING WILL TURN YOU FROM IT— *NOTHING*. I know you so well! . . . *You will remain*. I SHALL GO . . ."

Fisher was distraught. Perhaps he was having a breakdown. Sometimes he seemed almost unnaturally himself: he was amiable enough when he called on Asquith, and on May 18, while these catastrophic events were still unfolding, he made Hankey laugh till the tears came with the bubble of his hilarity. On the other hand he wrote a half-incoherent letter to Bonar Law, leader of the Opposition, which seems to show some fragmentation of his powers. It was scrawled this way and that, with afterthoughts and deletions everywhere, wild underlinings, capital letters and theatrical warnings, and drew upon the full Fisherian repertoire of Shakespearean quotations, biblical texts, Latin tags and injunctions to secrecy. It was headed "This letter and its contents must not be divulged now or ever to any living soul," and its most pregnant phrase was this: *"A very great national disaster is very near us in the Dardanelles."*

Out of the agony, the prophecy rings all too clearly. Fisher was right. Eight months later the Gallipoli operation ended in misery, more than 40,000 men lost in an operation that achieved nothing whatsoever. Nevertheless Fisher was always to be seen as shamefully abandoning his post, especially because at that moment news came that the German High Seas Fleet was about to leave its bases—that the new Trafalgar, in short, might at last be about to happen. It proved a false alarm, as Fisher guessed, but his absence from his desk at this crucial time fatally weakened his cause. "I consider," wrote Violet Asquith in her diary, "that he has behaved in a lower, meaner and more unworthy way than any Englishman since the war began." The magazine *John Bull* said Fisher had set a shocking example to the whole people. "Stick to your post like Nelson!" reproachfully wrote his old friend Queen Alexandra. King George V declared he should be hanged from the yardarm. Old 'Ard 'Art said his defection would be a national tragedy. From the Grand Fleet, Jellicoe implored him to return. He ignored them all, with one disastrous exception. His old confidant Reginald Esher, now a peer too and still moving in the highest circles with a silky confidence, wrote to "My dear, dear Jackie" with some calamitous advice. What Fisher should do, he said, was to revive for himself the office of Lord High Admiral, and thus become the supreme and absolute commander of the Royal Navy, immune to political interference.

Fisher's resignation, although it had not yet been accepted by the prime minister, had shattering political effects, and Asquith immediately set about forming a new coalition government. It was clear that Churchill, his reputation cruelly tarnished by these affairs and by the emerging fiasco of the Dardanelles, would be dropped from the Admiralty. Seizing upon Esher's rash suggestion, in a frenzy of pride and despair Fisher wrote to the prime minister a letter that was his downfall. These are its chief points:

- *If the following . . . conditions are agreed to, I can guarantee the successful termination of the War . . .*
- *That Mr Winston Churchill is not in the Cabinet to be always circumventing me . . .*
- *That there shall be an entire new Board of Admiralty, as regards the Sea Lord and the Financial Secretary (who is utterly useless). New measures demand new men.*
- *That I shall have complete professional charge of the war at sea, together with the absolute sole disposition of the Fleet and the appointment of all officers of all ranks whatsoever, and absolutely untrammelled sole command of all the sea forces whatsoever.*
- *That the First Lord of the Admiralty should be absolutely restricted to policy and parliamentary procedure . . .*
- *That I should have the sole absolute authority for all new construction and all dockyard work of whatever sort whatsoever,*

*and complete control of the whole of the Civil Establishments of
the Navy.*

· *These conditions must be published verbatim so that the Fleet
may know my position.*

It was a deranged letter. It was the worst letter Fisher ever
wrote. It made the mild Asquith declare that Fisher ought
to be shot, and even old friends were ashamed—"Jack's
got megalomania," reported one devoted member of the
Fishpond, "and done for himself." Jack himself bitterly
regretted writing the thing, when he had recovered from this
period of hysteria—"Moses spake unadvisedly with his
lips—*so did I!*" But by then it was too late. His career with
the Royal Navy was over. Without waiting for an answer to
his fulmination he took the train to Scotland, and at Crewe
Junction the stationmaster handed him a telegram formally
accepting his resignation.

He had behaved less than Nelsonically—less than Fisher-
ianly, indeed. *Mad things come off?* Out at the Dardanelles, the navy was ready to try again, and it was indeed
possible that one more remorseless, relentless assault upon
the strait, risking great risks, sacrificing ships and men, might
have taken the fleet to Constantinople. The operation would
have succeeded, wrote Roger Keyes, naval chief of staff at
the Dardanelles, who was desperate to try again, "if that
wonderful old man had devoted all his fierce, ruthless energy
towards supporting,   instead of thwarting [it] . . ." The
Turkish commander, Enver Pasha, thought so too. "If the

English had only had the courage to rush more ships through they could have got to Constantinople." Von Tirpitz himself thought that if the Dardanelles had fallen, Germany would have lost the war. *Caution in war is imbecility?* At the time when Fisher was agitating for the return of his ships to the North Sea, the Grand Fleet always had a decisive superiority over the High Seas Fleet. *Any fool can obey orders?* Asked why he had not spoken out more forcibly at the War Council against the Dardanelles operation, Fisher replied limply that it was not his place: he had already made his views known to the prime minister, and it was Churchill who must speak for the Admiralty.

To this day historians argue about the possibilities of the Dardanelles, and Churchill never doubted that the campaign could have been a famous victory rather than a tragic defeat—"I came, I saw, I capitulated" was his bitter apothegm about the eventual withdrawal from Gallipoli. Fisher never allowed the thought to trouble his conscience, and instead maintained to the end of his days that some variety of the Baltic Project could have won the war.

Smoldering, resentful and regretful, feeling no doubt that he had let himself down at this supreme moment of a marvelous life, his face a mask of bitter hauteur at the window of his sleeper, our Jacky steamed away into his closing chapter.

Concerning Pathos

Pathos haunted the last years of Fisher's life, and drew its threads together. His spirit remained marvelously resilient, and he soon recovered from the worst traumas of the Dardanelles crisis, but never again was he to perform at center stage (except at his funeral, when even Admiral of the Fleet Earl Jellicoe was seen to shed a tear . . .).

It was certainly not for lack of trying. He may have regretted his Lord High Admiral ploy, but he never doubted that he was the best man to run the navy, if not the country, and for the rest of World War I he schemed indefatigably for a recall to power. The nearest he got to it was an appointment as chairman of an impotently advisory Board of Inventions and Research, nicknamed by Fisher's enemies the Board of Intrigue and Revenge, and said by Philip Guedalla the historian to be "like a kind of inverted Mr Micawber waiting for something to turn down."

His enemies rejoiced at his ignominy, but he had many powerful supporters still, and propagated his own cause as shamelessly as ever. He likened himself to Cincinnatus, Jephthah the hero of Gilead or the great fighting Doge Enrico Dandolo—"Oh! for one hour of blind old

Dandolo / The octogenarian Chief!"—and almost everything he did in his last years can be construed as the mis-
guided efforts of a man of power to regain a lifetime's lost
authority.

It was not to Kilverstone that Fisher took his train that day.
From Norfolk, Kitty anxiously watched the dramatic events
in London, kept in touch by brief notes from Fisher: when
the denouement came she and her daughters were terribly
hurt that Jack, instead of coming home, sped away almost as
far and as fast as possible. He was hastening to the comforts
of another woman, the Duchess of Hamilton, who was intel-
lectually more exciting, who bore a sacredly Nelsonic name,
who was rich, whose religious fervor equaled his own, whose
social and political clout might serve Fisher better than the
mere love of a devoted family, and who was thirty-eight
years his junior.

Like most of his extramarital relationships, Fisher's affair
with Nina Hamilton was variously interpreted, seldom flat-
teringly. Most people probably assumed it to be carnal (even
within the Hamilton family there was uncertainty), many accused Jacky of feathering his own nest (the Hamiltons had
mansions all over the place) or of trying to use the dukely
family for political ends. There was nothing sudden to it—
they had known each other for years. The thirteenth duke,
Nina's husband, had been one of Fisher's midshipmen in the
Mediterranean, but had been invalided from the navy. When
the duke was a boy Fisher described him as being "small as a
rat with a voice like a bosun's mate, and more oaths than one

of Cromwell's troopers." By now the duke was confined to a wheelchair, and his propensity to foul talk was so grotesquely extended that he could be a distinct social embarrassment ("I think His Grace is tired," Nina would say to the footman, I am told, having him hastily removed from the dining room). Willy-nilly, then, he played the part of the complaisant husband, and Jack threw himself into an infatuation for the duchess with no attempt at secrecy. When Augustus John painted his portrait, Nina came along to the sittings—"You won't find as fine a figure of a woman," Fisher proudly told the artist, "and a duchess at that, at every street corner." As for Nina, who looks in her photographs bright, agreeable and ingenuous, and who was passionate in her devotion to animal rights, she was besotted by the old sailor and spoke of him with an extravagance uncannily like Emma Hamilton's before her. He was the Great Admiral. He was a giant among pygmies. He was a hero, a saint, greater than Nelson.

Together they explored the mysteries of religion. The Hamiltons were Presbyterians, and the duchess was a devout evangelical, besides dabbling in Spiritualism and Christian Science. They invited a different minister to preach every Sunday at their private chapel in Scotland, a luxury indeed for Fisher. "Look out for hearing of me preaching at street corners and the Duchess with a tambourine!" he wrote after a visit from the celebrated American evangelist Paul Moody. Nina and Jack loved swapping holy thoughts and conjectures, and some of the religiosity of Fisher's young manhood returned to his geriatric prose. Was it not true that shadows but serve to show up the sunshine more clearly? Do we not have Realities unperceived all about us? Did not Revelation 13, verses 4 and 5, make it clear that the war would end on February 4, 1918, it being given unto the beast with seven heads and ten horns to continue forty and two months? In return the duchess seems to have provided an element of whimsy. She encouraged her children to call Fisher "Uncle Jacky," and once described her daughter Mairi (who died in childhood, and was somewhat suggestively subtitled Star of the Sea) as "the little fairy who hugged him and climbed up his knee."

Fisher confided everything to her. He thought her a genius of perception, and gloried in her social eminence—*"I wish I'd been born a Duchess."* The Hamilton children adored the old man, and he used the various family establishments as his own, though sometimes referring to the duchess as his landlady. He became a trustee of the enormous Hamilton estates, and his letters of the period are variously written from Dungavel or Hamilton Palace in Scotland, from Balcombe in Sussex, from Knoll House in Dorset, from 19 St. James's Square, London, or from Ferne House near Salisbury—all agreeable Hamilton properties. If we had been in Wiltshire in 1918, wandering about the sweet stone village of Berwick St. John, we might have heard a tinkling of sleigh bells and a trotting of small hoofs down a narrow hilly road: and merrily into sight there would come a little basket trap, drawn by four well-groomed Shetland ponies, with a bright-eyed duchess and an aged admiral in it. Up the road today, in the purlieus of Ferne, little Mairi the Star of the Sea lies buried within the same enclosure as some of the family pets, and people in the village still wonder if Jack was really her father.

Kitty Fisher must have cursed the name of Nelson, for of course it was by the example of the Immortal Memory that Jack justified himself. Without *his* Lady Hamilton, Nelson would not have been what he was—as Nelson had said himself, *"If there were more Emmas there would be more Nelsons."* Nelson, too, had yearned for enthusiasm and emotion and passion, and didn't find them in his wife. Fisher still wrote frequently to Kitty, with tenderness always, but all too often with excuses for his absence. All the long years of friendship and separation, the endless letters from sea, painting the cabin of *Inflexible,* dinner beneath the stars on *Renown,* entertaining admirals and princesses beneath Abraham's cedar at Ham Common—all seemed to have been put out of mind. Once at least Fisher took Nina to Kilverstone, but the atmosphere, so another guest reported, was distinctly uncomfortable. However, when in the summer of 1918 Kitty fell fatally ill at her daughter Beatrix's house in Gloucestershire, all Jack's tendency to romantic remorse flooded over him. Was he remembering his mother? He rushed to be at Kitty's sickbed (writing frequent letters to Nina to report on the progress of the illness) and some of his most moving prose was written in her memory. "A most perfect, peaceful, blissful end," he reported to the duchess when Kitty died on July 18. "May your saintly end be the same!" There seems to have been no irony in the hundreds of letters of sympathy that reached him—it was accepted perhaps that though Fisher might now be riding around in pony traps with the Duchess of Hamilton, Kitty Delves-Broughton was his true and life-long love.

On her gravestone at Kilverstone, where one may still read it, he placed the text "Her children rise up and call her blessed, and her husband also, and he praises her." She was, he wrote, "for 52 years the wife of Admiral of the Fleet Lord Fisher of Kilverstone, having married him as a young lieutenant without friends or money or prospects, and denied herself all her life long for the sake of her husband and her children: to them she was ever faithful and steadfast, and to such as condemned them she was a Dragon!" She had brought into their marriage the blood of the Plantagenets, and left him with a coronet. He directed that when he himself died, his name should be placed below Kitty's on her memorial plaque inside Kilverstone Church, with the words: "Who hopes, through the mercy of God, to be united with her in spirit hereafter."

Jack claimed in his memoirs that no woman would ever appear against him at the Day of Judgment. I find it difficult to think that the Painted Frigate, Clementine Churchill or the virulent Violet Asquith will actively give evidence on his behalf, but in general I believe what he said. Most women will acquit him. I accept that his relationships with them were essentially innocent, and I do not doubt that Kitty forgave him even his last infidelity. He knew very well, all the same, that he had behaved badly toward her in the last years of their marriage, neglecting her when she must have needed him most, and after her death he wrote to the duchess, with some reason: "I am going to St James' for communion tomorrow. I hope to get help and forgiveness just once more. 'Seventy times seven' I get forgiveness . . ."

It was astonishing what forgiveness the admiral still found in the country, anyway, from much of the press, from part of the navy, from many friends and colleagues, from the great public. People seemed willing to forget his desertion from duty, ignore his age and overlook his increasing grotesqueries, and there were frequent calls for his return to office. He was given a heartwarming welcome at the Lord Mayor's Banquet of 1916. Jellicoe invited him to visit the Grand Fleet. "With all my heart I wish our great Sea Lord joy of his birthday," wired Queen Alexandra when he turned seventy-six, "and may his good advice be followed everywhere and bear fruit." Even so, the whole nation was astonished when Churchill himself, his career apparently ruined by Fisher's defection, brought his association with the admiral to a last climax with a gesture that I like to interpret as a gage of passion, spectacularly thrown upon the floor of the House of Commons.

Everyone knew that each man blamed the other for the disaster of the Dardanelles (though when it came to a Royal Commission of Inquiry, they blended their evidence), and Churchill often spoke of Fisher with bitter reproach. "I expect the old rogue will realize increasingly as time passes the folly of his action. Together we could have ridden out every gale, and sure of our strength, we could have afforded to run those risks which alone open the gate to victory." All the more theatrically heightened, then, was the surprise that

Churchill sprang upon the Commons on March 7, 1916. Since leaving office in the previous year he had been commanding a battalion of the Scots Fusiliers in the French trenches, but he was still an MP, and being on leave in London decided to speak in the debate on the navy estimates. His theme was to be the ineptitude of Arthur Balfour, his own successor as First Lord, and he would take the opportunity to defend his own record, and at the same time (as he told a friend) "teach that damned old Oriental scoundrel Fisher what it meant to quarrel with him." Before the debate, however, a reconciliatory lunch was arranged by some of Fisher's supporters, and once again the admiral's charisma prevailed. Once more Churchill fell under his spell. Mrs. Churchill was horrified. "Keep your hands off my husband," she snarled at Fisher. "You have all but ruined him once. Leave him alone now."

Fisher was overjoyed at the renewal of their friendship, and vehemently pressed Churchill not to return to France, but to make a supreme effort to get back into government. It was like the old days! He assured Churchill that he was bound to become prime minister, said that Fate had him in its Grasp, reminded him that no David had yet come along to the Cave of Adullam, quoted I Samuel, chapter 22, verse 2, adjured him to think in oceans, shoot at sight, assured him that the Country wanted a Man, and promised him that together they could "take gigantic steps for fresh gigantic doings with Big Conceptions that will end the War!" Churchill went to the debate charged with the old Fisherian fire.

His attack on the Admiralty was severe. He accused it of unimaginative passivity. He said it was sluggish in the production of new ships. He warned of the dangers of submarines and zeppelins. And he concluded with this startling and totally unexpected coda: "I feel there is in the present Admiralty administration ... a lack of driving force and mental energy which cannot be allowed to continue, which must be rectified while time remains and before evil results. . . . *I urge the First Lord of the Admiralty without delay to fortify himself, to vitalize and animate his Board of Admiralty by recalling Lord Fisher to his post as First Sea Lord.*"

"*Splendid!!!* You'll have your Reward!" So Fisher thought, but nobody else did. Coming as it did at the end of a well-argued political speech, Churchill's resuscitation of lost loyalties struck most observers as perfectly crazy. The House of Commons reeled when it heard this quixotic declaration. Asquith was described as "positively speechless." Lloyd George said he could hardly believe his ears. The press was mocking. Clementine Churchill was aghast. The speech was generally regarded as political suicide, and Sir Hedworth Meux, MP, one of those limpets and parasites whose promotion, back in 1912, had created the first great rift between Jack and Winston, said maliciously of Churchill: "We all wish him a great deal of success in France, and we hope that he will stay there."

He did stay there for another couple of months, and he did not return to government office until July 1917. Fisher, of course, never returned at all, and the events in the House of Commons that night remain something of a mystery still. In the general view Churchill naively supposed that standing up for Fisher, still enormously popular in the country at large, would be politically advantageous to himself. I know better, though. He was declaring his love that day, recklessly, before he went back to war.

"When you have done your very utmost for your Country, then sit down under the Juniper Tree with Elijah and ask of God that you may die! and exclaim with the deepest humility and unutterable self-degradation and self-effacement: 'I am an unprofitable servant!' "

Fisher may have thought like this in his most despondent moments, but one would not know it from the eccentric gusto with which, even in his last years, he pressed his ideas, his complaints and his claims for office. His job at the Board of Inventions and Research may have been part-time and peripheral, but he threw himself into it as precipitately as ever. He renamed the board's headquarters Victory House, he called its panel of eminent experts variously the Chemist's Shop and the Magi, he plastered it with posters of Epstein's bust and a populist Fisherian slogan: "To HELL with Yesterday What's Doing *Today*." At the same time he pestered people for a chance to help more directly in the war—to return as controller of the navy, a job he had held in the previous century, or to be ambassador to the United States. He circulated a self-promotional booklet *(Some Notes by Lord Fisher for His Friends)* with a doctored frontispiece allegedly portraying himself in 1917, but really resurrected from 1904. He wrote long letters of advice or appeal to politicians—Asquith, Lloyd George, Balfour, Bonar Law. He even tried to justify himself with a rather too humble appeal to George V, "futile George."

He also wrote a famously provocative series of letters for publication in *The Times,* then edited by Wickham Steed. These chiefly concerned his ever more revolutionary ideas about naval warfare. By now he was quite convinced that the day of the battleship was over, and that sea war in the future would be dominated by the submarine and the aircraft. In a few years the whole navy would be obsolete, and not a single d——d fool at the Admiralty realized it. The Order of the British Empire ought to be the Order of the Bad Egg. Furious indeed were these Letters to the Editor, sometimes written in rough pencil, sometimes in huge penstrokes, and they were occasionally interspersed with telegrams of invitation, signed Johannes Piscator—HOPE YOU WILL COME HERE NEXT THURSDAY AND HAVE TWO DAYS GROUSE SHOOTING AND THE BEST PREACHER IN SCOTLAND ON SUNDAY IN THE PRIVATE CHAPEL. Some of the writing was full of pith still, some was tediously self-seeking, some childish (*The Times* did not print the bit about the OBE); and since the leitmotiv of the letters was the useless incompetence of nearly everyone, they became known as the Sack the Lot correspondence.

It seems unnatural to feel sorry for Jack Fisher, but by now one does. Tragedy evaded him: pathos became bathos. Faced with an increasingly bizarre and repetitive torrent of letters from the admiral, and tipped off by the duchess that the old man was overtaxing his powers, Wickham Steed wrote him a letter gently advising him to remain silent, like a nurse to an almost senile patient. "You must keep perfectly quiet, and in order not to tempt you to misbehave yourself I shall not publish your last letter on 'Hares, tortoises and greyhounds.' In fact, you must not write a word until you are able to run at least as fast as a tortoise yourself! Meanwhile, be good . . ."

Only twenty years had passed since Jack Fisher in the prime of his manhood was Lord of the Mediterranean, and the crews of great warships trembled to his panther tread.

The strongest thread of Fisher's life turned out in these last years to be the most raveled of them all, and is not disentangled even now. Nobody denies that Fisher's prewar reforms revived the British Navy to meet the challenge of war. The Grand Fleet, which he in effect created, never did lose the war in an afternoon, but instead formed the basis of a blockade which in the end strangled Germany and won it. His dramatic building program of 1914 did much to save Britain from starvation when unrestricted submarine warfare began, as he said it would, in 1917. His victory at the Falkland Islands was a great *coup de théâtre.* His patronage of the engineering branch helped to ensure that the machinery of the Royal Navy worked magnificently throughout the war, his prophetic insights inspired it to brilliant innovations in aviation and submarine warfare.

Not much else could really be described as brilliant, though, in the navy's record in World War I. Its seamanship was fine, its courage and doggedness were not often in question, but it was short of panache. It lacked the gung-ho, let-'em-all-come qualities that Fisher had tried to instill in it: Nelson's inspiring signal "ENGAGE THE ENEMY MORE CLOSELY" had actually been removed from the signal book. The British public was sadly disillusioned when so few dashing victories were won to confirm all the epic prints and legends of boardings and grapplings of triumphant three-deckers wreathed in gunsmoke, which had so long fired its patriotism. So eagerly awaited from the first day of the war, the new Trafalgar never happened at all, and the one great clash between the battle fleets, off the Jutland coast in 1916, ended indecisively—if anything, it seemed, in the Germans' favor.

In fact the British achieved their object there, because after Jutland the High Seas Fleet hardly ventured out again, but for Fisher the battle was a terrible disappointment. "They've failed me, they've failed me! I have spent 30 years of my life preparing for this day and they've failed me, they've failed me!" His beloved battle cruisers, used not in small task forces but as part of the battle fleet, had proved more vulnerable than he had ever imagined: "There's something wrong with our bloody ships today," said David Beatty their commander, as he saw three of them blown to pieces before his eyes. His decision not to adopt Pollen's system of fire control had denied the British ships the advantages he always planned for them—the faster ship and the bigger gun did not necessarily win. Worst of all, the Grand Fleet did not even seem to try to achieve the annihilation which was, in Fisher's eyes, always the purpose of a naval action. The fear of mines and torpedoes, the conviction that keeping his own fleet intact was more important than destroying the fleet of the enemy, restrained Jellicoe (known in his youth as "Hell Fire Jack") from hurling his ships into battle come what may. Forgetting his own caution over the Dardanelles, Fisher said that his prize protégé had been "congealed in discipline," and that Jellicoe's declared objective of "Keeping the Ring" was "the saddest thing ever said by a British Admiral."

Nevertheless the fleet that Jack built won its war, and in November 1918 its victory was symbolized in a grim and theatrical ceremony at the Firth of Forth in Scotland. At 9:00 A.M. on a gray day a forlorn procession appeared out of the North Sea: the entire German High Seas Fleet, 14 capital ships, 56 cruisers and destroyers, coming in line ahead to be interned. Its ships were battered, dingy and rusted. Its crews lounged demoralized around their decks. At the mouth of the Firth the Grand Fleet awaited it in very different shape: 370 ships in perfect order, commanded by 20 admirals, manned by 90,000 disciplined men, flying from every mast and staff all available White Ensigns. The British ships formed themselves into two parallel lines, and escorted the Germans into the Firth implacably, guns trained and all crews at action stations. It was a moment of high drama, and the greatest naval capitulation in history.

This should have been the crowning moment of Fisher's life, the justification of all his work. For all his errors and excesses, he was the architect of the Grand Fleet, and the real creator of its victory. He was not, however, at the Firth of Forth to share in the triumph, having received no invitation. As he complained in his memoirs, nobody said thank you.

. . .

Cheer up. As usual, Jack did. Elijah was desolate and deserted, after all, "and then he saw all those chariots and Angels, etc." Six months after the surrender we find him with his duchess in spirited unofficial attendance upon the Versailles conference, amusing luncheon parties with tales of his love affairs—"The Saints were all sinners to begin, so what I say is, 'Sin like blazes.' " He went to service at the American Church, sitting between Lloyd George the prime minister and Woodrow Wilson the president to hear a fine Presbyterian sermon and sing the "Battle Hymn of the Republic." Winston Churchill lent him a Rolls-Royce, in which he and Nina trundled majestically around the countryside, and Fisher's indefatigable dancing at the Majestic Hotel was delightedly recalled for me, forty years later, by Lloyd George's secretary and lover Frances Stephenson (who thought Nina "rather a stupid woman . . .").

He never gave up. In his seventy-sixth year he was threatening to run away to Palm Beach with a delightful American, in his seventy-ninth he proposed marriage to Nellie Melba the opera singer. He was still pressing upon Lloyd George his claim to be "a dictator at the Admiralty—*ruthless, relentless, and remorseless.*" He was still dreaming of airpower, submarines, an ultimate battle cruiser of 40,000 tons with 20-inch guns and a speed of 40 knots. He wrote letters all over the place, investigated new realms of theological debate, waltzed whenever he could. He dictated his highly idiosyncratic memoirs, *Memories and Records,* to a charming young stenographer; the first volume was published on the anniversary of Trafalgar, the second on the anniversary of the Battle of the Falkland Islands. He felt himself to be "on the crest of the wave . . . illustrating Jeremiah's saying 'It is good for a man to bear the yoke in his youth!' "

In 1920 he underwent five operations for cancer, but even then his gift for enjoyment did not fail him. His memoirs had earned him some £4,000, one of the few financial windfalls of his life. On the strength of it he ordered for the duchess a Rolls-Royce of her own, and in almost his last enterprise, before dying at 19 St. James's Square on July 10, 1920 (or as she would have it, "passing to a fuller life"), he took Nina and her young son off for a holiday in Monte Carlo. "*It's Paradise!!! And fancy my not finding it until my 80th year!!!*"

VALEDICTORY

Well, what d'you think of our Jacky now? For myself, having tracked him so closely and affectionately down the years, and having actually acquired by osmosis some of his lesser characteristics (for example his exclamation marks and his use of the deliberately expressionless expression), I have decided that on the whole I would rather love him than be him, and have settled for an affair with him in the afterlife, if he can fit me in.

He got a grand funeral. Great silent crowds lined the processional route to Westminster Abbey, under the Admiralty Arch and down Whitehall. Marines with reversed arms headed the cortege, to the slow beat of a drum. The coffin was drawn on a gun carriage by bluejackets and attended by admirals. *The Times*, which had so often been a friend to Fisher, said that only the funeral of his beloved master, Edward VII, could match it for emotional impact. The body was cremated at Golders Green cemetery—Fisher had no more feeling for a cast-off body, he used to say, than for a cast-off suit of clothes—before being taken to Kilverstone.

The obituaries were lavish. Sir William Watson published a valedictory poem:

His ageless eyes burned with unsquandered power;
    His countenance, when that magic smile came o'er it,
Was like a sea-crag breaking into flower
    Though all the tempests gore it . . .

And I behold him still—though but in dream:
    Fighting the thunderous battle his fate denied him:
Fighting for England her dread fight supreme,
    With her great soul beside him.

Dorothy Loxton wrote to Cecil Fisher, now the second baron, to express her sympathy, and this is how he replied:

Lots of people loved the dear old man, & will never forget him.
Yours v. sincerely
His Son.

The Duchess of Hamilton had a memorial slab erected on a wall of the church at Berwick St. John, where we saw them trotting by in the pony cart that day. It is there still, above a large photograph of Jack and an empty metal deed box with his name upon it, forming a kind of shrine. "The Great need no advertisement," the inscription says, "their deeds seek no applause," but nevertheless the duchess pressed hard to have a public memorial erected in London. Fisher was a greater man than Nelson, she reiterated to Wickham Steed, hoping for the backing of *The Times,* and if he could not be com-memorated in Trafalgar Square in the presence of the

Immortal Memory, then it should be in Westminster Square, beside the statue of Abraham Lincoln, "whom he admired so much." Nothing happened, though. There are busts of Jellicoe and Beatty in Trafalgar Square, but none of Fisher. Perhaps George V prevented it, or perhaps the stacked prejudices of the fossils, parasites and slugs, Berkeley Goeben and Violet Asquith, Clementine and the pedantic Sturdee were too powerful. Fisher's decorations are in a strong room at the National Maritime Museum, his uniforms are in air-conditioned storage there (in 1994 I tried on his admiral's cocked hat—it was rather too small for me); but there is no public recognition of his service to the state, and no plaque to mark his passing in St. James's Square. He did appear on a postage stamp in 1982, but of all the pictures ever made of him, it was unquestionably the worst.

There are many still who think him undeserving of honor. To this day the name of Fisher arouses fervent loyalties and vehement skepticism. Historians and biographers are divided in their responses to his work. Navy buffs curse and bless him still. Admiral Hyman Rickover, USN, the father of the nuclear ship, was his declared admirer. So, it was said, was Admiral Sergei Gorshkov, who did for the Soviet navy in the 1960s what Fisher did for the Royal Navy in the 1900s. But he is blamed still for his blind opposition to a naval war staff, for the failure of the battle cruisers at Jutland, and for the tragedy of Gallipoli. I think it safe to say, though, that the subtle and complex nature of his genius is finding new recognition now, at least among academics. More and more it is realized that technically and even strategically he was often so far ahead of his time as to be almost a twenty-first-century man; and all too many of his prophecies have proved astoundingly true, down to Winston Churchill, his love and his nemesis, as prime minister of Great Britain.

Forty years since I first started to think about him, and sparked that first flood of correspondence, I still hear from people eager to share with me their views upon Jack Fisher. He can still provoke adoration, laughter, suspicion or detestation, and his face, as I know from experience, can still stop people in their tracks: when visitors come to my house I generally take them into the bedroom and with a theatrical flourish fling open my closet door to display him sneering astringently out at us. (It was the novelist Beryl Bainbridge who drew my attention to the smallness of his ears.)

He does not look anachronistic. His face is timeless still. If he had been born a century later, into a lesser Britain, I doubt if he would have been a sailor at all. Nineteenth-century fate sent him into the British Navy, but give him a liberal education instead of the harsh and narrow upbringing of a cadet at sea, and he would probably be something quite different. He might be a provocative churchman, declaring his disbelief in Virgin Birth, eagerly supporting the ordination of women, but certainly having no truck with any of those d—d new liturgies. He might be the president of an international conglomerate. I can imagine him as a Hollywood character actor, or a newspaper magnate, or a crusading cross-bench peer, or the notoriously wayward head of an Oxford college. He would relish the age of television and tabloids, I fear, and might well antagonize even me by his appetite for publicity. I can conceive of him wearing an earring and owning an airline. Like me, he would love fast and flashy cars. I'm sure he would be a European. I hope he would still be a republican. Perhaps he might be Welsh?

The nature of his charisma still puzzles people. How much of it was intellectual, how much emotional, physical or actually sexual? As the ill-used Arthur Pollen wrote of him in 1930, "His ascendancy over Court, politicians, Parliament and Press will never be understood by a generation that did not live through it." Pollen himself thought Fisher "paralyzed the intelligences" of others by his daemonic force, but I have come to conclude that his real strength lay in his childlike quality. His enormous energies, his powers of analysis, his plots and his visions, were all sustained by a kind of unworldliness—an innocence of sorts—and the greatest of his gifts was an ageless genius for delight. His love of fun translated into a particular kind of persuasion, having its effect upon all but the least susceptible or most unappeasable, and winning over statesmen, scientists, industrialists, courtiers, churchmen, kings and all.

Fisher played life as an artist might play it, and even now people respond to him with instant vitality, as though the field of his magnetism is still charged. Let me end my book with a last example of his lingering powers, drawn from the life. We are flying in a navy fighter from Beirut to join an American aircraft carrier, one of the most powerful warships in the world. In itself as formidable as many a lesser nation's entire air force, it is patrolling the Mediterranean with the United States Sixth Fleet. The sky is utterly cloudless, the sea below us a calm azure, and the sensations of the flight are heady. The aircraft fiercely vibrates, the sun blazes through our canopy, static crackles on the radio, there is a marvelous sense of space and freedom as we race into the west. Our course takes us south of Cyprus, leaving the snow mountains of Lebanon behind us. Alexandria lies to the south, Malta due west, the Dardanelles are a few hundred miles to the north.

These are Fisher waters, and we are somewhere south of Corfu when Jack exerts his last enchantment on us. Below our wings, we see without surprise, there sails his own proud fleet of fin de siècle. It puffs and chuffs its passage toward Grand Harbor, billowing black smoke and alive with ensigns. There are the battleships, wallowing beneath the weight of their preposterous cannon, with their funnels side by side and their prows gold-embellished. There are the burnished cruisers gleaming in the sun. White torpedo boats range around the fleet, their bow waves like arrows below us, and there is peculiar *Polyphemus,* and *Boxer* madly tossing, and poor old *Rupert* striving to keep up, and grandly in the van is *Renown* herself with her huge admiral's ensign at the mainmast. We can hear the thudding and hissing of the engines. We can almost smell the steam.

It does not last. They are not in sight for long. Now instead the immense carrier is below us, smokeless, silent, with her fighters ranged upon her deck, the rescue helicopters forever hovering around her stern, her radars twirling, her escort destroyers steaming port and starboard. We bank abruptly. A sudden crooked glimpse of destroyers, choppers, the deck of the carrier, the sea all blue and white—a violent jolt as the arrester wire catches us—a howl of our engines and we are down. "Welcome aboard!" shouts a smiling black sailor above the wind. Through gray steel doors he leads us, up a steep series of ladders to the bridge, and around us all is air-conditioned calm and concentration.

The captain courteously rises from his revolving chair. "Coffee?" he says, making for the automatic dispenser. Good-bye, Jacky, we must leave you, but we are not quite out of the spell. Fisher's fleet is far behind, Fisher's face is certainly nowhere on that bridge, but can't you hear somebody whistling?

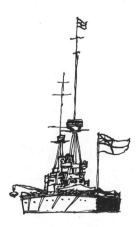

Thanks

This caprice has benefited from the kind and scholarly advice of Nicholas Lambert, author of the forthcoming *Influence of the Submarine Upon Naval Strategy, 1898–1914*, who read it in typescript; and it is heavily indebted to the published works of six other eminent historians and biographers, none of whom have read it, but all of whom gave the idea of it their generous encouragement. Martin Gilbert has been the official biographer of Winston Churchill since 1968. Richard Hough's *First Sea Lord: An Authorized Biography of Admiral Lord Fisher* was published in 1969, Ruddock F. Mackay's *Fisher of Kilverstone* in 1973. The late Arthur Marder published his collection of Fisher's letters, *Fear God and Dread Nought*, between 1952 and 1959, and his study of the Royal Navy in the Fisher era, *From the Dreadnought to Scapa Flow*, between 1961 and 1967. Richard Ollard's *Fisher and Cunningham: A Study in the Personalities of the Churchill Era* was published in 1991, and Jon Tetsuro Sumida's *In Defence of Naval Supremacy: Finance, Technology and British Naval Policy 1889–1914* in 1989.

Fisher's son and grandson have both been good to me—the second Lord Fisher at the start of my interest, the third

Lord Fisher more recently—and other members of the Fisher family kindly tolerated my intrusion into their affairs. And I owe my sometimes shamefaced gratitude to Lord John Kerr, Mr. Patrick Thursfield and the multitude of other people, living and dead, who have enriched me with material, reminiscence and often vehement opinion since I first contemplated *Fisher's Face* in 1951.

Trefan Morys, 1994

JAN MORRIS's thirty-odd books include works on the British Empire, Venice, Oxford, Sydney, Hong Kong, Manhattan and Wales, as well as six volumes of collected travel essays, two autobiographical works and a novel, *Last Letters from Hav,* which was a finalist for the Booker Prize in London. She is an Honorary D. Litt of the University of Wales and a Fellow of the Royal Society of Literature.

The text of this book was set in Janson, a misnamed typeface designed in about 1690 by Nicholas Kis, a Hungarian in Amsterdam. In 1919 the matrices became the property of the Stempel Foundry in Frankfurt. It is an old-style book face of excellent clarity and sharpness. Janson serifs are concave and splayed; the contrast between thick and thin strokes is marked.